SOCIALISM AND TRADITION

THE VAN LEER JERUSALEM FOUNDATION SERIES

SOCIALISM
AND
TRADITION

Edited by

S.N. Eisenstadt and Yael Azmon

HUMANITIES PRESS

ATLANTIC HIGHLANDS, NEW JERSEY

Library of Congress Cataloging in Publication Data

Main entry under title:

Socialism and Tradition

   (The Van Leer Jerusalem Foundation series)
   "Papers . . . originally given in 1969–1970 at the Interdepartmental
Seminar on Comparative Traditions at the Eliezer Kaplan School of Social
Sciences at the Hebrew University of Jerusalem."
   Bibliography: p. 241
   1. Communism and Culture – Congresses. I. Eisenstadt, Shmuel
Noah, 1923–   ed. II. Azmon, Yael, ed. III. Series: Van Leer Foundation
for the Advancement of Human Culture. The Van Leer Jerusalem
Foundation series.

HX523.S57   335   73-85036

ISBN 0-391-00375-5

CONTENTS

PREFACE

The papers presented in this volume were originally given in 1969—1970 at the Interdepartmental Seminar on Comparative Traditions at the Eliezer Kaplan School of Social Sciences at the Hebrew University of Jerusalem, in which members of the Departments of Sociology and Political Science and of the Institute for African and Asian Studies cooperated. The transcription of the proceedings and the preparation of the volume for publication were carried out under the auspices of the Van Leer Jerusalem Foundation. Jeanne Kuebler has been instrumental in preparation of the manuscripts.

S.N. Eisenstadt
Yael Azmon

Jerusalem
The Hebrew University
July 1973

SOCIALISM AND TRADITION*

S.N. EISENSTADT

I

It has been usual to view socialism and tradition as among the two most opposing forces in the modern world. Socialism (i.e., communism) has often been portrayed as perhaps the most extreme manifestation of modernity — as both the modern rebellion or protest against the first concrete force of modernity in terms of the basic premises and processes of modernity, as well as the fullest manifestation of the potentialities of development of the human race into a new civilization which would constitute the culmination of human history.

This civilization was viewed as consisting of several basic components: a scientific explanation of nature; a social ideology and possible scientific explanation of social development; a complete political program. It was assumed that these components, each of which was presented in intellectual and programmatic terms as a "total" dynamic whole, tend to coalesce naturally and in such coalescence to constitute the essence of a new dynamic civilization, transforming and changing the first forms of modernity and obliterating the old, traditional fetters of mankind.

The fulfillment of socialist vision was predicated on its victory in its struggle with its direct enemies, the bourgeoisie, and beyond this on its overcoming the perhaps more pervasive forces of traditionalism. But while socialism's struggle with its direct modern enemies, the bourgeoisie, often seemed to be the hard necessity of history through which the victory of socialism will necessarily come, the other more

* This paper was also presented at seminars of the Institute for Advanced Study at Princeton and at the Australian National University in Canberra. I would like here to record my indebtedness to the discussion that took place at these seminars.

1

traditional forces were seen as the major obstacles to the chances of
such success and to full development of the dynamic modes of civilization.

The full realization of the premises and processes of socialist
civilization was seen as impeded by "traditional" peasant groups, by
national religious or regional identities. The interests of these traditional groups were seen as necessarily opposed not only to the
revolutionary goals of socialism, but to the very conception of the
possibility of revolution. The attachments to traditional identities were
viewed as impediments to that broader international or class identity
on which socialism was allegedly based, and traditional habits as
impediments to the economic developmental goals of socialism.

Truly enough, with the continuous spread of socialist and of
communist ideology and movements it became quite clear that if they
could not destroy such traditional forces they had very often to come
to some accommodation with them. Moreover, with the spread and
institutionalization of socialist and communist movements, parties,
and regimes in Russia and Eastern Europe — and with the spread of
the socialist movements and ideology to Asia and Africa — the pattern
of such accommodation and the relations between these movements
and ideologies and local traditions became more and more variegated,
giving rise to a very great heterogeneity of ideologies and organizations
in the socialist camp.

But such accommodations — whether seen as temporary or as lasting — did not obliterate, in the perception both of many socialist and
communist leaders and of their opponents alike, the basic antithesis
between socialism or communism on the one hand and tradition on
the other. Similarly the growing heterogeneity of socialist ideologies
and organizations has been perceived as due to internal splits and
differences of opinions in the relatively unified fold of socialism conceived as either a philosophical-scientific "Weltanshauung" and/or as a
relatively unified, homogeneous political doctrine and program.
Accordingly, the many "local" differences which developed within the
socialist camp were seen mainly as subdivisions within such a unified,
universal, closed framework and, at most, differences in the evaluation
of different local situations.

And yet, a closer look at the process of development and spread of
socialism and communism points out that the relations between
socialist or communist regimes, ideologies, or political programs that
developed and became institutionalized as a party, a movement, or a
ruling elite in any given country and the traditional social and cultural

structure of this country were much more complicated than envisaged in this view. It became apparent that these relations could not be fully understood if one looked at socialism as a sort of new total universal civilization composed of all the components mentioned above and constituting a total break from preceding history and tradition.

Thus it could become evident, first, that to some degree the different socialist or communist parties or regimes tended to evince rather great similarities to the preceding − both modern and premodern − regimes in their respective countries. Such similarities could be discerned not only in some marginal customs or folklore but in certain crucial aspects of, let us say, the Soviet Union and the traditional Russian regimes; in some of the very basic modes of social and political symbolism, behavior, and organization of the Chinese Communist regime and those of the Chinese Empire; or in the "socialist" regimes of U Nu or Ne Win and some central aspects of traditional policy of the Burmese Kingdom.

Thus, in Russia, both regimes tended to emphasize a strong power orientation, the supremacy of the state over society, the crucial place of the bureaucracy, and the strong control by the state of most aspects of society. In China a similar continuity could be found in the strong emphasis on a "Mandate of Heaven," on the mechanism of thought control, and on the "educational" mission of the center, while in Burma the distributive welfare activities of the military regimes of both U Nu and Ne Win were very much in line with those of the traditional Burmese Kingdoms.

Such similarities and continuities did not mean, of course, that there were no changes at all − that "plus ça change plus c'est la même chose." Obviously, the great structural alteration due to industrialization, to political unification and mobilization or centralization are only too evident examples of far-reaching changes − to say nothing of the uprooting of aristocracies and of the bourgeoisie or of growing secularization and emphasis on scientific development. But in a sense these very changes tend only to emphasize even more the continuity in some of the modes of working of the political system or in some of the crucial patterns of stratification in both "traditional" and socialist regimes in many of these societies.

Similarly, many of these regimes maintained many central − not just marginal − symbols of collective, political, and cultural identity which were prevalent in their "traditional" settings. In some cases, such as many of the West European countries (e.g., Scandinavia or England under the Labor Party) such identity or continuity extended even to the symbols of the political regime, even while the new regimes attempted to change the old order's concrete policies. But even in revolutionary regimes such as Russia, where the very act of revolution created a new political regime with new symbols, there tended to develop — at first perhaps against the intentions of the revolutionary leaders though later with their encouragement — a continuity in some basic components and symbols of the political and the cultural identity of the collectivity, even if these continuities were never fully and consciously elaborated.

With the spread of socialism in South Asia (especially, but not only, in Middle Eastern and African countries), a new element came into the picture — namely, the effort to emphasize consciously the affinity between the symbols of socialism and the specific traditions, or what was constructed as constituting such traditions, of their respective civilizations or countries.

In these countries socialist or even communist movements often tended to pick up some of the traditional symbols of collective identity, even at times to create such symbols and turn them into rather central components of their own political symbolism. Thus the ideology of Arab socialism tended to emphasize the close affinity of socialism to some basic tenets of Islam — those of community and social justice; while the ideology of African socialism tended to emphasize its affinity to basic African traditions — the harmony and cohesion of tribal community, the lack of differentiation and conflict, and the like.

Obviously, in all these cases there did not take place just an automatic process of continuity of the modes of operation of political systems or of symbols of collective identity. Rather there developed here a continuous process of selection and even reconstruction of different elements from within the "traditions" of these respective societies.

But this process of selection took place, in each such case, not only from within the reservoirs of local tradition but also from within the repertoire of socialist symbols, orientations, and political programs. In some cases such selection emphasized those symbols or orientations from within the socialist repertoire which were most congruent with the central traditional symbols or orientations of the respective societies. In other cases — especially in some of the revolutionary societies — it might have been symbols which were more congruent with the traditions of rebellion and protest in these societies that were developed.

II

Such process of the creation of wider repertoires of socialist symbols and images and a continuous selection from within them started even before the very initial development and earlier spread of socialism in Europe. Already in reformist and revolutionary European movements and regimes, the institutionalization of socialist regimes, policies, or tenets was closely connected with such a double process of selection. They constituted not only an external accommodation to the local indigenous tradition; new cultural and political models also were forged out through such processes of selection of themes from socialist tenets and from the "local" traditions alike.

This process of the selection of themes from within the socialist repertoire was even more evident in the spread of socialism and communism to societies — as in Africa, Asia, or Latin America — where it became institutionalized in entirely different social and cultural settings and conditions than those in Europe. Here it became evident that the acceptance of socialism was not dependent simply on the same conditions as in Europe, as it spread to countries which were not industrialized — or which, in a broader sense, were not even modernized.

Indeed in these countries it is only in relatively exceptional cases that the progress of industrialism has given rise to the development of classical types of socialist movements. This fact emphasized even more that socialism was not accepted as a scientific Weltanschauung or political program. The varieties of socialist ideologies, theories, and practices which developed in these societies went beyond the "transplantation" of a given fixed socio-cultural political model to a new setting.

Nor can the spread of socialism to these countries be understood — as John Kautsky has claimed — only or mainly as a program for economic development and political mobilization. In many countries — Burma and many Middle Eastern states — the emphasis on development or industrialization was not only a sort of "symbolic" lip service; in other countries it was not the developmental or mobilization aspects of socialism that have been emphasized but the communal and distributive ones. Very often, instead of being very clearly focused on problems of development, the socialist ideology tended to emphasize some aspects of protest against modernity — such as colonialism or imperialism.

In many of these societies the orientation to socialism became dissociated from either any concrete political or economic program or from the acceptance of any of the tenets of the so-called "scientific" socialist Weltanschauung; and sometimes, as in some African societies, it seemed as if the political program was not taken very seriously. The major differences between socialist and non-socialist regimes would often be less in terms of concrete policy and political organization, and rather more in terms of ideologies and symbols.

Thus, a birdseye view of the spread of socialism — a view to be more fully elaborated and illustrated in greater detail in the various case studies presented later — indicates that, first, socialism is a movement, a modern one, which has spread throughout the world in one of the most far-reaching ways and scope that has occurred in history. And second, that this spread or diffusion consisted of a continuous selection of different aspects of the existing tradition as well as of different themes from within it, and that this selection was often influenced by various aspects of the traditions of the "receiving" societies.

And yet these symbols did constitute an important element in the social and cultural ambiance of these societies — even though its relative importance did, as we shall yet see in greater detail later on, vary greatly from case to case.

III

The preceding illustrations indicate that the simple view of the relation between socialism and tradition as that of two completely antithetical — even if sometimes mutually accommodating — forces is at most a half truth. They indicate that in fact there developed a much closer interaction, an interplay, between these two "forces"; that there takes place a process of mutual selection of elements from the traditions of these respective societies or civilizations and from the repertoire of socialism. They also indicate that this mutual selection is perhaps not only just a passing adjustment between two fixed entities — a fixed closed socialist or communist system and a fixed traditional economic and political reality — an adjustment which will disappear in the fullness of time with the ultimate victory of socialism.

Thus they indicate that what has been called socialism or communism as it has developed in Europe from the early nineteenth century on, while containing political programs and ideologies and scientific or philosophical Weltanschauung, is not exhausted by these aspects. Beyond these it contains also other elements or components which are more pervasive and forceful and influential in the diffusion of socialism.

What then are these components?

First of all, those socialist movements and ideologies contained, in a model or models of society, a social and often also a cultural order which attempted to provide not only specific political programs or scientific explanations of social or cosmic reality but also broader answers to some of the questions of the meaning of human life and destiny.

Second, beyond any such concrete model the socialist movements contained also several broader cultural orientations addressed to such basic questions which could become associated in different ways in different groups. Among the most important of these orientations was, first, a strong future orientation, a strong attempt to relate the future to the present; second, a strong emphasis on the primacy of the collectivity and on social justice, coupled with negation of the more individualistic approaches.

The third component was the emphasis on strong close relations between the social, political, and cultural orders, and on attempts to construct the new social order and to justify it according to some transcendental criteria and ideals inherent in it.

Fourth, there was also by definition a very "this-worldly" orientation, an emphasis on activity in this world — not through an acceptance of the existing order but rather an attempt to reconstruct the existing order in terms of some transcendental value beyond its given reality.

Fifth, socialism tended to emphasize strongly the possibility of active participation of social groups in the formation of a new social and cultural order, as well as a high level of commitment to such orders.

Sixth, socialism tended to emphasize very strong universalistic orientations — in principle negating the importance and significance of any specific political or national boundaries, but at the same time attempting to define a new, basic socio-political order with broad, yet relatively definitive boundaries. These boundaries were defined as those of the "workers" and the "intellectuals" — potentially embracing all mankind, or at least those parts of mankind willing to accept the basic premises of the "gospel" and define themselves in terms of such attributes.

Seventh, socialism developed also a specific mode of legitimation of the social and cultural order proposed by it — a very "modern" one, i.e., a legitimation based on combinations of charismatic and rational orientations or values shared by the broad groups of society and making, in principle at least, the leaders of the movements or the rulers of socialist regimes accountable to broad groups as representatives of these values and orientations in the creation of which all could and should participate.

But however modern and future-oriented it was, socialism also had reference to a past, to an imaginary human communal past, the symbols of which became very important components in the definition of the collective identity of socialist collectivities. It had as well a strong evangelistic and chiliastic trend, which, together with its "this-worldly" orientations, have given it the impetus to expansion.

All these different orientations could become combined in the socialist camp in many different ways — with the more overt aspects of socialism in the constitution of modes of social and cultural order, of political programs, of so-called "scientific" interpretations of society and nature. Each such construction involved the selection of different themes from the reservoir of socialist orientations and symbols and different combinations of such themes could become crystallized. But often socialist symbols could also serve and command a high degree of commitment without being infused with any such cultural model or political program.

Moreover these various orientations could coalesce, in different situations, in the different components of socialism — political programs, scientific theories, or general cultural symbols and orientations. But any such coalescence into a given organizational or doctrinal form could be rather transient, even this transiency only attesting to the strength of these symbolic elements of the socialist tradition.

IV

The social and cultural implications of these socialist orientations as well as some of the dynamics of their diffusion can, however, be understood only in the context of the basic structural and symbolic framework within which they developed and acquired, as it were, their concrete meaning. The most crucial fact here is that socialism and communism constituted a movement and ideology which combined within itself orientations of rebellion, protest, and intellectual antinomianism together with strong orientations to center-formation and institution-building — and that all of them were of specifically modern flavor and orientations.

The themes of protest and rebellion were, of course, central in the socialist repertoire. Indeed they constituted one of the major foci and symbols of identity that developed from within it, and it is not pure chance that almost all the great socialist leaders — Engels, Kautsky, Bernstein, and others — were ardent students of peasant and slave rebellions and of millenarian movements. It is not only that the analysis of the social determinants of such rebellions was important for the "scientific" understanding of social dynamics according to the tenets of Marxism. One cannot but be aware that the fascination with these movements has been at least partly due also to the attempts to find the roots of the identity of their own movements and especially to find, in the model of primitive communism or of communal and millenarian rebellions the paradigm for the combination — to use van der Lieuw's term — of "Uhrzeit" and "Endzeit" within its vision of new society.

Similarly, most socialist movements contained within themselves also very strong ambivalent attitudes toward the great intellectual movements of Modern Europe — especially to the Enlightenment and to the scientific-technological developments — accepting many of their orientations and premises but at the same time developing a very strong antinomian trend, a trend of heterodoxy and of negation against many of the premises of these movements.

However, socialism was not only a movement of rebellion, protest, and intellectual antinomianism. The various socialist and communist groups and movements developed also very strong orientations to center-formation and to concrete institution-building. It was indeed this strong connection with concrete institution-building and with formation and institutionalization of centers which distinguished socialism from other movements of protest in the history of mankind, and which gave socialism its specific modern revolutionary connotation.

To bring out the specific characteristics of socialism from this point of view, it might be worthwhile to compare them with the Great Religions or Traditions of the past, on the one hand, and with the other movements — such as the revolutionary movements related to the English, French, and American Revolutions which developed in the first stages of European modernity, or the other.

Like the founders of Great Religions and like the revolutionary movements which ushered in modernity in Europe — and in contrast to other movements of rebellion or of millenarianism and heterodoxy in the history of mankind — the socialist movements tended to connect protest, rebellion, and heterodoxy with active political institution-building and with the formation of centers. Organized political protest was joined with more elaborate intellectual heterodoxy.

Unlike, however, the Great Religions, the major emphasis of socialism was "this-worldly" — politically, socially, and economically. It was "this world" that served as the focus and source of socialism's major transcendental orientations — usually undermining the validity of any other-worldly legitimation to these orientations. And unlike other revolutionary movements of modernity — such as the English, French, or American Revolutions or the Enlightenment — socialism was the first overall modern movement of protest which was oriented not only against the premises of traditional systems of authority but also against the modern institutional systems — political, economic, and ideological — which developed in the first phase of modern European society.

V

It was this tendency to continuous combinations of these various orientations and elements and the fact that it was these elements that were the most pervasive ones in the spread of socialism that indicate that socialism and communism, as it developed in Europe from the beginning of the nineteenth century, very quickly crystallized into tradition of sorts, composed of many different elements and components which can indeed be, to some degree, "decomposed" in different situations, even if retaining some basic common cores.

It crystallized into a tradition, insofar as we view tradition not just as a burden of the past, the "cake of custom" and the like, but as the reservoir of the most central social and cultural experiences prevalent in a society; as the most enduring element in the collective social and cultural construction of reality.

This reservoir, however, is not an undifferentiated one; it has a structure of its own and it focuses primarily around:

1. The major ways of looking at the basic problems of human existence and of social and cultural order, of posing major questions about them, especially concerning such problems as: the definition of the relative importance of different dimensions of human existence and their bearing on cultural and political identity; the perception of the interrelation and mutual relevance of the cosmic, the cultural, the social, and the political orders; the patterns of participation in the formation of social and cultural orders; the cases of legitimation of such orders.

2. The possible answers to these problems that develop within a given society or civilization. And,

3. The organization of various institutional and symbolic structures for the implementation of different types of solutions to these problems.

The concrete parameters of this tradition were set up by the combination of the basic symbolic orientation codes and the model of society analyzed above, together with the different emphases on protest and institution-building and center-formation.

Indeed, from its very beginning, symbolic and organizational aspects of socialism developed all the major characteristics of "tradition," attempting to provide full answers to the basic problems of human and social existence. It became a truly international — inter-European — tradition, very much akin to the Protestant "international," or to some degree to that of the Enlightenment, although because of its political orientation, much more fully organized than the latter. In its fullest articulation it developed the major character-istics of a secular religion and all the trimmings of a theological system or doctrine disclosing some tendency to closure in the organizational and symbolic spheres alike.

This tendency to become crystallized as tradition was evident in the tendency of supporters and opponents alike to combine socialism's political program, Weltanschauung, with its scientific program, into one overall design, and the tendency to interpret any differences in terms of such overall doctrinal and "model" differences.

But from the very beginning it had certain elements of flexibility and heterogeneity built into it. These elements were built into it both by the very nature of its orientation and symbolism, as well as by its basic patterns of organization. This tendency to heterogeneity in the interpretation of socialism was built into it by the double orienta-tions and emphasis on protest and on institution-building and center-formation; and by the uncertain definition of the boundaries of this tradition as related to boundaries of political and cultural collectives.

These general tendencies to flexibility, to some heterogeneity, were intensified by its specific characteristics as a "modern" tradition in general and by some of its own peculiar brand of modernity in partic-ular. Being a modern tradition it had in-built organizational and symbolic correctives against any closure and a concomitant predica-ment to openness. In some of its organizational features it tended to evince some characteristics which showed some affinity to the structure of the modern scientific community.

Ultimately it was not successful in developing a fully sanctioning body; it had no single locus of authority that could continuously re-examine dogma. Its major tenets were not included in any single book or body of doctrines and no single personality — not even Marx — became the fully accepted ultimate symbol of sources of this doctrine. Although many attempts to establish such a single center or single basis of personality were indeed made in the socialist and communist camps — especially with regard to Marxist doctrine — they were never fully successful even in the Marxists' own camp, to say nothing about the wider socialist camp.

Moreover, the very bases of the legitimation of its premises — i.e., open acceptance and sharing of the doctrine by broader groups — in terms of secular, "open," "modern" values made this legitimation vulnerable to continuous criticism from within the elite as well as from the broader strata of the members.

But, however open this tradition was, it did not necessarily abate the possible sectarian nature of the debates and discussions in the socialist camp. Rather, the combination of all these elements made for a strong tendency to the development, within the socialist camp, of many differences of opinion, of interpretation, of heterodoxies.

The predilection to heterodoxy and to sectarian splits which was inherent in this tradition intensified with socialism's spread and with the attempt to institutionalize its universalistic-missionary vision in a great variety of settings, a consequence the new doctrine had in common with other Great Traditions. Any such attempt at institutionalization brought out strongly the problems and ambivalence of the boundaries of this tradition — of the place of the particularistic "national" ethics or cultural collectivity and its relation to the universalistic community of workers; it brought to the surface the tensions between the premises of potentially closed as against open creativity, as well as those of the relations between its different concrete themes and of its components — and especially those of the political program, scientific explanations, and cultural models.

VI

It was through various attempts to institutionalize some aspects of the socialist creed that the great variety of different socialisms developed, each of them selecting different aspects, or rather different combinations of aspects and orientations from within the socialist repertoire.

Such processes of selection and of consequent splits and tensions in the socialist camp have been taking place in Europe from the very beginning of the development of socialism. They were indeed part of the very processes of crystallization of this tradition; of its development out of the European traditions and its incorporation into them. And the concrete directions of such incorporation were greatly influenced by the context of development of socialism in Europe and of its spread beyond it.

Indeed, the original development of socialism in its various forms in Europe was predicated on some specific conditions of the development of European modernity, and both in its origins and in its actual development socialism was, in more than one way, part and parcel of European traditions. Probably the most important of these was, in the words of G. Lichtheim and E. Kamenka, the specific reaction to the tension between the premises of the French Revolution and the realities or problems created by the Industrial Revolution: between the ideals of general universal brotherhood, justice, and universal participation in the social and cultural order and the realities of class division and social and economic dislocation created by the Industrial Revolution as already evaluated according to the premises of the French Revolution.

In other words, the original development of socialism was a reaction to the specific problems, to the forces and contradictions created by the great structural and symbolic upheavals of modernity as it developed in Europe and arising out of the breakdowns of the initial European constellations of modernity.

The structural and symbolic orientations which gave rise to the socialist movement and ideology, to the socialist traditions, were predicated on the acceptance of the premises of European modernity — the strong universalistic orientation, the combination of protest and institution-formation, the quest for the broadening of the scope of participation in the center, and the utilization of this participation for effecting changes in the formation of the center and for concrete institution-building.

This development of the specific combination of the orientation of protest together with the orientation to center-formation and institution-building was greatly in line with several other aspects of European traditions, and it was related to the fact that it was perhaps the only one of the Great Traditions in which some orientation of protest and center-formation was strongly connected with some orientation of rebellions and heterodoxies. It was this tradition which has also greatly influenced the development of some of the major specific themes which characterized the world-view of socialism and especially a view of history as changing toward the future: its strong emphasis on the temporal dimensions of human existence; its activist orientation, as well as the specifically scientific and "national" components.

Socialism and communism also incorporated into their traditions and symbols some of the eschatological elements of Christianity, of its vision of the course of history and redemption, of division between the City of Man and the City of God. And the original socialist movements were in line also with general ideological trends of European modernity, with the emphasis on the nation-state on the one hand and on the tension between state and society and the importance of "class society" on the other.

Even the specific socialist emphasis on class society has been very closely related to some aspects of the European tradition, especially to the combination of Imperial, feudal, and city-state active orientations to the social order; to the autonomy of the "estates"; and to the active participation of broader groups and strata in the formation of the society.

Most of the original European socialist groups — be they anarchists or communists, "scientific" or political — have indeed accepted most of these orientations. And they have accepted, or rather taken for granted, the existence of relatively strong centers and national communities. Even those, like the anarchists, who seemingly denied the validity of legitimacy of such centers and communities did neither deny its existence nor its importance — even if negative — for their program. Their very emphasis on the importance of the dissolution of the political realm — the dissolution of the dilemma of state versus society by a total victory of the latter — was only possible in a situation in which both political centers as well as national or ethnic communities were already existing. The existence of such centers was, of course, also a basic datum for the utopian orientations of the "withering away" of the state in some branches of Marxism.

But even in Europe socialism was not a uniformly closed tradition: already there has been a continuous process of selection of different elements of the tradition and of their incorporation in different ways in the modern European social and cultural life. And even in Europe socialism was not only a political program or a closed cultural model. Beyond that it had also an important symbolic element or component.

One of the most interesting illustrations of the force of this symbolic and sectarian aspect of European socialism can be found in its more recent developments or trends — in the more literary and artistic realm of Sartre or Althiesser or in the political events of May 1968 in France and the spread of the New Left thereafter.

While on the purely "intellectual," philosophical, or scientific level these developments are, as Raymond Aron has so well shown, rather feeble reinterpretations of Marx and while their political program proved to be rather ineffective — yet the great popularity and impact of these trends attests to the fact that their attraction is due to the strength of their symbolic dimension.

VII

Given these specifically European historical roots of socialism, the question arises: Why was it so successful in spreading beyond Europe to countries and civilizations where both cultural traditions and structural, economic, or political conditions differed greatly from those in Europe and within which the specific structural conditions which were so important in the spread of socialism — that is, the spread of industrialization — developed, if at all, but very haltingly?

Though a large part of the doctrinal disputes within the socialist and communist camps was devoted to attempts to explain this seeming mystery and all possible tools of dialectic were used in this effort, this anomaly was not abolished. The debate only emphasized it to a greater extent. Truly enough, the spread of socialism in its various aspects — be it a political unit, ideology, or symbolism — in these countries was rather uneven. While in some cases — as in China, Russia, to some degree Burma, and some African countries — it became incorporated into the major new symbols of the political collectivity or at least of political action, in others — Japan or until very lately Latin America — it became predominant only in more marginal sectors of the working class or among groups of intellectuals.

But all these differences notwithstanding, the fact remains that of all traditions, ideologies, or movements which spread out from within the Western and Central European centers, socialism was the one which became more widespread and continuous. Some European models, such as nationalism, became much more pervasive in these countries, but they did not entail the participation — even if a "superficial" one — in organizational or symbolic frameworks which to some degree were common to societies and movements both in Europe and outside it.

How can we then explain this success of socialism in spreading beyond its points of origin and into conditions seemingly entirely different from those of its origin? Why was socialism more successful than the "European" religions such as the different branches of Christianity, or than movements like liberalism? Why has it been even more forceful than indigenous movements of protest — sometimes even absorbing them into its own fold?

Here, even more than in the discussion of European socialism, it is clear that explanation of the attraction of socialism in terms of its being either a complete, total Weltanschauung or a concrete political program is, as we indicated at the beginning of this essay, inadequate. It is clear that even the political programs have to be understood first of all as points of crystallization of the more symbolic components of such tradition.

The clue to the special position of socialism and communism is to be found in some aspects of the encounter of the non-Western, non-European societies with modernity as it spread from Europe; in some of the unique aspects of the processes of modernization as compared with other situations and movements of change in the history of man-kind. The unique characteristic of this movement is the fact that it was based on the assumption of the possibility of an active creation by man of a new socio-political order, an order based on premises of universalism and equality. The spread of these assumptions through the world was combined with far-reaching structural-organizational changes, especially in the economic and political fields; and it took place through a series of social, political, and cultural movements which, unlike movements of change and rebellion in many other historical situations, tended to combine both orientations of protest and of center-formation. Through this spread there developed a tend-ency to a universal, worldwide civilization in which different societies — and especially the first, the European one — served as reference points, from which they judged their own place and each other according to these premises of universalism and equality, thus serving for each other as negative objects of protest as well as models of emulation in terms of these premises.

In this process there has indeed developed a symbolic parallelism — in terms of the perception of relative standing and relative deprivation according to the universalistic principles of modernity — between the development of the working class in Europe and of the new nations in the modern international system.

In this sense those who claim that "class" struggle, instead of being within a nation, has become international and that the "new" countries serve as the proletariat of this new international struggle, have indeed put their finger on a very important aspect. But it is not, as they thought or claimed, a concrete "structural" or organizational aspect, but rather a structural-symbolic aspect of this process and these relations.

The exact structure of the relations between different countries in the world is, of course, entirely different from those of classes within the same society: instead of being internal it is international; instead of being related to the internal division of labor, it is mostly related to the ideological international and political stances. Hence also, the whole dynamism of the spread of socialism in these countries differs from its initial development in Europe.

But with all these differences there has indeed taken place a symbolic transposition and parallelism between the conditions of development of socialism in its original European setting and the situation in which many non-European societies found themselves as a result of the spread of modernity. It is due to this symbolic transposition that the attraction to the socialist tradition in non-European countries can be explained. It is due to the fact that the socialist tradition is the one modern international tradition in which the protest against the concrete constellation of modernity may be worked out in terms of identity of participation in the premises of the modern world itself.

The special attraction of socialism in general lay in the fact that it proved to be the best channel through which it was possible to develop some active participation in the new modern (i.e. Western) universal tradition together with some selective negation of many of its aspects in general and of the West in particular. Socialism made it possible for the elites and strata of many non-European societies to combine the incorporation of some of the universalistic elements of modernity in their new collective identity without necessarily denying either specific components of one's identity or the continuously negative attitude toward the West.

This symbolic transposition of the initial ideology of socialism from European to non-European settings has been greatly reinforced by the combination, in the socialist tradition, of the orientations of protest with that of institution-building and center-formation. Thus the respective groups and elites in these societies were enabled to refer themselves both to the tradition of protest and to the tradition of center-formation in these societies and to cope with the problems of reconstruction of their own centers and traditions in terms of the new setting in which they were put.

To sum up, the general attraction of socialism or communism beyond its European origin is rooted in these threefold characteristics: the combination of tradition to protest and center-formation, and the specific combination or reorientation of these traditions into the encounter with the impingement of modernity on non-Western, non-European societies and their incorporation into a broader potentially universalistic tradition of modernity — developments which at the same time enabled the receiving societies to take some degree of negative, of critical, attitudes toward parts of this tradition.

ELEMENTS OF RUSSIAN TRADITIONS IN SOVIET SOCIALISM

GALIA GOLAN

To examine the extent to which Russian traditions have influenced Soviet socialist institutions, one must first ask the question: What was socialism in the eyes of the Russian of the early twentieth century? Traditional socialism contained elements both of Messianism and of science — and both aspects appealed to the Russians. There already existed in Russia a tradition of Messianism — the idea of the Russian people as bearers of the truth, that which is spiritually necessary for a better world.[1] At the same time there was admiration of the West's technological progress: The bringing of order — albeit a materialistic order — to a world of chaos was an idea which should properly be coupled with the Russian spirit.[2] Thus, socialism appealed to both these aspects of the Russian tradition.

However, socialism represented two other things in the non-Western world. For some, it represented socio-political change — revolution and, subsequently, an emphasis upon a strong state and centralized control to accomplish economic goals — and socio-economic change, that is, industrialization. While these two aspects of socialism are by no means mutually exclusive, socialist movements in different countries or at different stages of development tended to emphasize one or the other.

In the case of Russia the emphasis tended toward the political side, or revolution.[3] It was indeed natural that a socialist movement out of power should emphasize the political side, for its primary goal was to gain power. Nonetheless, those aspects of socialism which appealed to the Russians were the promises of political change rather than of economic changes. This may have been a result of the traditional state/people dichotomy in Czarist Russia, the almost total alienation of the individual with regard to the government as well as the peasant nature of the society.[4] Even the Russian workers were basically peasants recently moved to the cities, still deeply attached to their peasant

19

origins and suspicious of industrialization as well as of the state. Most
of the political parties of early twentieth-century Russia were, in fact,
anti-industrialization, reflecting the peasant interests and suspicions of
their supporters, and anti-state.[5]

Russia was at the time undergoing industrialization at the behest of
and under the guidance of the state, with all the social upheavals
attendant upon industrialization but without the introduction of corresponding changes in political institutions. A middle class was being
formed, and the traditional points of identification were breaking
down. However, the political organs introduced by liberals elsewhere
were still lacking. Early industrialization in Russia was introduced not
through private enterprise but by the state, with the help of foreign
capital, with the result that there was little need for a liberal (laissez
faire) philosophy. In time, however, industry and the social changes
which it brought about created demands in this direction; thus eventually industrialization, without the corresponding development of
liberal political institutions, led to a revolutionary situation.[6] Given
the lack of political experience and of liberal traditions or institutions,
however, Russian demands tended to be radical in nature. The major
demand was to destroy the state in favor of some sort of self-
government.[7]

Thus the Russian socialists were faced with a population inexperienced politically yet distrustful of liberalism because of their fear that
it might mean perpetuation of the state. They had to bring under
control the anarchistic leanings of the masses who, like the socialists,
wanted to destroy the existing state, but who, unlike the socialists,
wanted no new central organs in its place.[8] Thus we have the fundamental problem of socialism and the state handled differently by two
streams of socialist thinking. One stream, which might be called the
"etatist stream," seeks to preserve the state for the purpose of economic planning and control of distribution. The "anarchist stream"
seeks to destroy the state altogether in favor of some sort of, though
rather amorphous, concept of self-rule.

Marx, in a sense, straddled both streams. It is difficult to determine
just how much of a center he would have preserved, given his concept
of the withering away of the state. Both Marx and Lenin spoke of
central administration that was *not* to be a bureaucracy. They apparently had in mind some sort of non-institutionalized rule resembling
mere bookkeeping.[9] Yet, in time, Lenin, and more decidedly Stalin,
centered their efforts around the etatist political interpretations of
socialism.

The question we are interested in answering is: What role did Russian traditions play in the selection of this stream and the interpretation of socialism following, as well as prior to, the revolution? It may be that an "etatist" interpretation was necessary in order to introduce socialism *despite* tradition, i.e., to overcome the traditional passivity of the Russian peasant. On the other hand, this type of socialism may have been introduced *because* of the tradition of a strong centralist state, i.e., the fear of completely disrupting society by going against this tradition or, more simply, because there was no experience in any other type of rule. Still another hypothesis might be that this emphasis upon the state was not the result of traditions but of objective factors, i.e., the necessity of central controls for maintaining power and introducing extensive industrialization. In this, the tradition of strong central authority merely helped.

All of these hypotheses may be partially valid. Indeed they are not necessarily contradictory or mutually exclusive. The Russian "selection" of specific elements or streams of traditional socialism was probably influenced by the fact that the Russian socialists lacked all experience in liberal institutions or non-authoritarian models of rule, just as Lenin's central concept of the leading role of the Communist Party was in keeping with the traditional political organization in Czarist Russia. Nonetheless, one should not overlook the role of objective factors, whether the more specific underground conditions which determined Lenin's organization of the Party; the more general need for central control to restrain the popular tendencies to anarchy and possible disorder; the need to stay in power and conduct a civil war; or the need for organization of society for industrialization, since this could hardly be expected to come through private enterprise. Given these objective factors, however, certain traditional institutions could certainly facilitate carrying out the tasks facing the socialists. We shall return to this matter below.[10]

Having chosen the "etatist" political interpretation of socialism, the Bolsheviks eventually introduced an entire system of institutions connected with atuocratic rule and many elements of the Russian state which they were in effect perpetuating. The actual institutions of rule in the Soviet state greatly resemble those of Czarist Russia.[11] For example, the personal rule of the Czar has its counterpart in the rule of the Party leader (or leaders). In both periods, the entire hierarchy of authority is subordinate and personally responsible to the leader, and even the idea of parallel hierarchies has been carried over. For example, the Czar always maintained his own private secretariat parallel to the government cabinet; so, too, under Soviet rule, the Party secretariat is parallel to the Council of Ministers. The Czar installed this system because he did not trust his own ministers and sought a way both to maintain a check on them and to enforce his views. So, too, the Communist Party (CPSU) has an organization parallel to the government to provide a check as well as a means of enforcing the Party's will. Like the Czars, the CPSU uses "mixing" to assure control, i.e., the Czar placed "his" people in key government jobs, just as the Party places its own particularly loyal people into the government. In both periods this mixing applies to other spheres as well, e.g., the army, the local bureaucracy, and so forth. Insofar as any real decision-making occurs outside the Czar or the Party leaders themselves, it is done within the Czar's personal secretariat or the Party secretariat (or the politburo or the central committee, depending upon the period in Soviet development), not the government. Indeed, the Bolsheviks even refined this system by creating still another parallel hierarchy within the Party in the form of the politburo (personally-loyal shadow cabinet) versus the *apparat,* at times together with, at times distinct from, the secretariat.[12]

Significant here is not the exact structure but the principle involved — and maintained — of autocratic "personal" rule, independent of the government or other organs of the state. Both the Czar and the Party stand above all other institutions with no need or desire either to share power or to rely on persuasion for their rule. Indeed, the legal system was affected by this autocratic concept of rule, be it under the Czar or under the Communists. The legal institutions are not considered independent institutions, above the government or ruling clique, as in the West.[13] Despite what may be — and has been — nicely noted on paper or in Constitutions, Communist courts, like Czarist tribunals, are to serve the regime, their decisions to be guided by political considerations. Thus the law is subordinate to politics, and the liberal concept of judicial review of legislation is also lacking. In both Czarist and Communist Russia one sees a tendency to "administrative" measures, i.e., "justice" without benefit of courts or due process of law. The prosecutor-general of Czarist days has maintained his functions as the strong representative of the regime, able to control investigations and criminal procedures independent of any other government organ. Even the defense attorney under the Czars was limited, though he is still more so under the Communists, for his task is defined not as defending the client but as helping the court establish the truth — and the "truth" is usually contained in the indictment presented by the prosecutor-general's office.[14]

Insofar as Soviet society is concerned, much of the resemblance to the Czarist system in the political sphere emerged only slowly, after the revolution, and has undergone certain adjustments over the years. Nonetheless, the overriding tradition of the political regime setting the rules independent of, and above, all other institutions and controls has remained. This in itself is based on a traditional concept of rule whereby the regime makes rules so as to provide the smooth functioning of society, while the people are responsible for maintaining this smooth functioning by following the rules. This implies a more or less passive role for the people of merely obeying or implementing the regime's decisions. The regime is not responsible to the people but, rather, the people are responsible to the regime.[15]

This traditional attitude, found in the Soviet as well as the Czarist system, implies two additional phenomena: manipulation and paternalism. This view of rule sees citizens as mere cogs in a machine, to be organized, shifted, or manipulated, as necessary, for the functioning of society. This was the attitude in Czarist days and was even more so under Stalin. Paternalism was quite well known and widely accepted as an element of "the little father's rule" of Czarist Russia. For the simple, rough peasant the "Czar knew best" — just as today the Party knows best. Indeed Lenin's concept of the Party is permeated with this paternalistic attitude, developed as it were because of the very fact, in Lenin's eyes, that the workers did not grasp their real, as distinct from their immediate, interests.[16]

The police and the bureaucracy are two additional institutions of the political system in which marked similarities can be found between the Czarist and Soviet periods. Just as the Czar and Party built parallel hierarchies of authority, so too both systems sought to use the police in similar ways, i.e., for political purposes. Both systems see the police not so much as protectors of the public but of the regime. Thus, they both rely heavily on informers and police spies in the various organizations and groupings of society. They both are designed to prevent treason, to safeguard the status quo. There are some differences, which we shall see below.[17]

Autocratic rule also means centralism: local organs are severely limited by controls from the center; local authorities are strictly subject to central authorities which are themselves more tightly bound to the autocrat. Deviation or disobedience could mean the most severe punishment. The organ of this centralized system is the bureaucracy which has maintained its powerful position almost entirely intact under both systems. The bureaucracy is powerful because it is the link between the ruling center and the people. It dispenses to the latter the will of the center, be it through punishments or favors, taxes or rewards. It is because of its power that the bureaucracy was, and is, permeated with officials personally loyal to the autocrat. There was an effort to break up the bureaucracy immediately after the revolution, since it was particularly hated as the symbol of the state's position over the people. In time, however, Stalin took over the old bureaucratic culture — needed as it were for running things — and restored even the old customs of ranks, titles, and uniforms. Little if anything has changed with regard to the bureaucracy, except that now the Party *apparat* exists as a parallel, and controlling, bureaucracy at all levels; like their predecessors in Czarist times, most bureaucrats are corrupt and untalented people, picked for their political or personal loyalty to the ruler.[18]

Another institutional element of traditional Russian society — and a tradition in itself — is the Russian Orthodox Church.[19] The Church and socialism represent differing world views and different values, each claiming a certain "infallibility." Yet the two live side by side in relative peace today, apparently because there is something in the religious tradition not entirely alien to, or irreconcilable with, the Bolshevik regime.[20]

One characteristic of the Russian Orthodox Church, which made eventual accommodation with the regime possible, was the traditional position of the Church vis-a-vis the state. The Church always accepted subordination to (but collaboration with) the Czar or secular power. The tradition of "rendering unto Caesar" is strong in Orthodoxy, and the Church was willing both to serve and bless the Czar. So, too, in time, the Church blessed Stalin. Moreover, Russian Orthodoxy, in contrast with Roman Catholicism, places more emphasis on liturgy than on dogma. It is not the pure Church Militant of Rome; it is willing to accommodate so long as worship is permitted.

After initial efforts to destroy the Church, the Bolsheviks eventually were willing to arrive at a modus vivendi. Since the Church was willing to accept subordination, to concentrate on liturgy and refrain from interfering in the realm of secular affairs or even beliefs, the Bolsheviks apparently conceded that it could not constitute a serious competitor. Indeed, arousing the population by abolishing the Church might serve merely to reinforce it as a symbol of popular identification. More subtle methods could be used to weaken the Church's potential as a focal point outside the Party. Meanwhile, the Church might be useful to the Soviet state, for it nonetheless was a symbol of the Russian nation. Thus it could and did aid Stalin rally the people with appeals to nationalism in World War II and it has served since, in "peace appeals" and so forth.

On a more theoretical level, the Orthodox tradition had something else to offer the Soviet state, passively if not actively. With its emphasis on the spiritual world, the Church had become a symbol of the long-suffering Russian soul, with Messianic promises of a better world tomorrow. The Church taught the peasant forbearance and patience, the need for sacrifice, and a belief in the next world — the idea that a man's seemingly insignificant existence serves some greater purpose.[21] This was an appeal used by Czarist Russia for its international ventures and it was no less useful to the Communists. The latter took the forms supplied by the tradition and changed the content. Ideology was substituted for religion, bringing a new body of beliefs or catechism, and a new set of rituals. But the individual's continued suffering or sacrifices were deemed part of the building of a better tomorrow. The disruption of personal life caused by industrialization could be justified by this participation in something larger and more important. Even the change in content was not particularly difficult to achieve, given the already mentioned dichotomy characteristic of the Russians. There existed, on the one hand, an admiration for the material achievements and technological progress of the Western world, together, on the other hand, with a belief in the superior spiritual values of the Russian (the Russian soul). These continue to exist side by side in Russia: idolization of the machine but baptism and burial in the Church. Add to this a measure of peasant skepticism, and one has the possibility of a transferal of allegiance from one "religion" to another.

It is of interest to see what remained of traditional Russian society's class structure and elites, once the theoretically egalitarian philosophy of socialism became entrenched.[22] Traditional society was composed primarily of two classes, the nobility and the peasants (the few workers being only peasants once removed), with a growing merchant sub-class. The nobility, however, was not a closed aristocracy into which one had to be born. The Czar could place someone in this class, as he often did with merchants, or expel them from this privileged elite. There were, however, other elites which grew out of this basically two-class society: the bureaucracy, the intelligentsia, and the military. The bureaucracy came mainly from the nobility, since a certain education was required for these positions. As industrialization began in the late nineteenth century, however, and education became slightly more accessible, the bureaucracy became quite mixed. The same was true of the intelligentsia and the military elite as well.

In Soviet society, privileges of one group or another may be less ostentatious or extreme, and there may be more fluidity in society than in Czarist days. Nonetheless, the same basic elites have remained (or, rather, re-emerged after the early revolutionary years) in terms of prestige, income, and social status. Today we have the party *apparat* (bureaucracy), the intelligentsia (including scientists), and the military as elites distinct from the workers, who are perhaps the only new class, and the peasants, still on the bottom.[23] As we have already seen regarding the bureaucracy, many of the symbols and characteristics of these elites, as well as their functions, have persisted.

Although the peasant could, and did, enter the intelligentsia, there was a certain traditional distrust on the part of the peasant regarding the cultured or educated. The resulting gap has persisted even until today and has indeed been exploited by the Communists to facilitate their efforts at silencing the intellectuals.[24] The Russian intelligentsia, however, is traditionally political and activist.[25] By the late nineteenth century, most of the intelligentsia had little patience for the concept of "art for art's sake." Rather, they saw their role as educative, i.e., they were to open the eyes of Russia to the problems and evils of society. Their task was to help improve society or man's fate in that society. This tendency toward political activism, an "involved" art, was not created by the Communists, but it would appear to be at the root of the idea of "socialist realism" which emerged under Stalin. In Soviet society, however, the traditional tendency toward political activism was taken over by the state, for as the critical elite of society — avowedly political — the intelligentsia could not be permitted to remain independent of the regime. The Soviet regime also sought to exploit and even demand the traditionally political function of the intelligentsia, for it needed this group to propagate its view, to rally and indoctrinate the masses. Thus, an "involved" intelligentsia was demanded, but just as every other organization or grouping in society had to serve and reflect the proletarian basis of society, this "involvement" had to be of a certain type only, limited to "positive" political action or limited "criticism in service of the regime."[26] Even with these efforts to harness the intellectuals, this group has in effect retained much of its former role — as in the days of the Czar — underground. It is still the critical element of society, the spokesman for reform and justice, despite the Bolsheviks' offers of privileges in exchange for obedience.

One must include the youth, particularly the students, in this broad category of intelligentsia. The students, too, were traditionally politically oriented in Russia, if for no other reason than that education was the key to places in the bureaucracy.[27] The Czar was as aware of this as the Bolsheviks; both sought to use the youth for their political purposes. In the case of the Czar, the major solution, however, was to limit numbers receiving education. The Bolsheviks needed educated masses for industrialization, and therefore sought the solution in organization of youth. As with the intellectuals, the Soviets have not tried to destroy the politically activist nature of the youth, but rather to harness it toward their own ends and control it. This meant a certain change in content but, after the early years of revolutionary experimentation, the Soviets returned to many aspects of the Czarist educational system, not only in forms but also in content. For example, there was a return to the use of examinations, uniforms, and teaching methods. To be sure, education under the Soviets emphasizes technology and production, but — above virtually everything — there has been a reversion to the former highly nationalistic quality of content.[28]

With regard to the third elite, the military, much also remained the same. In Czarist Russia, the military was a privileged elite living in garrisons somewhat separate from the masses.[29] It was, however, clearly subordinate to the Czar and lacking political power. Today, too, the Russian military establishment is one of the few which has continued to live apart in a type of garrison life. It has the same prestige as formerly and has even returned to the former use of medals and ranks. It is still subordinate to the civil authority and it is still without political power.[30] Granted, the importance of the military — and with it, its ability to have its requests filled — has varied in different periods, just as in Czarist days the military was more important in time of war than in peacetime. Yet both the Czar and the Party took measures to assure continued subordination of the military to the autocrat. The Czar placed military people in civil administrative positions and personally loyal persons in military positions in order to create an interlocking of positions useful to maintain loyalty. The Party has followed much the same pattern: it demands that the important military personnel be Party members and that they work their way up — through the Party. Interlocking and control is further

assured by the system of political officers, i.e., representatives of the
Party in the army, whose task it is to maintain the Party's domination
and control of the military.

When dealing with the other major class of Czarist Russia, the
peasantry, it is more difficult to trace similarities and differences.[31]
There are those who see in the *kolkhoz* of Soviet agriculture nothing
more than a return to, or continuation of, the *obschina* or *mir* of
nineteenth-century Russia. The *mir* was an agricultural community to
which peasants belonged after the end of serfdom in Russia. The serfs
were given small amounts of land, for which they had to make payments and taxes over a period of fifty years. The individual farmer,
however, was not responsible for such payments. Rather the *mir,* or
"village" of farmers, paid as a collective. The Czarist regime used this
system, both to provide a certain stability in agriculture and to better
insure receipt of this money. The *mir* could, from time to time, redis-
tribute land according to family sizes. Members of a household, however, could not leave without permission from the *mir,* and persons
leaving were obliged to send payments back to the *mir.* Farming,
however, was not collective. Each household farmed its own strips of
land — which were more often than not scattered over large distances
— for the purpose of self-sufficiency rather than a market.

By way of similarity to the present status of the peasant, one can
see a continuation of the traditional lack of peasant freedom of movement. The peasant remains tied to the land, able to move only with
difficulty. That a collective or communal spirit — which might have
facilitated or acted as a basis for the formation of *kolkhozy* — was
generated by the *mir* is another question. Aside from the collective
financial obligation, the *mir* was divided individually — each family
serving itself. Indeed, Lenin and most socialists (with the exception of
certain populist schools) vigorously opposed the *mir,* because it was
not communal in any way. It was flagrantly a socio-economic-political
device of the Czars designed to maintain the latter's undiluted central
control. The peasants bitterly opposed it, for they wanted, first and
foremost, land.[32]

The similarity between the *mir* and the *kolkhoz* may indeed be a
merely superficial one, rather than evidence of the continued influence of a tradition upon modern institutions. On the other hand,
one might say that the tradition of autocratic control of the peasantry
conducted through the commune *(mir)* has had a certain continuation
in the autocratic control of the peasant through the *kolkhoz.* Thus
one might speak, not of a continuation of a tradition of collectivism

or a tendency toward collectivism in the tradition, but rather of a tradition, or tendency in the tradition, toward centralism and autocratic control of agriculture.

There are two additional related facets of Czarist society which may be said to have aided the introduction of socialism, but they were not so much elements of tradition as objective factors.[33] The peasant's lack of land was seen by Lenin as a reason the Russian peasant should be interested in uniting, and one might argue that, as they had no land to speak of, a strong tradition of private ownership in agriculture was one obstacle the Russian socialists did *not* have to face. The second factor was the breakdown of the family unit, which was occurring with nascent industrialization. The strong family unit was swiftly passing away and with it another obstacle to collectivism in the countryside.

The fact is that neither of these situations greatly aided the Bolsheviks with regard to the peasantry, although they may have contributed to the attitude of at least some Bolsheviks toward collectivization. However, the fact that the peasant had no land was to become an important factor in the introduction of socialism for another reason — one which Lenin on some occasions seemed to appreciate. The point was not that the peasants did or did not have land of their own and therefore opposed or did not oppose collectivization because of some private property at stake. The Russian peasant always felt that he *should* have land.[34] If there is any tradition among the Russian peasants regarding land, it is an anti-communal tradition, for the peasant believed that God meant for each man to have his share of land. There was a basic injustice afoot which had simply to be set right, i.e., the peasant should and would be returned his land.[35] It was this strong belief among the peasants which led Lenin to incorporate land reform in his program when he realized that an alliance with the peasantry was needed. Later, for both ideological and economic reasons, collectivization was introduced against almost all the natural tendencies or traditions of the peasants.[36] For this reason it was a violent and extremely costly measure. The only tradition "respected" and maintained was that of centralized autocratic control of the countryside.

The last aspect of traditional Russian society we wish to follow into Soviet society is nationalism. Socialism clearly has a universalist side, which may or may not be emphasized given the particular socialist movement. It would be inaccurate to say that Soviet socialism has no regard for this universalist side of socialism, but it has given it a particularly Russian characteristic. In effect, the Soviets pursue a type of "nationalist" universalism or a Messianic internationalism. This may be explained, in part, by the traditional Russian feeling (often nurtured by the Czars) of spiritual superiority to the rest of the world. The Russian felt that he might learn from other nations, but he would add something vital, more spiritually pure, of his own. The Soviets exhibit much of this same attitude. The Soviet Union (even if not by original intention) must be the leader of the international Communist movement. Moscow possesses the truth for the movement — and therefore for mankind — even if it still must learn from Western technology.

Thus Soviet patriotism, born of Russian nationalism, serves an internationalist goal.[37] The former basic point of identity, however, has remained unchanged. The Russian still feels Russian before all else, and he is still outspoken and deeply nationalist. There are numerous plausible explanations for the continuation of the strongly nationalist tradition into Soviet society, one of which may simply be that the Bolsheviks found these feelings too deeply and strongly entrenched to risk prolonged efforts of expurgation. It would have been difficult to ignore the average Russian's suspicion of foreigners and attachment to the country. Yet, even as early as their first year in power, the Bolsheviks actually exploited and encouraged this nationalism when they called for support of the "socialist fatherland" against the Germans and, later, against the intervening countries during the civil war.[38] Indeed, they often appealed to nationalism for the purposes of staying in power and strengthening their position. This, in Soviet rhetoric, implied strengthening the world movement, since Russia was the bulwark of this movement.

Both in the time of the last Czar and in the time of the Bolsheviks, industrialization itself had a nationalist element to it, an element retained to this day. In both cases it was closely connected with the need to be economically strong, so as to stand up to outside enemies, e.g., the Czar's pronouncements when wars were not going well; Stalin's "socialism in one country" to combat the capitalist encirclement; and even Khrushchev's great push to overcome the West in the 1960's. Both the Czar and the Bolsheviks appealed to nationalism to achieve this economic progress.[39] In both cases the initiative came from the center, from the government or regime, so that in both cases a certain private initiative to stir the people to work for this goal was missing. To remedy this, both appealed to the Russian's love of and pride in his country — with all the Messianic overtones of bringing the world

something more and better than mere technological progress. The
Bolsheviks also used the nationalist appeal to maintain a certain
internal stability (a device not unknown to the Czars), i.e., arousing
fear of outside enemies in order to gain domestic unity and support, as
well as a willingness to sacrifice, on the part of the people. Indeed, the
Soviets made what at least in hindsight appears to have been calcu-
lated efforts to appeal to the Messianic nationalism of the Russian
people in order to overcome the traditional tendencies toward passivity and resignation. These last would have been inimical to the
extensive industrialization of a vast country and the building of a new
society — which demanded the active participation of the masses.[40]

Until now we have looked at certain elements of traditional Russian
society, particularly with regard to their contribution to Soviet
society. It is, however, difficult to determine the specific reasons for
the continuation of this or that tradition. With the possible exception
of traditional nationalism and of the traditional roles of the intelligentsia and youth, it would appear that the Bolsheviks did not permit
this continuation out of hesitancy to combat such strong or deeply
entrenched traditions. Rather it would seem that the deep roots of
most of these elements influenced (be it consciously or subconscious-
ly) the selection of the type of system the Bolsheviks introduced.
Indeed, they may even have served as some sort of examples or guidelines, given the Russians' almost total lack of experience of any other
system. To be sure, the Soviets gave these traditional elements new
content; they would never admit to having continued or returned to
any of them. Yet, in many areas, the Russians had never known any
way other than the traditional autocratic one, and they tended, perhaps, to understand socialism in a specifically Russian way — a way in
which many of these elements of the tradition seemed perfectly
acceptable or logical even within the framework of socialism. Certain
traditions, such as the religious or autocratic traditions, may even have
facilitated the installation of what the Bolsheviks understood as socialism.

The above leaves us, however, with two major questions: What *did*
socialism provide the Russians with? (Or, is there a difference between
the two societies?) And, was there really a continuation of traditional
elements or, in fact, a break in the tradition and then a return to
earlier traditions? The latter is a reference to traditions which were
part of the traditional Russian society that had, in fact, largely
changed by the time the socialists came to power. The second question might therefore be put in this way: Was there not a return, under

the Bolsheviks, to earlier traditions which had already been replaced by "new" traditions or tendencies until the Bolsheviks came and reversed the process?

It is possible to define the term tradition in numerous ways. In this chapter we have referred to the term tradition both as something static — such as traditional society — and as tendencies or a process. In nineteenth-century Russia, from the 1860's onwards, the old traditions, or traditional society, was in the process of disintegration.[41] Industrialization was bringing enormous changes in the composition of the elites, in the importance of the family, in the authority of the Church. It was creating political demands and activism in the place of traditional peasant passivity. New tendencies were emerging, even though in reaction to, or at least as a result of, the old society.

Indeed, it would appear that traditions were but a part of an historical process, themselves constantly changing and developing in one continuous process of history. The society with which socialism was confronted in 1917 was a society straining away from the traditions — away from autocracy, away from the Church, away from "communes," away from the old elites, away from passivity and long-suffering patient obedience, away from centrally organized life. It was straining toward freedom from the restrictive bonds of any institutional framework, be it the *mir,* the Church, an ideology, the state, or even a class. At the same time the government itself was responding to these tendencies. It was moving — however limited the extent and pace — in the direction of innovations to satisfy these new tendencies by programs such as land reform and representational government. Just as the Czar tried to neutralize the revolutionary potential of the changing society by belatedly introducing some of the necessary changes in the political institutions, so too the Bolsheviks grasped these new tendencies among the population and sought both to exploit and encourage them in the interests of dealing a death blow to the old regime. Thus they encouraged the demands even of the peasants, and they could easily discredit the government's belated efforts at liberalism on two counts — first on the grounds that the people opposed the state or the very continuation of central government, and secondly on theoretical grounds whereby evolution was rejected in favor of revolution as the only way to introduce genuine change.

Prior to the revolution and for a brief time following it, everything that had made socialism attractive was connected with the "new" traditions, i.e., activism and revolution. The old traditions, however, proved stronger, and only that part of socialism which fit the old traditions was employed when the Bolsheviks finally began to institutionalize socialist society, i.e., centralism, paternalism, Messianism, futurism. What of those aspects of socialism which did not have a counterpart in the old tradition — collectivism, popular participation, universalism? In a sense they were discarded — in practice at least, although not in theory. There is no genuine collectivism in Soviet society, nor its opposite — individualism — though there is an appeal to and indoctrination toward collectivism, particularly in the educational system. Rather, there is centralism and paternalism. In the same sense, popular participation is merely a facade of participation based, in reality, upon obedience. There is not a genuine internationalism but national superiority (except insofar as is necessary for keeping subject nationalities subordinate).

Thus, in a broad sense, there has been a return to the old tradition in the interpretation and resulting selective application of socialism. The Bolsheviks went backward, as it were, breaking the natural direction in which Russian society was developing in the early twentieth century. They ended, for example, both the government tendency toward liberalism and, for obvious reasons, the people's tendency toward anarchism.

This break with and return to the past did, nonetheless, bring with it innovations both in form and content. These innovations came with the introduction of a new element in Russian society, that of totalitarianism, for Czarist Russia was merely autocratic. Marxism can provide the basis for this added element, if it is interpreted in a certain way.[42] Marxism is a "total" philosophy, in that it offers a view of society in its totality and as an indivisible totality in which *all* is connected with the economic base. There are no independent spheres of society in the Marxist theory of superstructure and base. Moreover, it is a total world view, universalist and "scientific," that is, a world view that presumably is objectively true and applicable to all. Indeed it calls for a return of man's universal human nature, necessary for the harmony of the classless Communist society freed of alienating contradictions and class-induced inhumanities. There is nothing in this theory, however, which necessitated totalitarianism or a political dictatorship. Indeed Marx sought primarily to free man in every sense of the term.

The Russian socialists were influenced, apparently, by what they knew: centralism, authoritarianism, paternalism. They introduced primarily political socialism as distinct from the economic stream, i.e., strong political control and central planning over the economic sphere as distinct from a preoccupation with economic equalization of distribution and political rights. In effect, the Bolsheviks took the totality of the Marxist economic framework and added to it the Russian tradition of strong political control from the center. Their interpretation of the base-superstructure (at least under Stalin and subsequently) might be described thus: If art as part of the superstructure is determined by the economic base and the base is subordinate to the political center, then art too is subordinate to the political center. This relationship has been formulated by Stalin in his *Problems of Leninism* to explain the center's role, for example, in the collectivization of agriculture and the whole concept of the "transmission belt."[43] This last concept maintains that all institutions of society (government, youth groups, the educational system, trade unions, etc.) are but transmission belts for the will of the Party, for the Party is the embodiment of the proletariat and in a proletarian society all institutions of the society must be proletarian in nature, i.e., representative of this group which is in fact embodied by the Party.[44]

This element of "totality," or totalitarianism, was added to traditional Russian autocracy. Czarist society had never demanded total integration. The Czar did not strive to bring under his command every area of life. Indeed, there were even certain limitations upon the Czar: e.g., occasionally revolutionary treatises did get published; courts often heard dramatic defense pleas and even judged, occasionally, in favor of the accused. The Czar did not demand conformity, but merely obedience. The Czar did not care, for example, if the peasants were passive, so long as they were obedient. The people did not have to think like the government; it was sufficient that they paid taxes and did not revolt. Thus it was not a direct threat to the Czar if the peasant had loyalties "outside" — to the Church, to the family — in addition to his loyalty to the state. Czarist government was a negative rule designed to maintain and protect the status quo.

There is a difference between this type of rule and the activist, Messianic ideology of Bolshevism. The latter demands not only obedience to and protection of the status quo but also the building of a new world. The difference can be felt, for example, not only in the different attitude toward the peasants — i.e., the demand for a total and exclusive commitment — but also in the use of the police. The police in Czarist times were used for preserving and bolstering the status quo. Although a political role, this nonetheless accorded them less power than that of a police used to seek out and destroy all vestiges of the former system in the name of building the new society — and the new man. The difference between preserving the status quo and building the "new society" is the demand for an active commitment on the part of the population. To ensure this, a degree of social control unknown in Czarist times had to be maintained.[45]

Thus the difference between Czarist autocracy and that of the Soviets would seem to be the element of totalitarianism introduced by the Bolsheviks as a distortion of Marx's view of the totality of society. Yet this very distortion would appear to be the contribution of the Russian autocratic tradition, a contribution seen under the Soviets in the emphasis upon political power as superior to economic organization, the economy subordinate to the political center.

What resulted is an integration of socialism with Czarism, the melding of "economic oneness" of Marxism with autocratic centralist rule. Together they formed Bolshevism, or a new tradition of Soviet totalitarianism. Like any tradition, this new one, too, has undergone changes and variations.[46] Nonetheless, this is the model identified with the Soviet Union and the type of socialism that the Russians have striven to introduce elsewhere in the world and subsequently preserve.

NOTES

1 Nicolas Berdyaev, *The Origins of Russian Communism* (Ann Arbor: University of Michigan Press, 1955), pp. 7–18.

2 Cf. F.C. Barghoorn, "Some Russian Images of the West," in Cyril Black (ed.), *The Transformation of Russian Society* (Cambridge, Mass.: Harvard University Press, 1960), pp. 574–86.

3 Berdyaev, *The Origins. . .*, p. 143, 127 ff.

4 R. Tucker, "The Image of Dual Russia," in Black (ed.), *The Transformation. . .*, pp. 587–605.

5 Cf. Franco Venturi, *Roots of Revolution* (New York: Grosset and Dunlop, 1966), passim; Adam Ulam, *The Unfinished Revolution* (New York: Random House, 1960), pp. 22–89; and Leopold Haimson, "The Parties and the State," in Black (ed.), *The Transformation. . .*, pp. 110–44.

6 For this and following historical material, cf. the histories of Russia: Michal Florinsky, *Russia*, Vols. I–II (New York: Macmillan, 1969); Michael Karpovich, *Imperial Russia 1801–1917* (New York: H. Holt, 1932); and George Vernadsky, *A History of Russia* (New Haven: Yale University Press, 1948).

7 Cf. Haimson's essay in Black, or his book *Russian Marxists and the Origins of Bolshevism* (Cambridge, Mass.: Harvard University Press, 1955). Cf. also Berdyaev, *The Origins. . .*.

8 Ulam, *The Unfinished Revolution. . .*, pp. 107–32.

9 For Lenin's view of the dictatorship of the proletariat and the stages of communism, cf. his *State and Revolution* and *What Is To Be Done*; for Marx on this subject, cf. his *Critique of the Gotha Programme* and *Capital*, Vol. III.

10 For Lenin's concept of the Party, cf. his *What Is To Be Done;* Alfred Meyer, *Leninism* (New York: Praeger, 1963); Leonard Schapiro, *The Communist Party of the Soviet Union* (London: University Paperbacks, 1970) and *The Origin of the Communist Autocracy* (New York: Praeger, 1965); Venturi, *Roots of Revolution. . .;* Ulam, *The Unfinished Revolution. . .;* and Haimson, *Russian Marxists. . .*.

11 On this and the following, cf. Derek Scott, *Russian Political Institutions* (New York: Praeger, 1961), pp. 21–29; John Hazard, *The Soviet System of Government* (Chicago: University of Chicago Press, 1957), pp. 169–82; Merle Fainsod, *How Russia Is Ruled* (Cambridge, Mass.: Harvard University Press, 1967), pp. 349–85.

12 Cf. Scott, *Russian Political Institutions. . .*, pp. 136–51; Schapiro, *The Communist Party. . .;* and Leonard Schapiro, *The Government and Politics of the Soviet Union* (New York: Vintage, 1967), passim.

13 Cf. *ibid.*, pp. 133–44; Harold Berman, *Justice in the USSR* (New York: Vintage Books, 1963); Ivo Lapenna, *State and Law: Soviet and Yugoslav Theory* (New Haven: Yale University Press, 1964); and Hazard, *The Soviet System. . .*, pp. 151–68, 193; and John Hazard, "The Courts and the Legal System," in Black (ed.), *The Transformation. . .*, pp. 145–63.

14 *Literaturnaia Gazeta* of August 18, 1964, tells of an interesting discussion between a judge and a local "prokurator." The judge says that the prokurator's office investigates and the court alone decides if a man is guilty and what his punishment should be.

The prokurator replies: Such a theory means that the prokurator's office sometimes brings innocent people to court. Is this possible? No, it is not. The investigators of the procuracy accuse and bring to court only those who are guilty in their eyes — the eyes of the authorities! The court merely decides the extent of the guilt and the proper punishment.

15 Cf. Zbigniew Brzezinski, "The Patterns of Autocracy," in Black (ed.), *The Transformation. . .*, pp. 93–109.

16 For a discussion of paternalism in Soviet law, cf. Harold Berman, *Justice in the USSR. . ..*

17 For police, cf. Schapiro, *The Government and Politics. . .*, pp. 133–44; Hazard, *The Soviet System . . .*, pp. 61–70, 194; and S. Monas, "The Political Police," in Black (ed.), *The Transformation . . .*, pp. 164–90.

18 For bureaucracy, cf. J.A. Armstrong, *The Soviet Bureaucratic Elite* (New York: Praeger, 1959); Fainsod, *How Russia Is Ruled. . .*, pp. 176–208, 386–420; and A. Edeen, "The Civil Service: Its Composition and Status," in Black (ed.), *The Transformation. . .*, pp. 274–91.

19 Cf. E. Benz, *The Eastern Orthodox Church* (New York: Doubleday, 1963).

20 John Curtiss, *The Russian Church and the Soviet State* (Boston: Little, Brown, 1953); M. Spinka, *The Church in Soviet Russia* (London: Oxford University Press, 1956); Sir John Meynard, *The Russian Peasant* (New York: Collier Books, 1942), pp. 452–77; Sergei Pushkarev, *The Emergence of Modern Russia, 1801–1917* (New York: H. Holt, 1963), pp. 90–95, 331–36; and J. Curtiss, "Church and State," in Black (ed.), *The Transformation. . .*, pp. 405–24.

21 Cf., for example, Berdyaev, *The Origins. . .*, pp. 158–88.

22 Cf. R. Feldmesser, "Social Classes and Political Structure," and A. Inkeles, "Social Stratification in the Modernization of Russia," both in Black (ed.), *The Transformation . . .*, pp. 235–52 and 338–52.

23 Cf. Hazard, *The Soviet System . . .*, passim; Alex Inkeles and Raymond A. Bauer, *The Soviet Citizen: Daily Life in a Totalitarian Society* (Cambridge, Mass.: Harvard University Press, 1959), pp. 67–100, 279–320.

24 Berdyaev, *The Origins. . .*, p. 141.

25 Cf. Richard Pipes, *The Russian Intelligentsia* (New York: Columbia University Press, 1961); Venturi, *Roots of Revolution . . .*, passim; Donald Treadgold, *Twentieth Century Russia* (Chicago: Rand McNally, 1964), pp. 28–39; and G. Fischer, "The Intelligentsia and Russia," in Black (ed.), *The Transformation . . .*, pp. 253–73.

26 Cf. Adam Yarmolinsky, *Literature Under Communism* (Bloomington, Ind.: Indiana University Press, 1960).

27 Cf. Venturi, *Roots of Revolution . . .*, particularly pp. 220–31.

28 For youth and education under the Soviets, cf. Allen Kassof, *The Soviet*

Youth Program (Cambridge, Mass.: Harvard University Press, 1965); and G. Bereday, "Education: Organization and Values Since 1917," in Black (ed.), *The Transformation . . .*, pp. 353–70.

29 R. Garthoff, "The Military as a Social Force," in Black (ed.), *The Transformation . . .*, pp. 323–37.

30 On the role of the Soviet military, cf. John Erikson, *The Soviet High Command* (London: Macmillan, 1962); Roman Kolkowicz, *The Soviet Military and the Communist Party* (Princeton: Princeton University Press, 1967); Hazard, *The Soviet System . . .*, pp. 138–50; Fainsod, *How Russia Is Ruled . . .*, pp. 463–500.

31 For peasants under the Czars, cf. Meynard, *The Russian Peasant . . .*; Jerome Blum, *Lord and Peasant in Russia* (Princeton: Princeton University Press, 1961); Karpovich, *Imperial Russia . . .*, pp. 35–61; Pushkarev, *The Emergence . . .*, pp. 28–44, 125–46, 202–18, 264–74.

32 For comparison, see L. Volin, "The Russian Peasant," in Black (ed.), *The Transformation . . .*, pp. 292–311.

33 Cf. Berdyaev, *The Origins . . .*, pp. 136–39.

34 *Ibid.*, pp. 135–37.

35 Amalrik describes the peasant's concept of justice as the feeling that "nobody should live better than I do!" Andrei Amalrik, *Will the Soviet Union Survive Until 1984?* (New York: Harper and Row, 1971), p. 35.

36 Cf. H.S. Dinerstein, *Communism and the Russian Peasant* (New York: The Free Press, 1955); Hazard, *The Soviet System . . .*, pp. 106–12; Fainsod, *How Russia Is Ruled . . .*, pp. 526–76.

37 Cf. F.C. Barghoorn, *Soviet Russian Nationalism* (London: Oxford University Press, 1956).

38 E.H. Carr, *The Bolshevik Revolution*, Vol. III (London: Macmillan, 1953), pp. 73–116.

39 A. Gerschenkron, "Patterns of Russian Economic Development," and T. Parsons, "Some Principal Characteristics of Industrial Societies," both in Black (ed.), *The Transformation . . .*, pp. 42–71 and 13–41.

40 For the issue of nationalism and the other nationalities, cf., for example, Richard Pipes, *The Formation of the Soviet Union* (New York: Atheneum, 1968); R. Schlesinger, *The Nationalities Problem and Soviet Administration* (London: Routledge and Kegan Paul, 1956).

41 For the pre-revolutionary period, cf. Ulam, *The Unfinished Revolution . . .*; the histories already cited by Florinsky, Karpovich, and Vernadsky; Meynard, *The Russian Peasant . . .*; Treadgold, *Twentieth Century Russia . . .*, pp. 105–117; Schapiro, *Government and Politics . . .*, pp. 15–56.

42 For differences between and combinations of Russian autocracy and Soviet totalitarianism, cf. Z. Brzezinski and C. Friedrich, *Totalitarian Dictatorship and Autocracy* (New York: Praeger, 1965); Schapiro, *The Origin of the Communist Autocracy;* Treadgold, *Twentieth Century Russia . . .*, pp. 3–10; Adam Ulam, *The New Face of Soviet Totalitarianism* (New York: Praeger, 1963); and Brzezinski, "The Patterns of Autocracy," in Black (ed.), *The Transformation . . .*, pp. 93–109.

43 Stalin's *Problems of Leninism* (Moscow: Foreign Language Publishing House, 1953), pp. 97-100, 102-18. Cf. also *Economic Problems in the USSR* (New York: International Publishers, 1952), pp. 7-22.

44 Stalin, *Foundations of Leninism* (New York: International Publishers, 1939), pp. 125-27.

45 E. Vogel, "Voluntarism and Social Control," in Donald Treadgold, *Soviet and Chinese Communism* (Seattle: University of Washington Press, 1967), pp. 168-84.

46 For a discussion of the possibilities of a new tradition developing in a "post-mobilization" period, see Alexander Dallin and George W. Breslauer, "Political Terror in the Post-Mobilization Stage," in Chalmers Johnson (ed.), *Change in Communist Systems* (Stanford: Stanford University Press, 1970), pp. 191–214, or Samuel P. Huntington, "Social and Institutional Dynamics of One-Party Systems," in Huntington and Clement H. Moore (eds.), *Authoritarian Politics in Modern Society* (New York: Basic Books, 1970), pp. 3–47.

NATIONAL TRADITIONS AND SOCIALISM IN EASTERN EUROPE: THE CASES OF CZECHOSLOVAKIA AND YUGOSLAVIA

GALIA GOLAN

THE DEMOCRATIC-LIBERAL TRADITION IN THE CZECH LANDS

I

The figure of Jan Hus, the man and his movement, stands as the greatest single influence upon the formation of Czech traditions, i.e., the character, values, and attitudes of this people. A Protestant movement which began 100 years before the Reformation elsewhere in Europe, the Hussite movement held equality as its major tenet. All men, not just the clergy, were capable of understanding the will of God. Moreover, all men were free, for there were no inherent differences between them to justify the subservience of one man to another. Thus there could be no justifiable privileged elites, including the Church. This tenet also implied tolerance of all men, be they Jews, heathens, or Christians, and from this belief in tolerance a devotion to humanitarianism derived. Moreover, if all men were equal and might know the will of God, they had a certain intellectual capacity, i.e. reason; they need only use it.

Individualism, too, was involved, for if men were equal and capable of critical reason, their rights to judge for themselves were to be respected. No establishment or institution should presume to tell the individual what to do or think; each man's view was of value and, as a result, each man had a right to his say. The Hussite watchword, "Truth Will Prevail," was the expression of this, for it meant that there is a truth and that each man has the right to seek it — in other words, it is not that the authority has the right to dictate the truth, but rather truth which is more important than any authority.[1]

The above tenets had, of course, socio-political implications. Such concepts as individualism, the critical use of reason, truth versus authority (the issue of justice), equality, and the basic freedom of man were not exclusive to Hus but, in time, the foundations of modern liberalism.

Still another element of the Hussite movement which has been of importance in the formation of the Czech tradition is the element of nationalism.[2] This was not the romantic type of nationalism of later (nineteenth- and twentieth-century) conservative movements, but the type of nationalism more closely akin to the later liberal nationalism of Mazzini. Part of the idea of the reformation movement was to write in the vernacular so that all men might understand. Hus believed that if one values each and every man, the holy works must be presented in a language accessible to all. Thus Hus himself wrote simply and in the dialect of Prague. This was not purely a philosophical stand, for in those days there was a struggle between German elements and the Bohemians – in the University, in the kingdom, and in the church. In time, the reform movement became identified with the Czechs, and the Church of Rome with the Germans. Indeed, with the Hussite wars, it was the Czechs defending the reform against "foreign" protectors of the Church of Rome. Traces of this basic division may be seen even today in the generally anti-clerical attitude of the Czechs, despite the forced conversions to Catholicism during the Austro-Hungarian rule.

The Hussite wars introduced another element to the nascent tradition: the idea that the Czechs have a role to play or something to offer the world.[3] A type of Messianism, this was not the romantic superiority of Russian Messianism, nor an aggressive, proselytizing faith. The Czechs saw themselves not necessarily as better than the rest of the world, but as a unit in the world with something to contribute to the whole, with a positive role in the struggle for truth in Europe.[4] As in the case of Czech nationalism, so, too, Czech "Messianism" was permeated with the liberal values of tolerance, humanism, and a belief in the individual worth of man, as distinct from the romantic conservative notions of glory, superiority, and purity.

With the ideals of equality, humanism, and the value of man, in time there grew a tendency toward pacifism, a preference for the use of reason as distinct from the use of violence. This called for direct contact with the people and the use of persuasion rather than coercion, passive resistance instead of revolt, in the belief that Truth Will Prevail.[5] The idea was not, however, non-resistance; indeed, the Czechs fought many wars and won, until 1620. Having lost, however, the defeated must avoid futile violence. Instead of rebellion, patience was advocated. A strong feeling that "this too will pass" characterized the attitude connected with the belief in the ultimate victory of truth and reason.[6] Such an attitude did not mean no resistance, for this was to be a struggle for ideas. But just what form this struggle would take was debatable. The tradition contained both activist and pacifist elements, but nowhere does one find the passive resignation of the Russian peasant. The ideas of Hus were permeated with the idea of participation and indeed his movement was taken up by the people. The Czech attitude was, in fact, somewhere between the heroic rebelliousness of Serbian nationalism and the superior but passive resignation of the Russian. In the face of foreign domination, the Czechs strove to protect, preserve, and develop their national identity, resisting assimilation, so as to have something to contribute as a people.

Additionally, if one believed in the basic worth of the individual and individual use of reason, then one valued education as the means by which to develop and encourage the inborn ability to reason.[7] Thus education became an important attribute for the Czechs and under the Austro-Hungarian Empire, it took on a national aspect, as the way in which to be worthy, as a people, of freedom. It was argued that one must continuously revitalize the qualities being offered as a people so as to justify the demands for a separate existence as a nation.

In the eighteenth century, the Czech nation began to show signs of apathy, the passive resistance side of the tradition gaining the ascendancy and emerging as resignation. The enlightenment in Europe, however, brought a revival of the positive-activist ideals of the Hussite tradition.[8] This included the long-lived opposition to the Church of Rome, opposition to German culture or rule, and opposition to enforced authority (e.g., the Austrian police). With these came the idea that one must not only protect that which is Czech but fight for it. This was still not a cry for revolt, but it was a cry for the reawakening of the Czechs for a disciplined struggle for independence. The revival focused, again, on the idea of the Czech contribution, based on a background of humanitarianism and regard for justice, reason, and education.[9] The emphasis was on content and the need for a program, as distinct from mere demagogic cries for nationalist identity.

In this, one could see still another element of the Czech tradition as it developed under the Austrians — realism, which, combined with the value of education and the emphasis on content, produced an interest in discipline as distinct from anarchy. It was the idea of discipline which stood behind the formation of the Czech Sokol gymnastic organization in the nineteenth century. This discipline, implied perhaps by Hus' belief in reason, was to be physical as well as mental, so that the Czechs might be ready in all aspects for freedom.[10] While the Sokol was to be the preserver of the nation's heritage or identity, it maintained that the past was no guarantee of a nation's right to exist. Only the present activity and health, both physical and spiritual, of a nation could re-earn for a people the right to independent existence. This element of discipline was not to be confused, however, with simple obedience, which was repugnant to the whole tradition of reason versus arbitrary authority and of individual worth.

II

Many of the above-mentioned characteristics distinguished Czech nationalism from that of the Russians, for example. The Czechs were aware of this distinction, yet they sought to identify themselves as Slavs, in opposition to the Germanic influences of their history. Aware that their national traditions included certain positive qualities missing in the great Slav nation, they saw this as their contribution to "Slavdom."[11] As the nineteenth-century Czech journalist Karel Havlicek put it, the Czechs "can also work for ourselves to develop our nationality, and in thus serving the idea of liberty which Russia does not know, exercise a good influence upon her."[12] The identification with Slav nationalism or Pan-Slavism was problematic for the Czechs, however, for Pan-Slavism, with its romantic notions of a great Slav state, was a rather conservative movement.[13] Indeed, T.G. Masaryk struggled to maintain liberal values as an integral part of Czech nationalism and the struggle for independence, much as the Czechs had represented these values within the Austro-Hungarian Empire itself.[14]

The structure of Czech society was both influenced by and played a role in the formation of Czech tradition. The Czech tradition was fundamentally democratic or egalitarian. Hus spoke to all classes and opposed all privileges, hierarchies, aristocracies, and "establishments." So, too, the Czech revival of the nineteenth century, as the continuation of the liberal ideals of Hus, was an anti-aristocratic, multi-class movement. More accurately, it was a movement of most of the people: there was no category such as "the masses."[15] Sokol, for example, was opposed to elitism and open to all. Moreover, given the emphasis upon education and reason, a relatively high cultural level was attained among all elements of even the pre-industrial society. As a result, the philosophical-cultural and even material gaps between classes, as they formed, were not as large as elsewhere in Eastern Europe.

Industry came early to the Czech lands, and in the nineteenth century there was a highly developed Czech bourgeoisie.[16] In time, society was composed of only a small landed aristocracy which quite early lost its power to a large bourgeois middle class. In addition, the first Czechoslovak Republic contained a large and relatively well-off working class, and a similarly well-off peasantry which was small by East European standards. The ruling elite was the large middle class, which included the commercial interests, intellectuals, and bureaucrats. The commercial interests or capitalists were associated with German and Hungarian nationals who dominated, though not in numbers, this class. Thus, what might have been a class conflict often found expression in the broader nationality issue.

The intellectuals, who formed part of the middle class, came from both the workers and peasants. The gap was therefore not as large as elsewhere, particularly given the high cultural level of the population as a whole. The bureaucracy displayed greater similarity to a Western civil service than to the corrupt and powerful bureaucracies of the East. The very fact that the peasants were less backward than elsewhere reduced the potential for power of the bureaucrat, as did the traditions of participation and anti-autocracy.

The relative homogeneity of the society (with the exception of the small aristocracy), due both to the identity of values and ideals born of the Hussite tradition and to the common struggle for national independence, was of significance for the later confrontation with socialism.[17] Also important was the gap between the people (bourgeoisie, workers, peasants, intellectuals) on the one hand, and the Church on the other hand. The Church was denied a significant role in society, not only because of the traditional disdain for arbitrary authority, but also because of the historical association of the Church with the Germans and, subsequently, the Austrian Empire.

Another significant aspect of Czech society was the dominant role of intellectuals in the national liberation struggle.[18] The Hussite movement began and even centered in the University; the nineteenth-century revival was led by intellectuals; and the movement for a state also found its leadership among the intellectuals, e.g., T.G. Masaryk. While intellectuals traditionally played a political role in Eastern Europe, the long history and depth of the Czech tradition, given the relative homogeneity of Czech society both in terms of cultural level and values, gave its intellectuals still greater possibilities than elsewhere, Certainly the philosopher-President "tradition" was both a manifestation of and an influencing factor in the attitude of the Czech society to the Communists of the 1960's.

III

The last element of the Czech democratic tradition of importance to this discussion was the "concretization" of the tradition in the state created in 1918. The figure of T.G. Masaryk stands out in this connection, yet Masaryk was but the modern embodiment of the traditional ideals. His was a conscious effort to keep alive the best of the Czech tradition against the pitfalls and influences of romantic nationalism.[19] Thus he advocated all of the Hussite values, with the added elements of discipline and realism. He looked to Western liberal institutions as the most suitable counterparts of the tradition. Thus he built a strong parliamentary democracy based on a humanitarian program of social welfare, land reform, educational reform, tolerance and respect for individual rights.[20]

As distinct from Russian paternalism, however, Czech democracy nurtured, for example, a strong trade union movement, based upon the traditional Czech attitude of struggling for and earning one's rights. The legal system of the Republic was patterned after the French and the British.[21] It contained a Constitutional Court which placed the law above the political powers, in the form of an institution independent of the government. Likewise, an Administrative Court to protect individuals from administrative injustice constituted still another check on the political organs. Given the relative homogeneity of society and the relatively high cultural-economic level of all the classes, class warfare was limited, even insofar as the political parties were concerned.[22]

The tradition provided a strong thrust toward progressivism and enlightenment values, which led to the establishment of one of the earliest comprehensive state social welfare programs, including unemployment and social insurance, etc.[23] It also led to certain features common to socialism, such as government aid to industry, particularly during the depression of the 1930's. While government-directed industry was a feature of autocratic Russia, however, Czechoslovakia differed in that state intervention came not so much to gain control or profits or to strengthen the state for ventures abroad, but rather to help local (as distinct from foreign) capital and to ensure egalitarianism through the use of tax reform, so that economic progress — or crises — would not be at the expense of the peasant, as so often was the case elsewhere in Eastern Europe.[24]

The same marked progressive tendencies could be observed among the peasants, among whom the idea of cooperative farming gained a good deal of support.[25] Yet because of the individualistic tradition the type of cooperativism advocated was more similar to Western, i.e., United States, cooperativism than to Soviet collectivism. The peasant was willing to go into a cooperative because he did not see this as a threat to his individualism. He entered on the terms of what he, as an individual, could contribute. He did not build a collective above the individual, or some sort of bureaucracy or *apparat* which could destroy him as an individual or stand above him in a relationship of alienated power.

This same attitude could be seen in the foreign policy of the first Republic.[26] There was a strong internationalism, but not at the expense of nationalism. It was, rather, the idea of international cooperation, of individual nations working together, each contributing what it is qualified to contribute. Thus, national identity or sovereignty was not denied in the name of some higher institution or authority, nor, however, was nationalism emphasized to the exclusion of genuine cooperation. This attitude was not a simple one and is often confused with the traditional romantic nationalism of the Poles or the Russians.[27]

Thus the "nationalistic" aspect (or lack thereof) of the Czechoslovak Communist reform movement has often been misunderstood. Indeed, during the 1968 liberalization, Slovak nationalists blamed the Czech's "internationalist" concept of nationalism for the latter's failure to appreciate Slovak demands.[28] Prague's foreign policy in the first Republic was also Western-orientated, despite the sympathy for, and identification with, the Slavic world. The general feeling in interwar Czechoslovakia was that there was little to learn from the Slavic east. The Bolshevik experiment was considered an interesting one, of no particular relevance or applicability to the advanced and progressive Czech society. Indeed, Soviet terrorism made it repugnant to the humanistic tradition of the Czechs, but this facet was not exaggerated or emphasized, given the basic, if somewhat condescending, sympathy for the Russians.

There were also tendencies in inter-war Czechoslovak society which ran counter to the democratic Czech tradition, particularly in the realm of the policy on nationalities. While tolerance was practiced regarding certain minorities such as Jews (and Communists), other nationalities were strongly subject to the rule of the Czechs.[29] On a practical level, this attitude toward the Slovaks and Hungarians, for example, was probably the result of the different levels of cultural-economic development of these peoples, as distinct from the advanced Czechs. This could not explain the attitude toward the large German minority, but relations with both the Germans and Hungarians was marked by the years of resentment during which the Czechs and Slovaks had struggled for independence from the Austro-Hungarian Empire and against Germanization and Magyarization (in Slovakia).

Thus, for many reasons, the long struggle for Czech independence — with all its liberal values and tradition — led to a situation in which the liberal promises of T.G. Masaryk regarding most non-Czechs were not implemented.[30] Moreover, the new Republic was highly centralistic with only limited self-government, despite the traditions of participation and democracy.[31] Here, too, the reasons may have been the relative backwardness of Slovak and Hungarian institutions, such as their lack of political experience and cadres, as well as the desire to preserve and bolster the independence of the Czechs.[32]

The Czechoslovak parliamentary system was also characterized by strong party discipline and party government.[33] Party members were bound to support party decisions, and government decisions were determined by voting according to party. Disagreement, for the individual, meant resignation; for the party, it often meant the fall of the government.[34] The roots of this system may be traced to Czech participation in the Austrian parliament, in which the Czechs' national struggle demanded solid unity and discipline. It does not necessarily constitute a non-democratic feature, but it does provide historical roots for the Communist system of party discipline which, under Lenin's successors, has indeed constituted a violation of democratic principles.

There was much in the Czech tradition conducive to the adoption of socialism such as the tendency toward extensive welfare, born of the humanitarian tradition and the tendency toward cooperatives and an inclination for egalitarianism. There were no obstacles from religion: the Czechs tended to be free-thinkers and anti-clerical. These same traditions, however, influenced the type of socialism applicable to or desirable for Czech society.

Owing to traditional humanitarianism, egalitarianism, and individualism (with the Hussite disdain for arbitrary authority), the Czechs tended toward the economic-distributive side of socialism, rather than the political-strong central planning type. Moreover, because of their liberal tradition and discipline, they tended toward evolutionary democratic "social democracy" rather than revolutionary-autocratic Bolshevism. Even in the nineteenth century, socialism in the Czech lands was disciplined, moderate, reformist. The general Czech reaction to authority was not rebellion or anarchy but disciplined efforts to induce change through the use of reason, although, in view of the Czech revolution of 1848 for liberal-national values, it is difficult to say that there was no revolutionary strain altogether.[35] In the first Republic, Social Democrats and Communists alike emphasized welfare and the economic aspects of socialism, they advocated evolutionary, legal changes rather than revolution, and they were pro-Republic.[36] Indeed, an anti-Republic policy would probably have alienated the large Czech working class which was nationalistically loyal to the newly-formed Republic and united in a strong trade union movement.[37] If this group were to be mobilized for socialism, the goal had to be worker rights and benefits not revolution and the overthrow of the Republican government, for both the desire for national independence and the existing traditions created a preference for peaceful, gradual change.

The adoption of this policy by the Communists — be it because of the political necessities of the day or their own inclinations as inheritors of liberal Czech traditions — was the source of almost constant difficulties between the Czech Communist Party and the Comintern. The Czech Communists were "internationalists" in much the same way as the government of the first Republic, i.e., their approach was that of seeking a "Czech contribution" or a "Czech way" to socialism, without submerging themselves in a universalism which denied national sovereignty. The "Czech way" they advocated was non-violent "revolution" through persuasion, reform, and parliamentary changes.

Thus the Czechs would not fully accept the Leninist type of party dictated by the Comintern. The Leninist party was based upon paternalism and autocracy. The Czech worker, however, was not an ignorant peasant once removed; he was the educated recipient of the Hussite values of reason and persuasion. He would accept and value discipline, but not blind obedience or autocracy. Indeed, in response to criticism the leaders of the Czech Communists informed the Comintern: "The Czech worker grew up in national struggle against the authority of the state and any authority at all. . . The path to the Czech worker does not lead through assertion of authority and discipline from the outside. . . He needs to be convinced and won over. . . The method of command will not win him."[38] The role of

the Party, therefore, was not to give orders; it was not paternalistic
and autocratic. Nor did it see its task as the activist organization of
violent demonstrations and revolt. Rather, the role of the Party in
Czech eyes was to persuade: to listen to and represent the workers; to
gain seats in parliament in order to forward the interests of the
workers. More important than revolution was popularity and large
numbers of supporters or votes. Thus, when a Czech voted Communist
he voted for workers welfare and egalitarianism, not revolution.

To this attitude and the above policies the Comintern objected,
attributing the shortcomings of the Czech party to the "tradition,
training, and orientation of many of the members and an even greater
proportion of the leaders"[39] and the influence of too strong a democratic tradition.[40] The Comintern instigated purges in the Czech
Party, "bolshevizing" it by the replacement of many leaders in the
1920's.[41] While this did produce a certain change, it did not reap
lasting or complete success.

IV

The same problems persisted after World War II. The direct encounter
with Bolshevism had perhaps been facilitated by generally positive
feelings for the Russians as Slav brothers, and by the progressive, even
leftist, leanings of the well-organized working class. Certain elements
of the tradition (e.g., egalitarianism) could also facilitate the imposition of Bolshevism. But as we have seen there were even more
elements in the tradition which dictated a type of socialism different
from the Soviet model. The Soviets, apparently, were aware of this,
given the quarrels between the Czechs and the Comintern during the
inter-war period, and tailored their plans for Czechoslovakia accordingly. In the 1945-47 period, Soviet policy regarding Eastern Europe
was relatively flexible, and Stalin permitted each national Party to
employ the methods most suitable to gain and hold power, within a
certain framework laid down by Moscow. This was a period of transition when many of the old institutions were maintained in Eastern
Europe and "many roads to socialism" or variations on the Soviet
model emerged. The Czechs were, therefore, permitted to institute
their own way; indeed, the Soviets encouraged them to use methods
strikingly different from those of the other East European parties, i.e.,
their traditional, parliamentary way to socialism. In part, Stalin saw in
Czechoslovakia an example useful for the promulgation of socialism in

certain Western countries, such as France and Italy, where Communist strength held potential for legal assumption of power.[42]

Yet, once again, the Soviets (or the world movement) had to put a stop to the "Czech way," losing its patience and faith in Czech gradualism. Among the reasons for the Cominform's orders to the Czechs to change their tactics was the decision to consolidate the Soviet "camp" in accordance with the new "two-camp," cold-war line.[43] Yet, a contributing factor to this line, and even to the formation of the Cominform in 1947, was the disdain of such conservatives as Tito and Zhdanov for the Czech use of "bourgeois" tactics — even to the point of agreeing to the Marshall Plan. Despite the decision not to await the 1948 elections — as they were well aware that they were farther than ever from their projected goal of 51 per cent of the electorate — the Czechoslovak Communists came to power through parliamentary party maneuvering and a minimum of violence, though strong-arm tactics and the threat of violence were not entirely missing. As a result until this day the Soviets, and Chinese, refer to the Czech way as an example of a "peaceful" road to socialism.[44]

Once in power, the Communists still demonstrated a certain awareness of the strong liberal traditions of the Czechs, leaving intact, in theory though not in practice, a number of the former institutions. Whereas the other East European countries moved to Soviet-style Constitutions in the late 1940's,[45] the Czechoslovak Constitution of 1948 was similar — on paper — to the Republic's Constitution of 1920. Thus the importance of the Presidency and many parliamentary forms were preserved.[46] Only in 1960 was a "socialist" Constitution adopted. In practice, however, Bolshevism was introduced in its entirety in 1948: the courts were subordinated to the political power, the Constitutional and Administrative Courts were abolished, the Prosecutor-General was given expanded powers, and the Party ruled through a system of terror which took a toll larger than that of any other country in Eastern Europe.[47]

Indeed, this very extremism may have been a reflection of the tenacity of liberal Czech traditions. Because of its own liberalistic tendencies, the Czech Party was subjected to more "guidance" from Moscow and thorough purges to cleanse the Party of these tendencies. Moreover, the strength of the democratic tradition amongst the public necessitated an even stronger hand so as to maintain the dictatorial regime. Thus, as a Czech Communist historian later explained it, the use of terror created a need for more terror until, in time, the regime was entirely dependent upon it.[48] Even in 1956, when certain other parties began a cautious "thaw," the Czechoslovak Party could not afford the luxury.

The popular reaction to Communist rule was not unlike that of the Czechs under the Austro-Hungarian Empire — passive resistance and, eventually, apathy; a feeling that this too can be "out-lived." The gradualist-rationalist approach still prevailed. Even the "revolutionary" developments of 1968 were the result not of rebelliousness but of methodical Czech gradualism and democratic reformism in a period of revival.

In the late eighteenth and early nineteenth centuries, the Czech revival was brought about through the catalyst of the enlightenment. In the 1960's the catalyst came not from outside the society but rather from inside, from the practical as well as theoretical failure of Bolshevism to work in Czechoslovak society. The realization of this failure came in 1962 and 1963 when the regime saw that the once-prosperous Czechoslovak economy was on the brink of crisis; the public was apathetic, unwilling to work and uninterested in "socialism"; the educational system had deteriorated and the youth were both ill-prepared for, and little interested in, the future; the internal "national" problem was no less divisive than in the pre-Communist days; and even Party members felt alienated from the regime. The (proportionally) largest Communist Party in the world could not rally support and had, in fact, lost the youth and the workers, as well as the intellectuals and the farmers.[49]

In their own investigations of the reasons for this failure, Party intellectuals found that Bolshevism simply had not been suited to the society into which it had been introduced, i.e., a Western-type and Western-orientated, highly developed economically and culturally, democratic society. In the economic sphere, Bolshevism went against the traditional Czech emphasis upon the distributive, humane, and egalitarian aspects of the socialist economic system, rather than the autocratic emphasis upon organization and state-planning of the "command economy" of the Bolsheviks. The Bolshevik economic system might, Czech Communist economists argued, be suitable for a country on its way to industrialization, in which an emphasis upon extensive development was needed, but not for the already industrialized Czechoslovak economy.

Bolshevism had run counter to the cultural-political traditions of the country as well. These included a basic respect for freedom of speech, persuasion, and regard for the individual (and the individual as a creator); a high premium on education and the critical use of reason.

Terror and autocracy replaced justice, the rule of law, humanism, and democracy. Bolshevism had also run counter to the social traditions of Czech society, for the traditional Czech egalitarianism was not of the Soviet variety. The latter was enforced, rather than based on the idea of individual work or merit. Indeed, the Soviet system was paternalistic and even condescending, proffering welfare instead of individual freedoms and rights. The Soviet system offered collectivism based on obedience rather than individual voluntary cooperation, and it offered phony participation. Indeed, it created gaps and social conflicts where few had existed before. Thus, it set the worker above the peasant through discrimination and the "cadre system." It tried to set the workers against the intellectuals in order to control the latter,[50] while even the worker lost his right to speak out as he had in pre-Communist society. Moreover, Soviet "egalitarianism" had brought with it privileges and a bureaucratic elite, which formed an arbitrary authority or "establishment" above the people. Finally, even the moderate liberal nationalism of the Czechs was repressed by the denial of sovereignty or the idea of a Czech role. The country was isolated from its former international functions and partners and forced to submerge itself, not in a new organizational framework for cooperation but into a universalist "idea" to which it was forbidden to make a unique contribution.

Such reformers as the economist Ota Sik, the writer Ludvik Vaculik, the philosopher Karel Kosik, Professor Eduard Goldstucker, and Party leaders Josef Smrkovsky, Josef Spacek, and Alexander Dubcek himself pointed out the above contradictions between Bolshevism and Czech traditions. They argued that the system imposed upon Czechoslovakia in 1948 did not suit the country: the system fitted neither its stage of development nor its democratic-humanitarian traditions.[51] This argument was contained even in the Party's official program.[52] They put the matter thus primarily so as to avoid saying that the Soviet system itself was wrong, objectively and for any society, and also so as to avoid presenting Prague's new ideas as some sort of challenge to the Soviet model. Rather, they simply said that the Soviet model did not and could not work in Czechoslovak society. Perhaps the case would be the same in other Western countries; perhaps Czechoslovakia could provide a model for socialism in developed or advanced countries in which a strong parliamentary tradition and a high educational-cultural level existed. As Dubcek put it, in words themselves reminiscent of the tradition, perhaps this could be Czechoslovakia's contribution to international communism.[53]

It may be argued — despite the Czechoslovak Communists' own

references to the binding nature of their traditions — that Czech democratic traditions were not at the root of the development of socialism in Czechoslovakia in the 1960's.[54] There were indeed those who rejected Bolshevism because it was categorically and morally wrong, and still others who rejected it merely as a distortion of Marxism, without any particular reference to Czech or any other traditions.[55] Whatever the explanation, the values which prompted this rejection, as evidenced by the proposals offered for a new model, were identical with those of the Hussite tradition as it developed over the centuries. Just a few examples from the 1968 demands demonstrate the relationship: the rejection of arbitrary authority and privileged elites; the proposals for a return to the rule of law with the re-institution of Constitutional and Administrative Courts and independence of judges; government responsibility to the parliament and parliamentary responsibility to the courts and the people; respect and tolerance for individual opinions and the right to express them, be it through elected organs, representative interest groups, or individual creativity; Party leadership of society through persuasion and an appeal to reason; the Party's need to "re-win" or earn anew, continuously, its leading position through development of a realistic program; a return to Europe and a Czechoslovak "contribution"; and the very concept of "socialism with a human face" which summed up the demands of the reform movement.[56]

Indeed, the very nature of the Czechoslovak reform movement reflected the Czech traditions. Unlike the speedier, but more nationalistic-orientated "revolts" in Poland and Hungary after the death of Stalin, the Czechoslovak movement concentrated on legalistic programmatic achievements. Led by the intellectuals, it developed a philosophy and undertook institutional change.[57] The Czechoslovak movement was a much more protracted affair, moving slowly and gradually, mainly from 1963 onwards. It was, however, more thorough, disciplined, and realistic than the Polish and Hungarian movements. Although it gained a great deal of emotionalism when it became a mass movement in 1968, it still demonstrated a great deal of discipline and concern for legal, institutional change. Indeed, in the heady atmosphere of 1968, there were those, particularly among the young, who objected to this gradual, legalistic approach, but, for the most part, emotionalism was channeled to programs rather than anarchy. Thus, as in the nineteenth century, the Czech revival of the 1960's appealed to reason, not revolt; public participation but not anarchy; legal change, not violence. Unlike the nineteenth-century revival, it was more socialistically than nationalistically orientated, seeking only sovereignty and the right to a socialism suitable to its own traditions — even those of the Party — i.e., a democratic socialism.[58]

NATIONAL TRADITIONS IN YUGOSLAVIA*

I

Regarding Yugoslavia, one cannot speak of a national tradition so much as of various national or ethnic traditions — the difference and conflicts between which constitute the major traditional problem of Yugoslav society. The country of "southern Slavs" is composed of some five major nations, some of which are ethnic groups, such as the Serbs, Croats, and Slovenes, and some of which — specifically the Macedonians and the Montenegrins — are "nationalities" composed of one or more nations, such as the Serbs or Bulgars.[59] Yugoslavia also includes such minorities as Albanians, Slovaks, Muslims, Magyars, and Germans. Aside from minor language differences among the five major nations, there are significant differences of religion and of historical experience. For example, the Serbs and Croats are basically one people which split between Rome and Byzantium. Thus, very generally speaking, the Croats, like the Slovenes, are Roman Catholic and were the recipients of a basically Western influence, particularly in the Austro-Hungarian Empire. The Serbs, like the Macedonians and Montenegrins to some degree, are Orthodox and came under the influence of the East, particularly of the Turks. There are, however, many mixed areas, and the nationality picture is far from clear.

During their five hundred years under Turkish rule, the Serbs developed a strong yearning for their former days of glory as an empire, developing a cult of heroes. The Orthodox Church, traditionally a state church, was the rallying point for this nationalist longing, the result being an intense religious nationalism.[60] Moreover, as the Serbs under the Turks were isolated from the Western world, Western ideas barely entered the society, and the Serbs remained culturally and

---

* A major revision of this section is based on research conducted in Yugoslavia with the aid of a grant from the American Council of Learned Societies.

economically undeveloped. Having no native aristocracy, they were a relatively egalitarian nation of peasants. Only in time, a type of elite emerged, consisting of richer peasants and Orthodox priests; later, the sons of these groups who became traders and townsmen constituted the elite.

Certain characteristics developed among the Serbs during, and in reaction to, Turkish rule, such as secretiveness and rebelliousness. Theirs was an activist mentality, guided by a strongly anti-authoritarian attitude. Yet their experience included nothing but the Turkish example of oppression and corruption. Despite the cruel and demanding central authority from Turkey, however, the peasant community had a certain autonomy through the basic peasant unit, the *zadruga*.[61] Originally it was developed as a defensive unit with nationalistic-cultural overtones, to protect the Slav culture of the Serbs. Together with the Church it was the basic point of identification. Yet with the development of trade, the village replaced the *zadruga* as the focal point and center of local autonomy. Thus this large communal unit, based on patriarchal-autocratic rather than democratic rule, disintegrated with the changing structure of society, the emergence of individualism, and, eventually, with the diminished threat to Slavdom.

By the late nineteenth century, when the Serbs had achieved independence, their society reflected many of the conflicting characteristics their traditions had spawned. Political rule was autocratic yet the political scene was chaotic, torn by anarchistic, i.e., anti-authoritarian, tendencies. They looked to the West, particularly France, for ideas but, inexperienced as they were in anything but despotic rule, they had difficulty making Constitutional monarchy work.[62] Moreover, the peasants were dissatisfied, for they had believed that the end of foreign rule would mean the end of bureaucracy and interference from the central authorities. Instead, the town-country rivalry continued, along with bureaucracy and high taxes. The Serbs, peasants and townsmen alike (with the exception only of certain intellectual circles), remained romantic nationalists. Independence notwithstanding, they continued to long for the former glory of a "Greater Serbia." Indeed, they were not even sympathetic to Pan-Slavism because of their strong Serbian identification.

The Croats, also a primarily peasant society, developed differently, both as Roman Catholics and as subjects of the Austro-Hungarian Empire. Their cultural-economic level was higher than that of the Serbs and they were less isolated from Western ideas. They had an aristocracy and, in time, their own bureaucracy within the Austro-Hungarian Empire. The intelligentsia which developed with the bureaucracy was strongly nationalistic. Some were Pan-Slavic, though the religious differences between them and the Russians tended to operate as an obstacle to Pan-Slavism. Some were more Western, influenced by the German ideas of a state; others leaned more toward the mystic "Slav" state.

In addition to the religious differences between the Croats and the Serbs, the former tended to look down upon the latter. By and large, the Croats were more liberal in outlook than the Serbs and through their bureaucracy had a slightly greater degree of influence in the Empire; this tended to aggravate Serb-Croat relations even within the Empire.[63] Croat nationalism was no less intense than that of the Serbs, but it was somewhat more controlled, probably because of the influence of Austrian institutions. Among the peasants of the two nations, however, the differences were less substantial. The *zadruga* of the Croats was somewhat less autocratic than that of the Serbs, but it was no more democratic. The Croat peasant suffered from the strong centralism of Vienna (and of Budapest), but in time a degree of semi-autonomy was achieved. One could speak, therefore, of something resembling federal rule, although this did not quell the Croat peasant's desire for full autonomy or independence. Like his Serbian counterpart, the Croat peasant distinguished primarily between village and town, his loyalty and identification being to the former, his enemy − the "foreigner" − being the town or center which collected taxes and interfered in his life.

The Slovenians are similar in many ways to the Croats, though still more Western, and influenced more directly by a German aristocracy and their relationship to Austria. The Montenegrins resemble more the Serbs, for although they succeeded in maintaining their independence from the various empires, they fought for this almost to a man. The Orthodox Church was still more dominant in Montenegro: indeed the priests ruled what was in fact a theocracy. Macedonia, too, was orthodox and basically a tribal society. It was sorely split throughout its history between the Serbs and the Bulgars, with the Macedonians frequently unsure of their nationality. In time, a "Macedonian" idea developed, and when it did, it was a violent, passionate, right-wing nationalism.[64]

In contrast to the Czechs, the nationalism of all these groupings was of the romantic, conservative type born of foreign domination and the struggle for freedom. Even in the case of the Croats, in which there were strands of more Western rather than mystic-Slav orientation, the nationalism was of the Germanic-romantic type rather than liberal. And even among the Croats, these strands were less prevalent than Slavic-mystic nationalism. Rivalries between the nations were strong, principally on the issue of religion, but also in the economic and cultural realms, given the varied levels of development. Yet, as basically peasant nations their nationalism was intricately involved in the town-village conflict. The burning desire for independence was often no more than a desire for village autonomy vis-a-vis the town, carried over later in the form of opposition to any center or bureaucracy — somehow always seen as foreign by the villager.

In the pre-World War I period, the idea of a southern Slav (Yugoslav) state appealed mainly to the intellectuals, and of these particularly to the Croats in the Austro-Hungarian Empire.[65] The Croats tended to see a Yugoslavia as a way out of the Empire, though many also saw union with the Serbs as a cultural-economic step downward. The peasants' aspirations tended in the direction of Pan-Slavism but, above all, they were interested in a peasant state rather than a Yugoslav state as such. The Serbs, for their part, were more interested in a Greater Serbia.

The idea of socialism was also regarded in varied ways, and was of interest almost exclusively to the intellectuals of the Austro-Hungarian Empire. Nineteenth-century social democracy failed to satisfy the desire for national independence among these peoples and had only a limited appeal to peasant nations. Where there was interest in socialism — it tended toward a reformist socialism, with an emphasis upon democratic rights more or less synonymous with national self-determination.[66] In this can be seen the basic conflict that plagued both the Serb and Croat socialists in the twentieth century as well as the nineteenth: a revolutionary policy tended to ignore or even rule out the national issue, while emphasis upon the national issue dictated cooperation with the bourgeois nationalist parties for reform. The Serbian socialists tended to the revolutionary side, perhaps because there was an independent Serb state which they wished to join. One might also see in this more activist attitude of the Serbs something of the Serbian disdain for all things German — including reformist German social democracy — and admiration for the Bolsheviks.[67] On the whole, however, the only kind of "socialism" which appealed to both Serbs and Croats was not social democracy but populism, with its mystique of the "people" or the peasant.

II

During the inter-war period, the new Yugoslavia was almost torn apart by conflicts between the different member nations.[68] The nationality problem, however, was intricately connected with the peasant and his position. As a result of land reforms, the landowner class of Croatia, connected in part with foreign rulers, was more or less destroyed. In Serbia there had been no genuine aristocracy traditionally so that in fact both nations were in time characterized by a growing middle class. This middle class was composed of peasants who had become bureaucrats, intellectuals, or merchants — in short the new bourgeoisie. It was they who dominated the parties of inter-war Yugoslavia, and it was the parties which constituted the focal point of nationalist aspirations in this period. The primary interest of this class was not necessarily improvement of the peasants' lot, but rather the development of industry. This was to be accomplished centrally, as in Russia, through the state with the aid of foreign capital and from many points of view at the expense of the peasants.

As this was, nonetheless, a peasant society, the new bourgeoisie being only once removed from their peasant origins, the traditional aspirations of the people for equality and freedom (for so many centuries synonymous with national independence) were discernible in the new state. Yet the gap between the village and the town, between the people and the rulers, became so great that one could hardly speak of popular participation. Indeed that aspect of democracy, as distinct from equality and freedom, had never been notably present in either native Serbian or Croatian traditional society. Indeed, rule in inter-war Yugoslavia, for all its early aspirations and attempts at Constitutional democracy, was autocratic and centralistic, dominated by the Serbs. The central rule tended to be bureaucratic and corrupt, in the Balkan style, reminiscent of Turkish rule — the only type of rule in which the Serbs had any experience. The strong centralism was permeated with Serbian nationalism, often justified as some sort of "Yugoslavism." It may be argued that autocracy and centralism were necessary to the forging of a new "national" identity, but this was most likely an excuse for the realization of the Serbs' dream of a Serbian Empire.

The other nationalities, specifically the Croats, Slovenians, and Macedonians, strongly — even violently — opposed this "Greater Serbian" centralism. They saw in it an effort by a less cultured, less educated, less developed group to dominate people of a higher level.

The central questions, therefore, of inter-war Yugoslavia were not so much democracy versus autocracy, or liberalism versus conservatism, but federalism versus centralism, Roman Catholicism versus Orthodoxy, and peasant versus town. The peasant, be he Serb, Croat, or Slovenian, saw the central authorities as outsiders. Thus the peasant considered himself under continued foreign domination.

It is difficult to gauge the readiness of the peasants to accept socialism, or the type of socialism attractive to them. Among the Serbs there was a complete alienation from the government, from the political parties, and from the towns. Yet, on the other hand, there was also the breakdown of the *zadruga,* of the influence of the Church, and of village autonomy with the coming of industry and the growth of the towns. The result was a tendency, as in Russia prior to the revolution, toward radicalism and anarchism. Only among the Croats was there a movement of any significance toward cooperatives similar to that of the Czech peasantry. Nationalism was still strong and passionate, oriented toward a peasant state. As the Serbs had a state, they tended toward some amorphous Slav nationalism with a sympathy for Russia.

It is equally difficult to determine exactly what socialism meant to these nations; the peasant probably saw that side of it which represented opposition to the center and promised egalitarianism. The Yugoslav peasants, probably even more than those of Russia, were not interested in the promises of industrialization of one stream of socialism, but rather in revolution; they were not interested in the stream which focused on the political aspects – the stream emphasized by the Bolsheviks – but in the stream concerned more with egalitarianism and distribution. This similarity to Russian society just prior to the revolution is striking, but the matter is complicated by the nationalities issue. In Serbia the peasant could turn to the socialists as the only party which did not represent the continued rule of the town-bourgeois interests, even if there was nothing specifically "peasant" in its appeal or platform. In Croatia, however, the Peasant Party more directly expressed the interests of the peasant, as well as the whole nation's opposition to the center.[69]

The major problem for the Communists in Yugoslavia was that of the traditional feelings of national identity which, coupled with the peasant question, threatened to destroy the country.[70] Thus, the issue facing the Yugoslav Communists was, as in Czechoslovakia, how to cope with the inherited traditions, but the order of priorities was reversed. Whereas in Czechoslovakia the democratic-egalitarian tradition came face-to-face with the autocratic-political stream of socialism, with the centralism-federalism issue only a secondary (though problematic) part of this, in Yugoslavia the nationalist tradition came face-to-face with the universalist aspects of socialism, and the problem of federalism versus centralism took priority over those of reform versus revolution, democracy versus autocracy.

During the first years of its existence, the Communist Party of Yugoslavia was a "Yugoslav" party. Yet, internally, this all-national party reflected the situation in the country as a whole: the Serbs dominated, and the Party was torn by factionalism along national lines. The Party line maintained that the nationalities issue was more or less settled, and that any change was simply a matter of Constitutional adjustment. This was in effect a conservative reformist line, reflecting perhaps the fact that the Serbs were in power both in the country and in the Party. Thus the Party supported the Yugoslav idea and opposed nationalist demonstrations as a threat to the unity of the new country. The dominant Serbs in the Party saw nationalism as a divisive and superfluous factor, and they advocated a strong center and the need for discipline, i.e., autocratic political socialism, to counter the harmful effects nationalism might have upon the struggle for power. Theirs was a legitimate Leninist position: first secure the national aspirations, then go on to the universalist socialist revolution. They were now ready for centralism and Bolshevism. Their position on the peasants resembled that of the Bolsheviks just prior to the revolution. Emphasizing the center in the need for discipline, they made appeals to Slav unity, for they knew the Serbs would not be attracted by a line which conflicted with their Greater Serb aspirations. One might also argue, however, that because their national problem was "solved" they could now emphasize the universalist side of socialism, appealing for the Croats and others to overcome their nationalist passions. Thus they spoke of a socialist Yugoslavia and a Communist Commonwealth of Nations.

This appeal to universalism and socialist Yugoslavia was one side of the second stage: the bourgeois nationalist aspirations having been fulfilled, time was now ripe for the move to the proletarian revolution. Thus the Party, dominated by the Serbs, pursued a radical, revolutionary policy with promises of social justice; they sought to channel the peasants' revulsion for the center into revolutionary action. When dealing with the Serbs this could perhaps succeed, but to encourage the Croats or other nationalities to revolt against the center might threaten Serbian domination. Moreover, to support Croat nationalism meant supporting a bourgeois nationalist peasant party which was anti-center — and thus anti-government, favoring federation rather than gradual adjustments — but reformist rather than revolutionary when it came to social change.

The Comintern and Stalin saw fit to oppose the Serbian Communist line, decreeing a policy which would ally the Communists with the peasants, supporting all actions and demands, including those of a nationalist nature, that would weaken the bourgeois governments. Just as the Comintern decreed for the Party in Czechoslovakia, Moscow ruled that the Yugoslav Communists should encourage even violent nationalist outbursts, oppose "Yugoslavism," and play down the universalist aspects of socialism, so as to gain the support of dissident nationalities. The idea was to exploit, not overcome, the traditional conflict.[71] This entailed, also, alliance with nationalist but non-Communist forces, i.e., the peasant parties, which in fact meant a different line and possibly a different kind of "revolution." It clearly meant support of "separatism" and opposition to centralism. There were innumerable conflicts, shifts, and purges in the Yugoslav Communist Party over this issue of self-determination and nationalism. The Party accepted the Comintern line only in 1924–25. Moreover, this line was not particularly successful outside the Party, for the peasant nationalists were not willing to pay the price of alliance: socialism.

III

While there were certain adjustments in the Comintern line with the approach of World War II and Stalin's popular front policy, the war itself presented a complex situation for the Yugoslav Party.[72] There was to be unity with the peasant-nationalist forces in the struggle against the Nazis, but such a union demanded respect for, and even exploitation of, the nationalist feelings of the various national groups. The policy was, therefore, to be "above" nationalism by neither supporting nor condemning nationalist manifestations. There were exceptions to this, however, as in the case of Macedonia, where the Communists expressly encouraged nationalist sentiments in order to gain support. Yet the Communist underground sought to be an all-national movement, as distinct from Mihajlovich's distinctly Serbian underground, emphasizing the common struggle against the Nazis and opposing the break-up of Yugoslavia.[73] The Partisans had little hope anyway of gaining the extremist nationalist groups, for these tended to be fascist (the Ustashi) or violently anti-Communist (the Chetniks).

The Partisans in fact became a peasant movement whose rank and file cut across national and even political lines. The peasants saw the movement as one for national liberation, not so much to save "Yugoslavia," but to free themselves from foreign rule, be it Nazi or Croat fascist. It was to the Partisans' credit that they grasped the essence of this hostility toward "foreign" rule and sought not submersion in "Yugoslavism" but national liberation for each and every ethnic group.[74]

IV

Tito's approach to the nationality problem from 1944-49 reflected the tolerant attitude of the Partisan period, but in effect copied the Soviet model of federal centralism, which itself had evolved in Russia in answer to conditions and certain traditions there. Given the relatively loose policy from Moscow in the 1944-47 period, Tito's copying of the Bolshevik model at this time was more out of conviction that this was the valid approach to socialism than out of enforced subservience.[75] Tito may have seen the need for centralism and autocracy to overcome the centrifugal thrust of nationalism, and he, like the earlier Bolsheviks, had no other model or experience from which to learn — even with regard to the nationality problem. Like the Bolsheviks, the Yugoslav Party in Tito's time was an underground movement, for which autocratic-centralist methods were most suitable. Unlike the Bolshevik case, however, the element of paternalism had been missing. Nor was there a traditional passivity that had to be combated. The centralist, autocratic rule was designed rather, to cope with nationalism, semi-anarchistic individualism, and peasant opposition to the town (or any center), and it was to provide, as in Russia, the necessary controls for a unified development of the country.

The Bolshevik nationality policy was, in fact, a balance of nationalism and universalism.[76] Based on Leninist principles, federalized-centralism recognized the national identity of a people and, therefore, permitted a federation.[77] Indeed, the Bolsheviks even appealed to national sentiments at certain stages to rally the peoples for the building of socialism. Thus, technically, most nations within the Soviet federation have the right to national self-determination, i.e., the right to cultural-educational organs of their own language, "government" organs, and even the right to secede from the Union.

Yet, the theory maintains that once nationalist aspirations have been thus fulfilled, the problem will have become more or less neutralized; one can then build on what is mutual or "above" nationalism and move onto the second, universal, aspect of socialism. Indeed, the theory continues, the rise in the educational, cultural, and economic level of all the peoples will eliminate the differences between them. With the coming of socialism, nationalism or particularism, which was a phenomenon resulting from and nurtured by bourgeois society to keep the workers subservient and loyal, will disappear.

Centralism then becomes the counterpart of federation, for it supplies the vehicle for progress to the universalist, supra-nationalist stage. It is needed to overcome the centrifugal forces of nationalism on the road to universalism and to combat the particularism and disputes among the nations on the road to supra-nationalism. This is accomplished by vertical organization of the nations, each distinct and separate from each other, having minimum contact with one another. Each has its own bureaucratic hierarchy, loyal to the center or central bureaucracy. The center then represents that unit of supra-national identity as well as being a guiding hand for uniform development and harmony.

Here, again, we see the emphasis upon the political side of socialism, which was attractive because of the need for central control and a strong plan. The more liberal, economic, egalitarian-oriented stream (distribution) would have left too much room for centrifugal nationalist tendencies.

In the Soviet system there is, technically, equality between all nationalities, but in fact one nationality is "more equal" than the others, for Russia is the center. There was, and is, a definite appeal to Russian nationalism in order to mobilize the Russian masses, for the Russians were the mainstay of the new Bolshevik regime. The universalist appeal was used for the other nations, who were told that they had reached the second stage. Yet, even force was permissible to keep them in the Union, given the fact that all the characteristics of the second stage were somehow missing. Centralistic federalism seemed adequate to achieve the necessary unity, but continued and renewed problems of dissident nationalities in the Soviet Union indicate the inadequacy of this system.

In Czechoslovakia, too, one has had the superiority of one people despite the theoretical equality of nationalities, in part because of tradition, in part an effort to gain support of the important Czech working class. Here, too, centralism was the instrument of uniform development and counterforce to centrifugal nationalism. Here, too, the Communists were content to rely on central control because of their underestimation of the nationality problem. They believed that nationalism, particularly of the Slovaks, would "wither away" with the social reorganization and economic development of society.

There was no less centralism in the system Tito introduced in Yugoslavia after the war than in the Soviet Union, probably because of a similar need for uniform development and control of centrifugal forces. [78] Yet owing to the traditional depth and nature of the nationalities' problem in Yugoslavia, Tito could not afford to permit centralism in the form of superiority of one nation over the other — as had been the case in the past as well as in the Soviet Union. [79] Thus he copied the vertically structured federalism, to appeal to each nation in order to gain its support for the building of socialism, and to minimize international frictions, but he tried to avoid centralism by Belgrade or the Serbs. [80] The center was the Party and the mutual goal as represented by the Party. For the first time, there was equality between the Yugoslav nations; no nation was subject to "foreign" rule. This "adjustment" was indeed in keeping with Yugoslav experience and, in part, suited certain aspects of the country's traditions.

Nonetheless, as nationalism in Yugoslavia demanded autonomy, not just equal subordination to a center, the centrifugal tendencies were probably bound to reappear in the form of rebellion against even the non-national center. There was no essential difference between the Yugoslav and Bolshevik systems as regards the emphasis on the political, centrally enforced, autocratic side of socialism, as distinct from the liberal, economic, non-enforced, egalitarian side. This was possibly because — as in Russia so, too, in Yugoslavia — this type of socialism was most suitable and was the selection most in keeping with the traditions of autocratic-centralist rule, whatever the wishes of the masses.

The Bolshevik elimination of political parties and the subordination of the Churches also served Yugoslavia's battle against nationalism. The political parties had been traditionally identified with the nations and national aspirations. Indeed, the Communist Party had been the only "Yugoslav" party, though its own federative structure prevented it from being truly universalistic at various stages of Yugoslav history. Nonetheless, the elimination of the other parties eliminated a significant aggravant to the nationality problem and broke down at least one unit of national identification. The same was true of the Churches, which had also constituted a significant focal point for national identification and frictions. As the Churches declined in importance — in part even before the Communists came to power — the religious distinctions which separated and operated as rallying points for conflicts between the nations also declined in importance. The tenacity of the nationality problem, which we shall discuss below, indicates, however, that neither the parties nor the Churches had constituted an essential element of the problem, but rather that they had served as irritants which could be more or less contained.

V

It is difficult to determine to what degree the system introduced in Yugoslavia following the break with the Cominform constituted a response to specific Yugoslav conditions or national traditions. Tito had been free in the 1945-47 period to introduce certain variants to the Soviet model (*viz.* Poland, Czechoslovakia) and had more or less failed to do so.[81] On the other hand, the system introduced in 1949-50 was a consciously, possibly arbitrarily, sought alternative to the Soviet model in order more or less to justify Yugoslavia's unexpected position outside the Soviet fold.[82] Nonetheless the choice of a particular system over another and the problems it encountered may well have been influenced by certain traditions within the country.

The basic principle of Titoism is decentralization. This was the answer to a series of interconnected complaints, which included not only nationalism, but also traditional peasant opposition to bureaucracy and "foreign" interference (i.e., from the center), and economic problems. Tito gradually came to the conclusion that only decentralization would bring the economic progress and popular commitment needed if Yugoslavia were to stand alone. If one wanted genuine popular participation and economic success, one must abandon the use of force; one must break the alienation of the individual and provide him a genuine stake or role in the building of socialism. This could be done, the Yugoslavs argued, only through elimination of the bureaucracy, or decentralization.[83]

As a result of this thinking, emphasis was shifted from the political, autocratic, centralized-planning orientated aspects of socialism (i.e., Bolshevism), to the economic, liberal, distributive-orientated aspects. Planning would no longer be the strict and restrictive concern of the center. Egalitarianism would be maintained, but, instead of coming through autocratic enforcement from above, it was to be the result of economic development from below. The basic assumption was that if the individual were sufficiently involved in the system, his personal interest in its success would outweigh and supplant national rivalry.

Decentralization was not to be simply federalism without centralism. It was to be something entirely new: local or self-rule through workers' councils and peoples' committees. These were not, however, to be mere transmission belts for the rule or will of the center. They were to be genuine decision-making bodies. This "self-rule" was designed, in a sense, eventually to bypass even the governments of each nation, for these governments also interfered in the lives of the people, operating as a bureaucracy or center and as a focal point for nationalism. The idea was to go directly to the people, involving them directly in the political-economic conduct of society, thereby avoiding almost all possible centers of identification, including nationalism. Even the Party, like the state, was eventually to wither away, though this remains within the realm of long-term theoretical goals.

Neither Tito nor his theoreticians presented the new ideas as an attempt to adopt socialism to Yugoslav traditions, or as the result of these traditions — although they did refer upon occasion to Yugoslav "conditions." Rather, the Party always presented the reform as the logical and genuine application of Marxism-Leninism, the Soviets having fallen into bureaucracy and state capitalism.[84] Nonetheless, one can see the influence of the traditional peasant opposition both to bureaucracy and to centralism, both intimately connected with the national problem.[85] Whether consciously or otherwise, the new system would seem to be a response, and possibly the only answer, to Yugoslav traditions. It could cope with the nationalist, centrifugal tendencies in a way suitable to the traditional peasant desires for self-rule.[86] Decentralization suited the "ethnic mosaic" without, however, rejecting the Marxist idea that economic development and Communism would render national allegiances or identification superfluous.[87] The difference between Stalin and Tito, however, was that this economic progress, and Communism, was to be accomplished in Yugoslavia through economic decentralization and individual commitment — thus the "de-emphasis" of political, centralistic planning and control.

Other elements of the tradition have persisted, however, and to some degree they constitute obstacles to the success of the self-rule system, at least at present. One such phenomenon, possibly explained by the lack of any democratic tradition in Yugoslavia and the predominance of traditions of individualism, rebelliousness (particularly among the Serbs), and near-anarchist behavior, is the failure of workers and others to fully exploit and implement the system of self-rule available to them.[88] People tend to prefer individualist and non-formalized means of achieving things as distinct from working through organizations and/or democratic channels. Politics, including economic politics, are conducted outside the appropriate organs and institutions, informally, individualistically, often boldly and at the same time conspiratorially. This may well reflect the heroic tradition long coupled with individualism, particularly among the Serbs, which leads to a certain disdain for cooperation and ignorance of — indeed skepticism for — democratic processes.[89] Indeed the most Western of the Yugoslav nationalities, the Slovenes, exhibit a much greater capacity for organization, order, and discipline, possibly as a result of their extended contact with German culture, although the absence of democratic, participatory traditions are noticeable in Slovenia as well.

On the other hand, the system of self-rule is also impeded by the influence of the autocratic tradition which leads to persistent centralism and authoritarianism at various levels and spheres of the society.[90] Despite the proclaimed decentralization and depolitization of power, the Party has only slowly begun to relinquish those controls believed necessary for the shaping of a new society. While these controls are by no means as ubiquitous or restrictive as those of the CPSU, for example, they do posit and maintain an actual monopoly of political and, to a lesser degree, economic power within the hands of the Party. Indeed with decentralization and the proclaimed withering away of the state, the Party, at many levels, is the only factor providing uniformity or consistency.[91] Moreover, the loosening of central controls has, in effect, released many of the old centrifugal tendencies, such as nationalism or particularism. Granted these are now within a socialist context, i.e., one no longer has significant religious nationalism rallied around the Church or political nationalism rallied around a political party, although the national units within the Communist Party do tend to fulfill this function of the old parties.[92] Today, however, one is faced primarily with economic nationalism, centered in republics, local representative organs, and the national components of the Party.[93]

The basic unit of identification has, thus, remained the nation, as was distressingly apparent in Croatia when the 1965 Constitutional amendments began to be implemented in the early 1970's.[94] Once again one has the phenomenon of Serbs (albeit through the Serbian Communist Party) opposing decentralization because of the advantages which might devolve on the other nations. Once again the Slovenes and Croats complain of subordination to Belgrade, mainly in the form of economic exploitation. And once again, the response deemed necessary to maintain union is re-centralization or at least efforts to limit decentralization so as to curb the centrifugal tendencies which have reappeared.[95] There is an effort to shift from economic egalitarianism back to political autocracy, in order to maintain control, uniform development, and unity. Thus, there has been the introduction and strengthening of a Constitutional Court as a central control organ on local decisions;[96] there has been a strengthening of central Party controls; and there has been a great deal of hesitation and backtracking with regard to the decentralization reforms and amendments of 1965. There have been some efforts at moving and mixing populations, though without much success, just as fear of a common external enemy has on occasions been used to quiet internal rivalries.

These, however, are but partial solutions. Yugoslavia is faced today, almost no less than in the inter-war period, with the serious danger of internal disintegration. Yet today the dilemma is perhaps more complicated than ever before, for the traditional solution (and that of the Bolsheviks) is autocracy, or strong central rule based on force. Titoism, however, regards this as an obstacle rather than an aid to the achievement of socialism, and, instead, espouses the withering away of the central bureaucracy.

Thus the dilemma: Can one have union with genuine local (national) autonomy? Owing to this dilemma, one has a certain dualism in Yugoslavia today — decentralization in the socio-economic institutions, but a tendency toward centralization of the political institutions.[97] One has a dual battle — on the one hand against anarchism or particularism at the expense of overall uniform progress, and on the other hand against bureaucracy or central interference in local affairs at the expense of self-rule. One has an emphasis upon unity and universalism, e.g., glorification of the joint Partisan experience and the joint stake in the future through Yugoslavia's independent road to socialism. Yet the regime is careful not to emphasize the dreaded "Yugoslavism" at the expense of local pride or sensitivities. This very dualism, however, testifies to the influence that traditions and the traditional nationality problem have had on the development of socialism in Yugoslavia. Moreover, the persistence of the nationality problem testifies, perhaps, to the failure of even this adjusted socialism to forge a new identity.

NOTES

1 Cf. J. Macek, *The Hussite Movement in Bohemia* (Prague: 1958); Matthew Spinka, *John Hus and the Czech Reform* (Chicago: University of Chicago Press, 1941); F.G. Heymann, *John Zizka and the Hussite Revolution* (Princeton: Princeton University Press, 1955); and S.H. Thomson, *Czechoslovakia's European History* (Princeton: Princeton University Press, 1953).

2 In addition to the above, cf. R.W. Seton-Watson, *History of the Czechs and Slovaks* (Hamden, Conn.: Archon Books, Shoe String Press, 1965), pp. 56—75.

3 *Ibid,.* p. 86, cites Kamil Krofta, whose book, *The Nationalities Development of the Czechoslovak Land* (Prague: 1934), deals with the question quite thoroughly.

4 For example, in the mid-fifteenth century the Czech King Podebad (an elected King and a Hussite) suggested that the monarchs of Europe form a League of Princes to fight the Turks, rather than leave such a matter to the Church of Rome. This was to be an international assembly or "parliament" to discuss a reform of the Empire. *Ibid.,* p. 80.

5 See the development of this idea with Peter Chelcicky's influence on the followers of Hus. Peter Brock, *The Political and Social Doctrines of the Unity of Czech Brethren* (The Hague: Mouton, 1957).

6 This attitude is often quoted as that of one of the Czech national leaders, historian Frantisek Palacky and of journalist Karel Havlicek. Cf. R.W. Seton-Watson, *History of the Czechs . . .*, pp. 183—84; Robert Kann, *The Multi-National Empire: Nationalism and National Reform in the Habsburg Monarchy*, Vol. I (New York: Columbia University Press, 1950), pp. 165—70.

7 The outstanding figure connected with the Czech national heritage and the idea of education is Comenius. Cf. Ernst Denis, *La Boheme Depuis La Montagne Blanche*, Vol. II (Paris: E. Leroux, 1903), pp. 219—32; O. Odlozilik, *Jan Amos Komensky* (Chicago: Czechoslovak National Council of America, 1942); Matthew Spinka, *John Amos Comenius* (Chicago: University of Chicago Press, 1943).

8 Cf. Denis, *La Boheme . . .*, pp. 3—86; R.W. Seton-Watson, *History of the Czechs . . .*, pp. 161—63, 170—84. Among the figures whose contributions to the revival were most noteworthy are the above-mentioned Palacky, Havlicek, and poet Jan Kollar.

9 Cf. particularly Palacky in Kann, Vol. I, *The Multi-National Empire . . .*, pp. 157—58, 165—70; and R.W. Seton-Watson, *History of the Czechs . . .*, pp. 178—80.

10 *Ibid.,* pp. 212—13.

11 Cf. Ferdinand Peroutka, *Jaci jsme* (As We Are)(Prague: 1924).

12 Cited in *ibid.,* p. 184.

13 For the rejection of the strong tendencies toward Russian-Pan Slavic romanticism, cf. Kann, *The Multi-National Empire . . .*, pp. 160—70.

14 Cf. Masaryk's *Les Problemes de la Democratie* (Paris: Riviere, 1924), pp.

26—137, and his *The Making of a State* (New York: H. Fertig, 1969); also Kann, *The Multi-National Empire* . . ., pp. 209—16.

15 *Ibid.*, p. 156; R.W. Seton-Watson, *History of the Czechs* . . ., pp. 183—249; and Hugh Seton-Watson, *Eastern Europe Between the Wars 1919-1941* (New York: Harper and Row, 1962), pp. 40—41.

16 *Ibid.*, p. 124.

17 Cf. C.A. Macartney and A.W. Palmer, *Independent Eastern Europe* (London: Macmillan, 1962), p. 195.

18 Cf. Kann, *The Multi-National Empire* . . ., pp. 152—62.

19 Cf. his words of caution regarding Russian nationalism in *The Spirit of Russia* (New York: H. Fertig, 1967), pp. 111—27, in addition to *Les Problems de la Democratie* . . . .

20 Cf. R.W. Seton-Watson, *History of the Czechs* . . ., pp. 309—12; R.J. Kerner (ed.), *Czechoslovakia: Twenty Years of Independence* (Berkeley: University of California Press, 1940); Edward Taborsky, *Czechoslovak Democracy at Work* (London: Allen, 1945).

21 Cf. *ibid.*

22 R.W. Seton-Watson, *History of the Czechs* . . ., p. 329.

23 *Ibid.*, pp. 316—18. Cf. also Kerner, *passim,* and Edward Taborsky, *Communism in Czechoslovakia* (Princeton: Princeton University Press, 1961), pp. 441—42.

24 Macartney points to the levy on fixed capital as a sample of the "leftist" or progressive nature of government policy. Macartney and Palmer, *Independent Eastern Europe* . . ., p. 192.

25 Cf. Ladislav Feierabend, *Agricultural Cooperatives in Czechoslovakia* (New York: Mid-European Studies Center, 1952).

26 For foreign policy, cf. Felix Vondracek, *The Foreign Policy of Czechoslovakia 1918-1935* (New York: Columbia University Press, 1937).

27 Cf., for example, the way Edouard Benes put it, writing during World War II: "We have instinctively expressed our age-old effort to avoid simply and slavishly imitating cultural and other values of a particular nation and to cultivate instead a general human, an explicitly *universal* culture and progress while clinging passionately and obstinately to our *national* forms. All our great national leaders are clear examples of this tendency." E. Benes, *My Memoirs, From Munich to New War and New Victory* (London: Allen, 1954), p. 282.

28 Cf. Anton Hykisch, "The Everyday Routine of the Younger Brother," *Plamen* (Prague), 1, 1968.

29 For the nationalities problems, cf. Elizabeth Wiskemann, *Czechs and Germans* (London: Oxford University Press, 1938); Jozef Lettrich, *History of Modern Slovakia* (New York: Praeger, 1955); C.A. Macartney, *Hungary and Her Successors* (New York: 1937); and R.W. Seton-Watson, *Slovakia Then and Now* (London: Allen, 1931).

30 Cf. the failure to recognize the Pittsburg agreement signed by Masaryk with

American Slovaks in 1918 as binding. Hugh Seton-Watson, *Eastern Europe . . .*, p. 175.

31 Cf. Edward Taborsky, "Local Government in Czechslovakia 1918-1948," *The American Slavic and East European Review,* Vol. 10, No. 3, pp. 202–15.

32 Benes' agreement, albeit reluctant, to Communist demands (in Moscow, 1943) for the foundation of local national communities was probably a result of his awareness of this flaw. Cf. *Memoirs,* pp. 270–71.

33 Cf. Paul Zinner, *Communist Strategy and Tactics in Czechoslovakia 1918-1948* (London: Pall Mall, 1963), p. 19.

34 For the party system and parties of the first Republic, cf. Josef Chmelap, *Political Parties in Czechoslovakia* (Prague: 1926).

35 On 1848, cf. Denis, *La Boheme . . .*, pp. 235–321. For socialism, cf. R.W. Seton-Watson, *Slovakia Then . . .*, pp. 236–37; Kann, *The Multi-National Empire . . .*, pp. 40–51, 154–78. Marx and Engels were not too sympathetic to Czech nationalism (cf. *Revolution and Counter-Revolution*). Bauer's socialism was much more palatable. Cf. Bauer's *Die Nationalitatenfrage und die Sozialdemokratie* (Vienna: Wiener Volksbuchhandburg, 1907).

36 I.e., they opposed the policy of minority (Slovak, German) agitation against Prague. Cf. Zinner, *Communist Strategy . . .*, pp. 25–67, for Czech Communists in the inter-war period.

37 Cf. also Franz Borkenau, *World Communism* (Ann Arbor: University of Michigan Press, 1962), p. 203.

38 Cited in Zinner, *Communist Strategy . . .*, p. 39.

39 *Ibid.*

40 Stalin himself to 5th Congress of the Comintern.

41 Cf. also Kermit McKenzie, *Comintern and World Revolution 1922-1943* (New York: Columbia University Press, 1964), pp. 33–34.

42 Cf. Josef Korbel, *The Communist Subversion of Czechoslovakia 1938-1948* (Princeton: Princeton University Press, 1959); Zinner, *Communist Strategy . . .*, pp. 99–224; and Benes' *Memoirs*, for the wartime agreement and views that set the stage for the Communist success. Benes' philosophy and lack of fear regarding the Communist challenge may be found in his book, *Democracy, Today and Tomorrow* (London: Macmillan, 1939).

43 Communist failures in Western Europe and the decision by the Czechoslovak Social Democrats not to ally with the Communists in the forthcoming elections were also contributing factors. Cf. Zbigniew Brzezinski, *The Soviet Bloc* (Cambridge, Mass.: Harvard University Press, 1967), pp. 3–83, for the periods of flexibility and consolidation.

44 Cf. Jan Kozak, *How Parliament Can Play A Revolutionary Part in the Transition to Socialism and The Role of the Popular Masses,* published in the West by Lord Morrison (London: Independent Information Center, 1961).

45 Poland was the last in 1952.

46 Cf. Taborsky, *Communism in Czechoslovakia . . .*, pp. 167–72, for other Western elements retained.

47 Taborsky, *Communism in Czechoslovakia . . .*, for new Constitution.
48 Karel Kaplan, "Deliberations on the Political Trials," *Nova mysl,* 6–8, 1968.
49 For this period, cf. Galia Golan, *The Czechoslovak Reform Movement: Communism in Crisis 1962-68* (Cambridge: Cambridge University Press, 1971).
50 Cf. speeches by Novotny to workers in Ostrava and in Prague, *Rude pravo,* 24 March 1963, and 16 February 1968.
51 Cf. reports of speeches by Dubcek in *Rude pravo,* 23 February 1968 and 2 April 1968; by Spacek, in *Rude pravo,* 11 April 1968; and Smrkovsky, over Prague radio, 20 March 1968. See also Galia Golan, *Reform Rule in Czechoslovakia* (Cambridge: Cambridge University Press, 1973), pp. 211–17.
52 "The stage of development of the socialist states at the beginning of the fifties and the arrest of the creative development of knowledge concomitant with the personality cult, conditioned a mechanical acceptance and spreading of ideas, customs, and political conceptions which were at variance with Czechoslovak conditions and traditions." *Action Program* published in *Rok sedesaty osmy v usnesenich a dokumentech UV KSC* (Prague: 1969), p. 105.
53 Dubcek speeches, reported in *Rude pravo,* 5 March 1968 and 21 April 1968.
54 Though the trade union daily, *Prace,* 15 June 1968, said that the "Prague spring" was bound to occur because of Czechoslovak traditions.
55 Cf. for example, Ludvik Vaculik, *IV Sjezd Svazu Ceskoslovenskych Spisovatelu* (Fourth Congress of the Czechoslovak Writers Union) (Prague: 1968), pp. 141–51.
56 One could even find similarities between the development itself of the Hussite movement and the Reform Movement of the 1960's, or examine the differences in behavior between Slovaks and Czechs in the 1960's as manifestations of the different national traditions. Some of the above proposals can be found in the documents compiled by Robin A. Remington (ed.), *Winter in Prague* (Cambridge, Mass.: M.I.T. Press, 1969). Cf. also Golan, *Reform Rule . . .*, or such documents as the draft Party statutes (*Rude pravo,* 10 August 1968), the Action Program (*Rude pravo,* 10 April 1968) or the "2,000 Words" (*Literarni listy,* 27 June 1968).
57 For a comparison with the Hungarian reform movement, cf. Tamas Aczel, "Spokesman of Revolution," *Problems of Communism,* Vol. VIII, No. 4–5 (1969), pp. 60–66.
58 For characterization of the movement cf. Galia Golan, "The Czechoslovak Reform Movement in Perspective," *Problems of Communism,* Vol. XX, No. 3 (1971), pp. 11–21.
59 For compact histories of these people and the development of their national traditions prior to the Yugoslav state, cf. the following: Stephen Clisshold (ed.), *A Short History of Yugoslavia* (Cambridge: Cambridge University Press, 1966); Chas. Jelavich and Barbara Jelavich (eds.), *The Balkans in Transition* (Berkeley: University of California Press, 1963); Hugh Seton-Watson, *Eastern Europe . . .*,; and Robert Wolff, *The Balkans in Our Time* (Cambridge, Mass.: Harvard University Press, 1956).

60 Cf. G. Arnakis, "The Role of Religion in the Development of Balkan Nation-alism," in Jelavĭch, *The Balkans in Transition* . . ., pp. 115–44.
61 For a thorough discussion of the peasants in Yugoslavia, cf. Ruth Trouton, *The Peasant Renaissance in Yugoslavia* (London: Routledge and Kegan Paul, 1952). Cf. also J. Tomasevich, *Peasants, Politics and Economic Change in Yugo-slavia* (Stanford: Stanford University Press, 1955).
62 For the influences from the Ottomans and from the West, cf. W. Vucinich, "Some Aspects of the Ottoman Legacy," and L. Stavoianos, "The Influence of the West on the Balkans," both in Jelavich, *The Balkans in Transition* . . .; and Vera Erlich, *Family in Transition* (Princeton: Princeton University Press, 1966).
63 Cf. Robert Kann, *The Multi-National Empire* . . ., pp. 241–59.
64 For treatment of other nationalities, cf. above histories and Hugh Seton-Watson, *Eastern Europe* . . ..
65 For this period, cf. works cited above by Clisshold, R.W. Seton-Watson, Wolff, Macartney and Palmer, and R.W. Seton-Watson, *The Southern Slav Ques-tion and the Habsburg Monarchy* (New York: H. Fertig, 1969). Cf. Kann, *The Multi-National Empire* . . ., pp. 241–59 for Croats and the Southern Slav ques-tion.
66 One must not exaggerate the support either for socialism, even of the reformers' (e.g., Bauer) brand, among Croat intellectuals, for almost all extremes of ideologies could be found among this group prior to World War I.
67 For another, more moderate albeit non-Marxist strain of socialism among the Serbs, cf. W.D. McClellan, *Svetozar Markovic and The Origins of Balkan Socialism* (Princeton: Princeton University Press, 1964). Cf. also Leonard Bushkoff, "Marxism, Communism, and the Revolutionary Tradition in the Balkans," *East European Quarterly,* Vol. I, No. 4, p. 382.
68 Material on this period, with reference to the development of the various nations, structure of society, and political identity, may be found in Hugh Seton-Watson, *Eastern Europe* . . ., and Wolff, *The Balkans in Our Time* . . .. Cf. also T. Stoianovich, "The Social Foundations of Balkan Politics, 1910-1941," in Jelavich and Jelavich (eds.), *The Balkans in Transition* . . ., pp. 297–345, and H. Roberts, "Politics in a Small State: The Balkan Example," in that same volume, pp. 376–95.
69 Though in time it moved away from purely peasant interests by concentrating more on the nationalist claims of the bourgeoisie.
70 The best treatment of the inter-war period of the Yugoslav Communists may be found in Paul Shoup, *Communism and the National Question* (New York: Columbia University Press, 1968), pp. 13–60. Cf. also Paul Lendvai, *Eagles in Cobwebs* (London: MacDonald, 1965), pp. 66–71, and Ivan Avakumovic, *History of the Communist Party of Yugoslavia* (Aberdeen: Aberdeen University Press, 1964).
71 Cf. J. Degras, "United Front Tactics in the Comintern 1921-1928," in David Footman, *International Communism* (Carbondale, Ill.: Southern Illinois Univer-sity Press, 1960), pp. 9–23; Kermit McKenzie, *Comintern and World Revolu-*

tion . . ., pp. 106–8; Shoup, *Communism and the National Question . . .,* p. 57;
George Jackson, *Comintern and Peasant in East Europe 1919-1930* (New York:
Columbia University Press, 1966).
72 Cf. Stalin, *Marxism and The National and Colonial Question* (Moscow:
Foreign Language Publishing House, 1935).
73 Cf. Shoup, *Communism and the National Question . . .,* pp. 60–100; D.A.
Tomasic, "Nationality Problems and Partisan Yugoslavia," *Journal of Central
European Affairs,* Vol. VI, No. 2, pp. 111–25.
74 Cf. Mose Pijade, in *Materijali za ideoloski odgoj clanova Narodnog Fronta*
(Zagreb: 1949), pp. 118–23.
75 Cf. Brzezinski, *The Soviet Bloc . . .,* pp. 3–66, for domesticism.
76 For a modern formulation, cf. *Programme of the Communist Party of the
Soviet Union* (Moscow: Foreign Language Publishing House, 1961), pp. 102–5.
77 For Lenin's views, cf. his *A Contribution to the Question of a National
Policy.*
78 Cf. Shoup, *Communism and the National Question . . .,* pp. 114–20.
79 *Ibid.,* p. 119.
80 Cf. G. Schopflin, "National Minorities Under Communism in Eastern
Europe," in Kurt London, *Eastern Europe in Transition* (Baltimore: Johns
Hopkins Press, 1966), p. 137.
81 As seen above, the very choice of Stalinism then may have been the result of
the autocratic traditions of Yugoslavia.
82 Cf. Adam Ulam, *Titoism and the Cominform* (Cambridge, Mass.: Harvard
University Press, 1952), pp. 69–140.
83 For a clear expression of Titoism, cf. *The Programme of The League of
Yugoslav Communists April 1958* (Belgrade: 1958).
84 *Ibid.*
85 One might see an influence of Tito's Croat origins on the system chosen: one
slightly less autocratic, and more federalistic in inclination. One must be careful
with regard to personalities, however, for in fact the theory was more or less the
product of Tito's chief ideologist, the Jew Mose Pijade. (When looking at the
personal elements, one is struck by the "Russian nationalist," Stalin, who was a
Georgian, and the "Czech democrat," Dubcek, who was a Slovak.) Moreover, in
the 1971 crisis with the Croats, Tito's origins did not prevent him from taking
drastic, autocratic, and centralistic action.
86 George Zaninovich, *The Development of Socialist Yugoslavia* (Baltimore:
Johns Hopkins Press, 1968).
87 For policies regarding the smaller nationalities, cf. Schopflin, "National
Minorities . . .," pp. 138–39.
88 A study is currently in preparation by Yugoslav sociologists on the question
of participation among the Yugoslav public.
89 Cf. Erlich, *Family in Transition . . .,* for discussion of the persistence of the
heroic tradition.
90 There are many additional factors such as the high percentage of peasants still

attached to the land but working in industry, the low educational level of workers, the natural growth of bureaucracies and technocracies, all of which constitute obstacles to full implementation of the self-rule principle. In my opinion, however, the element of political culture or tradition is paramount.

91 Cf. Adam Ulam, "Titoism," in Milorad Drachkovitch (ed.), *Marxism in the Modern World* (Stanford: Stanford University Press, 1966), pp. 151–54; Zaninovich, *The Development . . .*, p. 81. For the continued role of the Party, cf. also Nenad Popovic, *Yugoslavia, The New Class in Crisis* (Syracuse: Syracuse University Press, 1968), particularly chapters 4 and 6–9; George Hoffman and Fred Neal, *Yugoslavia and the New Communism* (New York: Twentieth Century Fund, pp. 183, 382–413.

92 Even the success regarding the churches is debatable. Cf. Lendvai, *Eagles in Cobwebs . . .*, p. 170.

93 Cf. for Tito's early admission of the problem, Tito, *Selected Speeches and Articles* (Zagreb: Napoijed, 1963), pp. 195–96. Cf. also Jack Fisher, *Yugoslavia: A Multi-National State* (San Francisco: Chandler, 1966), passim; Hoffman and Neal, *Yugoslavia and the New Communism . . .*, pp. 493–96; Shoup, *Communism and the National Question . . .*, pp. 227–60. The continued problem is also discussed in Lendvai, *Eagles in Cobwebs . . .*, pp. 140–72.

94 For pertinent discussions of national identity, see H. Isaacs, "Group Identity and Political Change," *Survey,* No. 69 (October 1968), pp. 76–98; Hans Kohn, *The Idea of Nationalism* (New York: Collier, 1944).

95 Cf. the Rankovic conflict, R.V. Burkes, "The Removal of Rankovic: An Early Interpretation of the July Yugoslav Party Plenum," Rand Corporation memorandum, Santa Monica (1966); cf. also V. Meier, "Yugoslav Communism," in William Griffith, *Communism in Europe,* Vol. I (Cambridge, Mass.: M.I.T. Press, 1964), pp. 59–76.

96 For a discussion of this, cf. Alvin Rubenstein, "Yugoslavia's Opening Society," *Current History*, Vol. XLVIII, No. 283, pp. 149-79.

97 Zaninovich, *The Development. . .*, pp. 109–10, 125 ff.

THE BASIC ASSUMPTIONS AND SOURCES OF MAOISM

YITZHAK SHICHOR

INTRODUCTION

The question of continuity and change in contemporary China has attracted the attention of many scholars and has been treated in numerous books and articles. Obviously, this subject is so complicated that oversimplified definitions designating the People's Republic of China as either the modern embodiment of a traditional Chinese dynasty[1] or a mere copy and variation of the Soviet model[2] cannot be valid. On the contrary, the very fact that such opposing evaluations have been adopted clearly demonstrates that contemporary China combines many elements of different origins, local as well as foreign.[3] Answering the question of continuity and change depends, therefore, not only on what aspect of Chinese society we examine, but on what period as well.

Such a formidable task is definitely beyond the scope of a short paper. Instead, this work is going to concentrate on Mao's authoritative values that have given — or at least have attempted to give — contemporary China its unique character.

Mao's thought, however, is built neither systematically nor in an organized manner. Still, one can distinguish a number of basic assumptions that form a kind of precondition on which the rest of the conceptions and doctrines are based. It is very probable that any attempt to explain the aspects of either Maoism or China will eventually arrive at one or all of the following basic assumptions: the universality and infinity of conflict; the need to reform man's nature and the possibility of doing so; the belief in man's superiority over his objective environment; and, finally, nationalism, populism, and a sense of global mission.[4]

Although Chinese Communism firmly and openly rejects Chinese tradition as well as Western values, there is no doubt that in Mao's

77

personality and thought, in particular, deep influences do exist whose origins lie both in the Chinese tradition and in the West.[5]

This work will examine Mao's basic assumptions while trying first to differentiate their various components; second, will explore the relationships between these components and the various traditions — the Chinese, the socialist, or the Western; and finally, will evaluate the influence of one tradition on the absorption, rejection, or change of elements from another tradition.

THE UNIVERSALITY OF CONFLICT

Mao's revolutionary world outlook reflects a continual dissatisfaction with reality — a dissatisfaction that explains his desire for incessant change, which in turn makes possible progress toward a better future. Thus, the essence of his theory of contradictions lies in the assumption that contradiction, conflict, and struggle exist everywhere and at any time, *ad infinitum,* and lack any final and absolute solution. On the contrary, the creation of new contradictions out of the solution of former ones is what advances society. The belief that contradictions do not exist or have disappeared, or that there is no need or possibility to solve them, leads to a standstill — to stagnation and, in fact, to a retreat.[6]

The Sources

Neither the concept of conflict and struggle as a dominant factor in human society nor the desire for future progress are characteristically Chinese values. On the contrary, the Chinese tradition saw the foundation of society in harmony, compromise, and cooperation. This definitely does not mean that traditional Chinese thought ignored the existence of change and contradictions. However, the traditional concept of change and contradictions was deeply influenced by the basic desire for harmony and unity. History, therefore, was in a constant state of flux but within a fixed cyclical pattern, while opposites were but two sides of the same coin, complementary and mutually dependent rather than isolated, contradictory, and antagonistic.[7] Change, in short, was formalized and limited; political and social protest was legitimate and expected;[8] and conflict was conceived as a personal philosophical matter, stemming from a fundamental and natural state of unity. Therefore, although it advocated harmony and compromise the Chinese tradition nevertheless influenced the Maoist concept of conflict and even gave to it its exclusive quality, primarily through two aspects: first, by admitting that conflict is focused in each individual's soul; and second, the traditional concepts of humanism and harmonized contradictions probably brought about a softening and moderation of the definition of conflict in Maoism.

Both conflict as a dominant element in society and the desire for progress are, in fact, characteristically pre-Marxist Western values. Marxism only defined the social struggle less in moral terms and more in economic-materialistic terms. At any rate, both the idea and the terminology accompanying it were absorbed into Maoism from the socialist tradition, though with considerable distortions. What caused these distortions apart from Chinese tradition is modern Chinese reality and Mao's realism as well as optimism vis-á-vis this reality. The acknowledgement of the existence of an enormous gap in China between reality and the vision necessitated the universalization of contradictions, while the national traits of Chinese Communism from the beginning led to the blunting of contradictions.

The Location of Contradictions

The first characteristic of the Maoist concept of conflict lies in the location of contradictions. The location is two-dimensional: on the one hand there is the time dimension — when and until when will the conflict take place? On the other hand is the space dimension — from where does the conflict spring and where does it exist? A universalistic view of both dimensions is what singles out Mao's theory of contradictions.

Conflict is perceived as external and infinite, for contradictions have always existed, do exist now, and will always exist. As conflict is a universal process, no socialist society — not even the communist future society — will ever escape from it.[9] The starting point of this concept is that conflict does not derive necessarily from objective class contradictions, but is a natural human phenomenon that can be found anywhere: in man's soul, between men, between man and nature, in nature itself, and so on in every aspect of human society — agriculture, industry, education, organization, military affairs.[10]

Compared with this universalist concept, conflict in the socialist tradition is limited to a particular historical stage as well as to a particular social group, since conflict develops from the existence of contradictions between economically-defined social classes. The abolition of classes, according to this traditional approach, would remove both contradictions and conflict.[11] This traditional Marxist approach has been accepted by the Soviet Union since the days of Lenin.[12]

The Chinese approach, however, is completely different. Class struggle, according to Maoism, does not mean a struggle between one class and another — that is, class in the sense of economically-defined social groups — but a struggle between subjective class nature contradictions. Therefore it means primarily a struggle of everyone with his own self.[13] Class nature is not necessarily the product of objective circumstances — ownership of the means of production, wealth, or poverty. It is the by-product of education, world outlook, and self-definition. The proletarian character, therefore, does not necessarily reside in the industrial proletariat. Furthermore, it is not even attached permanently to a Communist Party,[14] as the degeneration — from the Maoist point of view — of the Chinese Communist Party in the 1960's showed.

The independence of class nature and class contradictions from the objective economic context derives primarily from modern Chinese reality. Modern China not only lacks the objective economic conditions on which the concept of conflict in the socialist tradition is based, but also awakened wide national awareness, common to all social classes. Furthermore, classical Chinese thought, mainly Neo-Confucianism, saw man himself as responsible for shaping his own character and for solving the contradictions in which he finds himself. Although conflict in Chinese tradition is far from being universal, Maoism arrived at the universality of conflict from the very same traditional assumptions but through a popular supra-class view. Contradictions are basically internal as in Chinese traditional thought, but it is less a particularist phenomenon and more a general human one that has no exclusive connection with any class.

The Quality

In addition to its universalist element, the Maoist concept of contradictions is also unique in its emphasis on the non-antagonistic nature of contradictions. The distinction between antagonistic contradictions, those whose solution necessitates violence, and non-antagonistic contradictions, whose solution is non-violent, in itself preceded Maoism. It is drawn from the socialist tradition according to which, however, contradictions exist mainly in pre-socialist society, or between a socialist society and the outside. Mao not only applied the theory of contradictions to socialist society itself, but also relaxed the tension between contradictions within the society. This mitigation of the contradictions — that is, viewing them as soluble through education, persuasion, and criticism and not through coercion, suppression, or liquidation — demonstrates Mao's general tendency toward the moralistic-humanistic orientation.

Antagonism and non-antagonism is but one variation of China's oscillation between two basic orientations: the idealistic-universalistic orientation versus the materialistic-instrumentalist one. This oscillation had also existed in the Chinese as well as the socialist traditions and was solved by each one in a different way.

Traditional Chinese thought, particularly Neo-Confucianism, was full of dualisms distinguished by a clear hierarchy in which the moralist element always took precedence over the instrumentalist one. Thus, *li* (principle, spirit) was always preferred above *ch'i* (matter, material), although both were regarded as essential to maintain a harmonized and well-organized society; similarly, *t'i* (value, essence, content, inside) was always considered more important than *yung* (function, practical use, technology, outside), although the latter could never be discarded.[15] Accordingly, the highest status in society was granted to the scholar with general universal knowledge while the merchant, for example, with his specific materialistic knowledge, generally had the lowest social status.

The idealistic orientation was also dominant in pre-Marxist Western thought, with Hegel as one of its outstanding representatives. A balance between the two orientations could be discerned even in the writings of Marx, especially the early ones, for humanism was still as important to him as materialism. Marx's successors, however, gave priority to the deterministic "objective" and "economistic" orientation in the socialist tradition, making this orientation the orthodoxy it has been since then.

In Maoist China the basic contradiction between these two orientations splits up into an enormous range of contradictions that arise from them: morality vs. technique; will vs. knowledge; spontaneity and initiative vs. discipline, organization, and control; democracy vs. centralism; collectivism vs. egoism and individualism; society vs. state; village vs. city; and finally, "Red", that is, revolutionary and well-indoctrinated, vs. expert, that is, professional, inclined to be selfish and narrow-minded.

Mao to some extent follows both Marx and traditional Chinese thought in seeking a combination of the two orientations and the contradictions arising from them. Yet, despite his interest in the

fusion of mental and manual work, in the identification of the city
with the village, in the desire that the Red be also an expert, it is clear
to him as a realist that such a combination is still far off. Faced with a
choice he gives, therefore, all his preference to the moralistic, humanistic, and universalistic orientation, that is to the *Red.*[16] This preference means unwillingness to forgo moral values and frugality; it means
emphasizing revolutionism and moral incentive in exchange for economic development built on bureaucracy, egoism, and a materialistic
incentive. Such a choice may conform to and be influenced by the
Chinese moral-orthodox tradition of anti-economism, anti-specificity,
and frugality,[17] as well as the heterodox tradition of rebellion and
anti-bureaucratic protest. No less an important factor are China's
objective conditions: "The monetary incentive was not only 'revisionist,' but also expensive, whereas the moral incentive was both socialist
and cheap."[18]

It is from Mao's emphasis on the non-antagonistic contradictions
that the possibility for thought reform arises.

THE REFORM OF MAN'S NATURE

Mao believes that the correct class consciousness, i.e. "proletarian"
consciousness, is not connected *a priori* to any social class, social
origin, or economic status. Class nature is composed of characteristics
that can be acquired in different ways. It is possible, therefore, to
change man's nature and to direct him toward a correct world outlook
and a "correct thought." This second basic assumption in Mao's
thought is itself conditioned by two prior assumptions: first that it is
necessary to reform man's nature; the second "given" is that such a
change is indeed possible and can be realized.

The Need

The need to reform man's nature, through a subjective and guided
effort and in a systematically organized process, was unknown to
classical Marxism. As the universal revolutionary class the proletariat,
in any case, represented the best qualities and correct world outlook;
since this class and no other class or group was to carry out the
revolution, the question of reforming its class nature simply did not
arise. What remained for the workers was to complete their personality and to realize their political consciousness through revolutionary

activity; by shaping the environment they would inevitably and unconsciously also shape themselves.

Lenin, however, suggested that the socialist and revolutionary consciousness is not necessarily a characteristic of the proletariat. Under circumstances where there is no proletariat or where it is not yet developed, this consciousness may emerge in an intellectual minority group whose task it is, among other things, to inculcate the socialist awareness upon the proletariat. This reflected the situation in Russia where the proletariat was no more than "city peasantry." Therefore, the task of "proletarianization" of the society remained to be fulfilled even after the Bolshevik revolution.

Though Lenin was the first to emphasize that proletarian characteristics do not always belong to the proletariat, he nevertheless maintained that class nature is objective and cannot be changed by changing political attitudes. Lenin, and even more particularly Stalin, did not acknowledge the need for a dictated and directed human transformation.[19] There was always ideological education in the Soviet Union, but its scope, aims, and principles were considerably limited. In order to obtain the proletarianization of society, which is a precondition for realizing communism, the Soviet regime acted in two ways. The first was "negative" education by physical elimination and violent oppression of "anti-socialist" elements. The second way, which the Soviet Union follows to this day, maintains (as professed by orthodox Marxism) that economic development and extensive industrialization will necessarily and inevitably lead also to creating "proletarian consciousness" among the workers.

Both methods are entirely rejected by Mao's China. Neither physical oppression nor economic development lead to the proletarianization of society. The dominant condition for proletarianization — of course, only after the state has gained control over the means of production — is the need to reform man's nature. This approach derives from the awareness that elimination of the external class conflict does not yet eliminate the internal moral conflicts. Similarly, objective economic change does not bring about a parallel subjective change and does not automatically create proletarian virtues. The existence of the socialist relationships of production in themselves is not yet a guarantee for the fulfillment of communist aims: there is a continual need for permanent and successive processes of ideological transformation and political revolutionary activity.[20]

Giving preference to the socio-political revolution in China derives not only from abstract ideas but no doubt also from the objective backwardness of China.[21] In addition, the impatience of her leaders as reflected by their desire to accelerate the achievement of the revolution's final aims also plays a part. For, although the acknowledgement of the need for "thought reform" does not fit in with classical Marxist-Leninist concepts, it can, nonetheless, be seen in the context of the socialist tradition: the content of the aspired-to change is socialist as are the goals it intends to realize.

The Possibility

As important as it may be, the need to change human nature would have been meaningless and valueless unless accompanied by the belief in the possibility to achieve such a change. Indeed, this is exactly what Mao thinks *is* possible, and it is possible because conflict is mainly subjective and focused in the individual himself, while the dominant contradictions in society are the non-antagonistic ones. This belief is the cornerstone of Maoist China's efforts to transform Chinese society. Mao's words illustrate the advantages of this approach:

> There are unavoidably die-hard, obstinate counter-revolutionaries. But under our social conditions the majority of even these people will change one day. . . . Some are not executed, not because of a less serious crime, but because their execution would serve no useful purpose. It is better to let them live. What is the harm of not killing a lone wolf? If he can be reformed through labor, let him do that so that the useless can become useful. Besides, a head is not like a leek; it does not grow again once it is cut. If it is a mistake to cut off someone's head, there is simply no way to undo the mistake.[22]

Such an approach has nothing to do with the socialist tradition, since it didn't raise the need for thought reform and obviously did not discuss the possibility of realizing it. The certainty that man is able to reform his nature, whether on his own initiative or on others, is drawn, therefore, mainly from two sources: the Confucian tradition on the one hand and Chinese Communist revolutionary experience on the other.

The Chinese tradition, both the orthodox and the heterodox, assumed that natural equality exists between men: The importance of this assumption is that everyone is good by nature and can therefore be improved and perfected. This is perhaps the strongest unconscious influence of the Chinese tradition on Mao's thought and on Chinese Communism. Little wonder, then, that the effort to transform Chinese society had begun even before the People's Republic was established.

Most of the dominant trends in contemporary China, including the thought reform, were validated in the course of the revolutionary experience of the 1930's and 1940's. Thus the rectification movement in 1942—44 proved that man's soul can indeed be remolded through a dictated and subjective effort; it developed methods that feed these processes in China even until this day.[23]

Aims and Processes

Two complementary processes should, according to the Maoist conception, bring about thought reform. The first one is dictated from outside and implants into the individual the "proletarian" world outlook instead of his "bourgeois" world outlook. This alone, however, is insufficient to change one's class nature; a theoretical world outlook that is not put into practice has no value at all. Therefore a second process is needed that commits the individual to apply unremittingly the acquired proletarian world outlook. In other words, reforming human nature necessitates a continuous practical and revolutionary activity.

Without referring to the content of the change, the new terminology and the different objectives, we find the origins of both processes, as well as of several of the Maoist educational techniques, in the Chinese tradition.[24] Classical education was in fact the only formal way in which it was possible to change man's social status. Formally well-defined, very institutionalized and external, this process is known as "the examination system." In addition Chinese tradition required the realization of personal integrity as a complementary process to acquired education. Achieved through a continuous effort to conform man's behavior and deeds to his "class" world outlook and "knowledge," this process is mainly internal, subjective, and informal, and is known as "self-cultivation."

Self-cultivation in old China and self-criticism in new China are techniques aimed at arousing a state of mental tension. Feelings of unrest and discomfort with regard to personal integrity and feelings of guilt and shame are by-products of these techniques. The purpose is to encourage correct thought and activity in order to close the gap between behavior and action, on the one hand, and authoritative principles, on the other hand, through an incessant process of self scrutiny.

The traditional demand to apply acquired education through behavior and activity is very similar to Mao's principle of the unity of theory and practice and, of course, preceded the same socialist notion. Mao, in fact, fully accepted a traditional doctrine shared by most Chinese thinkers through the ages and particularly expounded by Wang Yang-ming (1472–1528).[25] Like them, Mao argues not only that there is no knowledge without action and, moreover, that true knowledge *is* action. But he insists also that knowledge alone is both meaningless and easy, while action is more important and decisive, and therefore more difficult. Mao has become more and more convinced, through experience, that education and indoctrination alone do not bring the anticipated results and that only revolutionary activity will complete the process and bring spiritual transformation. This definitely does not mean a disregard of knowledge. On the contrary, everybody should not act in blind obedience, but must fully understand theory and fit it to his surrounding circumstances, thereby making it his own knowledge.

The basic principles that guide "correct" behavior and "correct" action are found, therefore, in "correct" thought — and this truth is not detailed in the Holy Scripture from time immemorial (as in the Chinese tradition) nor fixed by any "representative" organization (like the Party in the Soviet Union). In China, "the source of the proletarian truth resides in no group or even organization but in the thought of Mao Tse-tung."[26] This is but one of the many differences between traditional education and cultivation and Maoist thought reform and indoctrination.

Whereas these processes, being rather the "confucianization" of individuals, were applied in traditional China primarily, and indeed only, to a tiny fraction of the population, Mao uses them to achieve the "proletarianization" of the entire society: It is not to create a specific class but a universal one. Furthermore, the dimensions of human change are completely different: Traditional China conceived change as directed to maintaining the personal integrity of the literati, being more a perfection of man's nature rather than a reform. In Maoism change is conceived as a much more fundamental process, as *fanshen,* a term that can be translated as a transformation of the identity." Traditionally, education and cultivation were aimed at bringing about a harmonious merger with the environment. In Maoist China, however, these processes are directed to the contrary objective of arousing an awareness of the existence of contradictions in order to prevent a state of satisfaction that leads to a standstill and to degeneration. Thus, self-criticism little resembles the traditional version of "watching oneself when alone," but is conducted more in the framework of a group in which a man is forced to criticize himself as well as others both orally and in writing. Also, the use of "human models" and "examples" is much wider than was the case traditionally. However, the continual repetition of authoritative principles that characterized traditional education is now carried out more vociferously, with an unrecognizable scope and intensity. Persuasion, that traditionally was carried out gently with dignity and manners, is today much closer to oppression, although in comparison with the Stalinist methods these are relatively moderate. Finally, whereas traditional education was formalized, in Maoism not only is change of man's class nature not institutionalized but it is also not defined and in many cases is even completely subjective.[27]

To conclude, both education and self-cultivation in Maoist China are collective, and not personal, processes: universal, not particular; radical, not moderate; public and vociferous, not private. Furthermore, their content is entirely different.

MAN'S SUPERIORITY OVER NATURE

One of the most impressive elements in the Chinese revolutionary experience that more than any other explains the victory of the Communists and their achievements in other areas was the belief that man, through maximum exploitation of his subjective forces, can overcome objective difficulties. On this belief is also based the goal of transforming China — which is, after all, developing and agrarian — into an industrialized socialist society, not necessarily in a slow, gradual way but rather quickly through leaps and short-cuts.

The Conditions

The belief in man's superiority over nature, in his ability to transform reality and overcome enormous difficulties, itself became a myth in Maoism. The impression received both from verbal pronouncements and the tasks the Chinese undertake is that this belief has no restrictions whatsoever.[28]

In fact, the Maoist belief in man's superiority fits well into reality, not only the subjective reality as Mao understands and sees it, but also the objective reality. Maoist voluntarism is limited and can be realized only when certain conditions exist. The first condition is an awareness of the existence of gaps and contradictions between man and his environment, between the objective circumstances and the desires and aims. In other words, it is the recognition of the need to struggle in order to overcome backwardness from which derives the view of nature as an enemy against whom one must fight.[29] The second condition necessitates the maximum exploitation of human spiritual sources and subjective forces and an organized application in practice of the principles of "correct thought," from which unlimited power can be drawn. The third condition calls for caution, deliberation, and full consideration of the objective circumstances. Maneuver, concessions, and even setbacks are legitimate in the short run and on the tactical level — because of the belief that, in the long run and on the strategic level, victory is inevitable.

The first two conditions are clear in themselves and in fact represent the two basic assumptions that were previously discussed — the recognition of the existence of contradictions and the need for indoctrination. The third condition clearly rejects the possibility that man is able to do everything, at any time and in any situation. On the contrary, superiority over the environment does not mean disregarding difficulties, or adventurism:

> If man wants to achieve success in his work, that is, to achieve the anticipated results, he must make his thoughts correspond to the laws of the objective world surrounding him. . . . . In seeking victory, those who direct a war cannot overstep the limitations imposed by the objective conditions; within these limitations, however, they can and must play a dynamic role in striving for victory.[30]

Notwithstanding the limitations imposed on the belief in man's superiority, it still forms one of the dominant elements in Maoism, especially on the operative plane. Theoretically, this belief sprang mainly as a reaction to the Chinese reality already in the beginning of the twentieth century but drew in addition from Western as well as Marxist-Leninist sources.

Influence of the Chinese Reality

The contribution of the Chinese inheritance to Maoist voluntarism is marginal and small. In orthodox Chinese tradition man was always perceived as inferior to nature, while the relationships between man and nature were complementary and not contradictory. Therefore, it emphasized the need for the individual's adaptation to his environment and his integration in the external harmony. In the heterodox tradition — that of the protest movements and of legendary heroes as expressed in popular novels — struggle against nature did play a central role.

Mao was greatly impressed by such novels[31] and even used some of them to illustrate the dimensions of man's superiority over his environment. However, what gave man his superiority in Chinese heterodoxy were neither his own subjective forces nor any sort of "correct thought" but superhuman, heavenly forces.

The belief in human superiority is rooted, therefore, primarily in the modern Chinese reality. The disintegration of the empire in the course of the nineteenth century and the beginning of the twentieth century ruined the foundations of Chinese tradition and forced the intellectuals to search out new truths. The starting point for these searches, whatever may be the direction to which they turned, was awareness of the need to rescue China from the depths into which she had been thrown and to raise her up as quickly as possible to the heights she had been accustomed to in tradition. From this desire had already emerged the belief — at this stage only theoretical — that despite objective inferiority, by relying on human power, a society can leap over historical stages and shorten the path to the final aims.[32]

This belief, which originated from Chinese national needs, was to combine later with the Marxist-Leninist context. The link was made available by Li Ta-chao, one of the founders and outstanding figures of the Chinese Communist Party. His ideas are marked by all-out activism and anti-determinism; even before he became a Marxist, he saw in these trends the only way to solve China's problems, a way that conforms both to her capabilities and needs.[33] Mao Tse-tung was deeply influenced by the theoretical assumptions of Li Ta-chao on this question as well as on many others. Toward the end of the 1920's Mao adopted these concepts: Since then he has worked to realize them. The Chinese Communist revolution, especially during the 1930's and 1940's, fully proved the truth embodied in the faith in human superiority. Without it the victory and achievements of the Chinese Communists would be hard to explain.

Foreign Influences

Though it is clear that the voluntaristic concept that fed Maoism preceded Leninist concepts, both in the chronological sense and in its scope, nonetheless Maoist voluntarism also absorbed Western influences, in general, and Marxist-Leninist ones in particular.

The concept that man dominates nature, changes it, exploits it, and suits it to his own needs is in essence a characteristic "Western" concept that was also absorbed into the socialist tradition.

Basically, even Marx, despite his "dehumanization" by later orthodox Marxists, saw history — though in economic terms — as the product of human efforts and not necessarily as a result of objective and ungovernable independent forces or "laws of nature."[34] This is evident from his willingness to sanction revolution in countries where political but not necessarily economic conditions seemed ripe for it. It must at the same time be remembered that Marx's restricted anti-determinism was only applicable to the European context where a high level of economic and industrial development was taken for granted. In China, therefore, he saw at best nothing more than limited revolutionary potential which was of more importance to Europe than to China.[35]

Lenin, who is usually regarded as the prophet of voluntarism in the socialist tradition, did not in fact go further than Marx, and drew closer later on to orthodox Marxist concepts. According to Lenin's theories on imperialism he recognized in China a more real revolutionary potential than did Marx, but not once did he agree to viewing Asia as an exclusive center for revolution, or the revolution in Asia as a precondition for revolution in Europe. Leninist voluntarism was applied mainly to the Russian context; it began in fact with the Bolshevik revolution and finished together with it. Lenin's anti-deterministic approach was, therefore, limited to the field of political strategy and in this area his imprints are the most marked on Chinese Communism. In China, however, anti-determinism has become unprecedentedly universalistic.

Lenin's recognition that a professional and disciplined revolutionary pioneering group is needed in order "to move" history and realize the revolution — despite the objective backwardness and absence of a proletariat — had a more prolonged and more extensive significance in China than in Russia. Leninist voluntarism, as was expressed in the October Revolution, was a short act from the point of view of time, narrow and limited from the point of view of scope. The Chinese Communist Party, though built on the Leninist model, faced much harder challenges within a much larger scope and within a longer period of time.

After the stage of political take-over, Soviet voluntarism expressed itself particularly in the economic field. This was a result of the assumption that the socio-political transformation had ended at the first stage and every effort was now to be dedicated to creating economic abundance, which is a primary condition for true communism. This assumption was based, in fact, on the orthodox concept that the complete transformation of society would occur together with the process of economic development and as a result of it. Therefore, in the Soviet Union priority was given to speed up economic development.

Although it was clear also to the Chinese that communism cannot be realized without economic development and industrialization (they even followed the Soviet path till 1957), they have since then emphasized socio-political transformation over economic change. The economic motive in man's struggle against his environment does, of course, exist in Maoism, but the meaning of this struggle at present is first of all political and ideological, involving mobilization of the population (a move that the USSR did not even take as an efficient means for economic progress), the breakdown of indifference, the implanting of collectivist consciousness, and the abolition of self and selfishness.[36] In China, therefore, priority was given to socio-political transformation.

To sum up, the Maoist theory of man's superiority over nature derives from motives other than those found in the West and in the Soviet Union. Immense human capabilities do not apply to a particular historical stage or to a particular area but are expressed throughout the whole of history and in every field — in the economy, the military, medicine, science, and so on. Contrary to the Western and socialist concept that sees nature as a stumbling block and nothing else, in Maoism the contradiction between man and nature is greatly intensified. The extreme concept of man's superiority over nature is also more emphasized in Maoist China compared to her traditional concepts. In the Soviet Union, on the other hand, the voluntaristic dimension which in itself is very narrow is not so contrary to tradition, for Russia was, to some extent, a "Western" society.

NATIONAL SOLIDARITY AND INTERNATIONAL SOLIDARITY

The emphases on non-antagonistic contradictions in socialist society, on the possibility of transforming man's nature, and on man's superiority over matter — all lead to the fourth fundamental concept in Mao's thought. This is the belief that the entire Chinese people can, and must, take an active part in the revolution. "Peasants," "Proletariat," "Communist Party," and similar concepts have never been exclusive foci for identification in the Chinese political system. They are, undoubtedly, sections of "the people" yet inferior to it. This desire for the maximum involvement of the population in political processes and in the national effort characterized the Maoist Revolution as early as the end of the 1920's.

The stress on the importance of the people as a whole — and not necessarily one class or another, or certain organizations or individuals — imparts to new China a unique character that is different not only with regard to Western societies but also to socialist societies of today, as well as to traditional Chinese society.

This Chinese uniqueness is manifested not just in the centrality of nationalism in general, but particularly in the Party's partnership with two classes (although in an opposite meaning with each of them) which, according to the orthodox Marxist tradition, have no importance and no positive function in socialist, industrial society. The first group is the peasants, who have a positive task of primary importance in the Chinese system. The second group, the bourgeoisie, is less defined and more subjective, and plays a somewhat negative role. The struggle between these two contradictory lines and the effort to integrate one with the other into one unity has created in China a dynamic, revolutionary energy whose meaning and influence has repercussions far beyond China's borders.

As a single unit without class differences and because of their national and revolutionary achievements, the Chinese people bear a mission to the world. China has created a pattern which, so she claims, answers the needs of other developing nations that have suffered from national humiliation, economic exploitation, and social disintegration in the same way as China. Chinese national solidarity has, consequently, developed into international solidarity.

The Positive Role of The Peasants

According to Mao's revolutionary conception, the peasants — and not the proletariat — embody the revolutionary potential. In China, the peasants are the universal class in two senses: firstly, the majority of the Chinese people are peasants; secondly, the characteristics of the peasants in China are, in fact, those that acquired for the proletariat, in the socialist tradition, its revolutionary quality as a "universal" class. Poverty, economic exploitation, suffering, ethical purity, and readiness to sacrifice — all these are the "proletarian" characteristics of the Chinese peasantry.

Similarly, orthodox Chinese tradition bestowed on the peasant class a special honor as the productive class that sustained the empire.[37] However, although agricultural employment was considered the basic occupation in traditional China, the peasants were really, despite their weight in the population, a passive group that shared no part in the government in any form whatsoever. But a more active and dynamic function was carried out by the peasants in the heterodox Chinese tradition. The protest movements in traditional China — though at times led by literati — were peasant movements in their essence and in their aims.

Li Ta-chao was, again, the first to believe that if there is any revolutionary potential in the Chinese people at all, it is latent in the peasantry and in no other class.[38] Mao, who was born and raised in a rural environment, began to believe relatively late in the revolutionary capability of the peasants: he came to this view only in the latter part of the 1920's.[39] Yet once he began organizing them he did so to an ever-increasing extent in comparison with his predecessors. The mobilization of the peasants and the acquisition of their sympathy bore fruit, and there is no doubt that the Communist victory in China was the victory of the peasants. In China there were no centers that could be seized quickly and so realize the revolution at a stroke, as was done in Russia. The Chinese revolution required the participation of large sections of the population for a much longer period of time. The response to the Communist call came, particularly after 1937, mainly as a reaction of national feelings.[40]

The participation of the peasants in the Chinese Revolution on such a scale — not as an excess, but in leadership and operational positions — differs totally from what is accepted in other socialist traditions. Ostensibly, Mao could have found the first hints at this — though very restricted ones — in Marx himself. The initial negative attitude of Marx toward the peasants changed gradually to a more positive view, but he never saw them (nor did his successors, including Lenin) as a group capable of independent revolutionary action, or even as a leading force in the revolution — much less the dominant one. At the most, he agreed to see them (as an implication of the French Revolution) as a force that is close, from the point of view of its interests, to the proletariat and not to the bourgeoisie. The peasants could cooperate, therefore, with the urban workers alone.[41] Marx naturally referred to the European context in which he saw as a given the existence of the industrial proletariat at this or that stage of development. The proletariat was the leading and dominant force of the revolution while the peasants could not act as a substitute since it is not possible to fulfill the revolution solely on the basis of proletarian virtues. These virtues exist, perhaps, among the peasants, but what they lack — considering the needs of the revolution and of the socialist society — is the concrete and professional knowledge.

Mao, on the contrary, saw the great advantage of the revolution in China precisely in the lack of real professional knowledge. Not only is it possible to build things anew but, what is no less important, the Chinese peasantry is still pure. It has not yet been exposed to the evils of the corrupting industrial society and has not yet tasted economic abundance. From this point of view, the peasantry is, in fact, more "revolutionary" than the urban proletariat. This approach, which is much closer to the ideas of Russian populism,[42] appears as a total denial of the holy concepts of Marxism-Leninism. Marx only hinted at the possibility of peasant participation in the revolution in Europe, while Lenin went further, in a sense, when he spoke of peasant partici-pation in the revolution of Asia. Yet, as both never doubted the leadership of the "city" in the revolution, they were ill-prepared to accept the idea of a Communist peasant party.

Mao's recognition of the revolutionary potential of the peasantry, therefore, does not have its origin in the socialist tradition, but in the identification with the Chinese protest-tradition, on the one hand, and in the circumstances of Chinese reality, on the other. An insignificant proletariat, the failure of urban uprisings, the seizure of cities by the enemy, and the absence of one governmental center — all these factors raised the peasants not just to the level of a revolutionary class but also made them the basis for national identification.

The Negative Role of the Bourgeoisie

A share in this Chinese national unity is also kept for the bour-geoisie.[43] According to Mao, not only in the socialist society but even in the communist future society, bourgeois thought will still continue to exist.

In the attitude of the Chinese Communist leadership toward the bourgeoisie, one can clearly distinguish two stages. Before the take-over of China in 1949, and in particular during the years of the Japanese occupation, the bourgeoisie was regarded as a "positive" factor. Not only was it a part of the "people" (in the broader sense of the word), but even a part of the "people's dictatorship" although, naturally, under the hegemony of the proletariat.[44] Cooperation with the bourgeoisie derived from their identification with the struggle against the invaders, when the common aim — and for the Communists the primary one — was a national aim. This bourgeois element strengthened the Communist ranks not only against Japan, but against the Kuomintang as well.

Yet, since the civil war and with the establishment of the People's Republic, the importance of the bourgeoisie has been gradually declining. After the nationalist aim had been realized for the most part — although it has not been fully realized even today — the Chinese regime turned its efforts in the social, economic, and political direction. From these viewpoints, the bourgeoisie is a "negative" factor. More and more the bourgeoisie is becoming an evil, but somewhat of a necessary evil — necessary, first, because it cannot be altogether disposed of and will always exist; and second, since even in its negative existence there is a positive element. By its very being, the bourgeoisie prevents the revolution from stagnation and stimulates the incessant struggle which is the primary condition for the progress of true revolution. Moreover, bourgeois thinking, as a subjective and personal phenomenon, can be reformed by suitable education and thus can even contribute to the revolutionary and national interests.

From both viewpoints, the nationalist and the socialist, the role of the bourgeoisie has altered from the way it was conceived in the other socialist traditions. Cooperation with the bourgeoisie in China, on the national-revolutionary plane, was on a much broader scope and for a longer period of time than ever imagined by Lenin or Stalin, not to mention their predecessors.

Hints at the possibility of inter-class participation, excluding the high aristocracy, as part of the national struggle that could serve revolutionary goals can be found in Marx and Engels. In inter-class cooperation they saw, however, only a marginal aspect of the revolutionary effort, significant to Europe alone.[45] Contrary to this, the idea of a "united front" became the cornerstone of Lenin's ideas with regard to revolution in colonial countries. Applied to China, his concept meant a continual pressure on the Communists to join hands with the Nationalist Party (the Kuomintang) and with the national bourgeoisie. Nevertheless, it is difficult to see in these tactics a long-range principle in the Soviet strategy. The Soviet leadership always placed the interests of the revolution in Europe in general, and those of the USSR in particular, above the interests of the revolution in China. In a "united front" Moscow saw but a temporary and passing need, a need that was negative in essence. Needless to say, the Chinese approach completely differs and did not spring, therefore, from the writings of

Lenin and Stalin, or the Comintern, but out of the local situation, perhaps even out of the Chinese tradition.

The priority given to supra-class national needs can be explained not only by the reaction to the humiliation of the Chinese people and the Japanese invasion, but also by the Chinese tradition of the unity of the empire and of social integration. Although traditional Chinese thought vindicated and legitimized the Chinese class structure, it nevertheless considered every component of the society as essential to the organized empire as a member to an organic body. Furthermore, times of national danger in Chinese history created identification between the gentry and the peasants. The leaders of peasant protest movements were frustrated intellectuals. Chinese scholars always had had a central role in the administration of the empire and their influence on the population in general, and on the youth in particular, was great: those who conferred the legitimacy on a new emperor to rule and to set up a dynasty were, in fact, the literati. These traditional influences presented the Chinese Communists with many dilemmas. On the one hand, they desired to gain the sympathy of the intellectuals, to draw them into the party ranks and to recruit them for revolutionary activity. On the other hand, especially after 1949, it became clear that the intellectuals were a bourgeois element and fear of them increased precisely because of their educational role and their influence on the youth. Actually, the repeated efforts of the regime to reform the intellectuals proved that precisely this group was difficult to change. Perhaps here lies the source of the dualism in the regime's approach: The bourgeoisie is, indeed, a part of the people, but it is a negative example.

Acknowledgement of the existence of the bourgeoisie, not necessarily as an economic class (this was already destroyed during the first stages of the Communist take-over in China) but chiefly as a subjective bourgeoisie, and of bourgeois thought is another proof of the realism of China's leaders and of Mao Tse-tung in particular. Such a realistic approach to the problems of socialist society does not exist in other regimes based on Marxist-Leninist theories. In China, bourgeois thinking is regarded as a universalist and even eternal phenomenon. One can find bourgeois, "revisionist" thinking not only in the ranks of the Party, but even at the top leadership; moreover, when all classes have been abolished, bourgeois thinking will continue to exist. This recognition derives from Mao's fundamental belief that the focus of contradictions is in the individual soul, and as long as men live contradictions and struggle will not cease.

Nevertheless, the struggle is carried out with a certain optimism that is based on the belief that man's nature can be reformed. Physical liquidation, oppression, and torture are not the means to achieve this goal; instead it must be accomplished through education and indoctrination, manual labor, and political revolutionary activity. In this way, one can harness additional forces to the wagon of revolution.

The belief that the realization of both the national revolution and the economic, social, and political revolution is the concern of all the Chinese and that this dual revolution must be realized without losing the national identity and the Chinese uniqueness is almost an axiomatic assumption in Mao's thought. Much more than in Soviet society or in the Chinese tradition, the idea of the responsibility of the entire nation for its fate exists in Maoist China.[46]

The Global Significance

The realization of the revolution in China is not the end. Mao, as a universalist, regards China as one of the oppressed nations and one of the exploited classes in the world, whose duty it is to serve the revolution on a global plane. Among these classes, the Chinese both implicitly and explicitly claim seniority in virtue of their revolutionary achievements, which they see as an example in which theoretical knowledge and practical revolutionary experience were combined.

The only thing derived from Marx in these conceptions is the final goal and the somewhat ambiguous recognition that the final victory is inevitable. In Marxism, global revolution will not be realized as the result of a struggle between nations but rather of internal class-struggle in every individual nation. The center of this process is found in Europe and not anywhere else. Lenin did not shift, in principle, from the Marxist position. He firmly opposed "Asio-centric" approaches and refused to see either the revolution in Asia as a pre-condition for the revolution in Europe or the role of the European proletariat as a passive and conditioned one.[47]

Mao, however, went further than both of them together. Firstly, he recognized the importance of the revolutionary potential not only in Asia, but also in Latin America and in Africa. Secondly, he conferred upon China an unprecedented position in the socialist tradition. Although this feeling of superiority was influenced, undoubtedly, by the national and, in particular, the revolutionary achievements of the Communists, in principle it could have been expected of any Chinese leader. Mao, therefore, is no different from other Chinese nationalists in this century in manifesting the desire to restore China to its former greatness — not only in a national sense but also in a global sense.

The Chinese today measure their greatness and their superiority — just as in the past — not necessarily in conventional terms like population, economic wealth, natural resources, military strength, and so forth. Since China is still regarded as a developing nation her superiority cannot yet depend on these objective factors. Thus, obviously, considerations of power and economy are secondary. What counts is the spirit, the virtues — what tradition meant and called "culture." Undoubtedly, the content of the culture is totally different today; the culture of the gentry has been replaced by the culture of the people, namely the peasantry and proletariat and all that is understood by this. However, some aspects common to both remain: whatever is good for China is good for the whole world. The traditional Chinese view was always universal and marked with a millenary and utopian dimension, both in the orthodox tradition and in the protest movements.

The Maoist contribution to the traditional concept of superiority is, of course, activism. Traditional superiority desired to bring redemption to the world — but without taking any practical action in this direction. This was a closed-in superiority, one of passivity, tolerance, and complacency. Maoist superiority is far more missionary: it is active, not satisfied with the status quo but desirous of changing it; displeased with reality and impatient. It does not wait, as in the more traditional era, for others to come to China to learn the truth, but is concerned with spreading the "correct" values in any possible way.

CONCLUSION

It was undoubtedly the Chinese reality that played the major role in determining the general course of the Chinese Communist revolution. In the first half of the twentieth century, China was no more than a backward, fundamentally agrarian society, disintegrated and humiliated. China's traditional empire, based for hundreds of years on the same social order, collapsed under the pressure of foreign powers. This situation in itself represented one of the deepest contradictions in world history.

Under these circumstances the new value-system required had to manifest at least three qualities: to offer a sound explanation for such turns of history; to provide the right strategy for overcoming national inferiority; and to assure China a brighter future in conformity with some traditional Chinese goals.

Contrary to other social ideologies, Marxism-Leninism embodied all these three qualities. It explained China's present decline as a passing historical stage, promising at the same time an inevitable better future that resembled, in general, traditional Chinese *Ta-t'ung* notions.[48] Furthermore, Leninism supplied the solution to China's most urgent problem — a strategy for terminating foreign exploitation and for achieving national unity. Pre-Lenin Marxism did not appeal to Chinese intellectuals not only, as is commonly accepted, because it was unsuitable for China's economic and social backwardness, but also precisely because it lacked the national dimension.

These, then, are the major elements Maoism has absorbed from the socialist tradition: its general direction (i.e., the terminology, aims, and ideals); its dialectics (extremely universalized to answer the immense gaps between the aims and the existing conditions); and finally, its principles of political organization and strategy.

From this point of view, it can be said that Mao's revolution up to 1949 was mainly carried out within the Leninist framework and according to its concepts, the differences being of emphasis rather than of substance. This definitely cannot be said about China after the takeover. While national objects had basically been achieved, most of the attention has since been devoted to socio-political and economic tasks. It is precisely here that the outstanding innovations of Maoism lie: on the one hand, the attempt to realize subjective proletarianization of the entire society, while ignoring the economic base needed for such a process; on the other hand, the attempt to build a modern and industrial economic base, while relying on these same subjective proletarian virtues.

These two attempts represent a complete deviation both from Marxism-Leninism and from Western experience in general. Paradoxically, it was the Chinese tradition that helped Mao devise the necessary methods and techniques and, moreover, insist on giving priority to socio-political transformation. Notwithstanding the reversal of stages, the objects remain Marxist and the approach is still dialectical, although much more subjective. This curious mixture of elements has been put to the test during China's long revolutionary experience, thereby making them legitimate and universal.

NOTES

1 See for example: C.P. Fitzgerald, *The Birth of Communist China* (Harmondsworth: Penguin, 1964), especially pp. 118—19, 143, 163, 190—91.

2 See for example: Karl A. Wittfogel, "The Legend of 'Maoism'," *The China Quarterly*, No. 1 (January — March, 1960), pp. 72—86 and No. 2. (April — June, 1960), pp. 16—34; Arthur A. Cohen, *The Communism of Mao Tse-tung* (Chicago: University of Chicago 1964), pp. 188—93. The conviction that Maoist China is totally a product of foreign ideas which have nothing to do with the Chinese tradition is, of course, widely held in Taiwan. See for example: Teng Kung-hsuan, "Maoism Vs. Chinese Cultural Tradition," *Issues & Studies* (Taipei), Vol. IV, No. 9 (June, 1968), pp. 1—8.

3 For example, see the different evaluations of "Stalinism" and "Chineseness" in Maoism by the various contributors to "Maoism: A Symposium," *Problems of Communism*, Vol. XV, No. 5 (September — October, 1966), pp. 1—30.

4 Cf. A. Doak Barnett, *China After Mao* (Princeton: Princeton University Press, 1967), pp. 44—45.

5 Stuart R. Schram, *The Political Thought of Mao Tse-tung* (Harmondsworth: Penguin, 1969), p. 30, and Benjamin Schwartz, "China and the West in the 'Thought of Mao Tse-tung'," in Ping-ti Ho and Tang Tsou (eds.), *China in Crisis*, Vol. I (Chicago: University of Chicago Press, 1968), p. 378—79. See also Franz Schurmann, *Ideology and Organization in Communist China* (Berkeley: University of California Press, 1968), p. 50.

6 See Mao Tse-tung, "On the Correct Handling of Contradictions Among the People," in R.R. Bowie & J.K. Fairbank (eds.), *Communist China 1955—1959, Policy Documents with Analysis* (Cambridge, Mass: Harvard University Press, 1962), pp. 275—94.

7 See Derk Bodde, "Harmony and Conflict in Chinese Philosophy," in Arthur F. Wright (ed.), *Studies in Chinese Thought* (Chicago: University of Chicago Press, 1953), pp. 19—80.

8 One author observes: "Chinese rebels from the most ancient times seem to have shared some fundamental beliefs with their natural antagonists, emperor and officials." Yuji Muramatsu, "Some Themes in Chinese Rebel Ideologies," in Arthur F. Wright (ed.), *The Confucian Persuasion* (Stanford: Stanford University Press, 1968), p. 248.

9 Mao Tse-tung, "On the Historical Experience of the Dictatorship of the Proletariat," in Bowie & Fairbank, *Communist China 1955—1959. . .*, p. 148. See also Schram, *Political Thought of Mao. . . .*, pp. 303—04.

10 Schurmann, *Ideology and Organization. . .*, pp. 102—03.

11 In Marx's terms: "Communism. . . is the definitive resolution of the antagonism between man and nature, and between man and man." T.B. Bottomore, (ed. & trans.), *Karl Marx: Early Writings* (London: C.A. Watts, 1963), p. 155.

12 Lloyd Eastman, "Mao, Marx and the Future Society," *Problems of Com-*

munism, Vol. XVIII, No. 3 (May — June, 1969), pp. 22—23; Schram, *Political Thought of Mao...*, pp. 72, 73, 89, 148 n.

13 "The Chinese Communists... believe that the arena of class struggle cannot take place abstractly within a class as a whole, but must be fought out within each individual human being": Schurmann, *Ideology and Organization...*, p. 32. Cf. Benjamin Schwartz, *Communism and China: Ideology in Flux* (Cambridge, Mass.: Harvard University Press, 1968), p. 21.

14 Benjamin Schwartz, *Chinese Communism and the Rise of Mao* (New York: Harper Torchbooks, 1967), pp. 191—95; "The Polemics Seen by a Non Polemicist," *Problems of Communism,* Vol. XIII, No. 2 (March — April, 1964), p. 106. Cf. Schurmann, *Ideology and Organization...*, p. 516.

15 Bodde, "Harmony and Conflict..."

16 Barnett, *China After Mao...*, p. 25. This does not mean, of course, that Mao underestimates the importance of expertise in general, and particularly of technical knowledge, for the achievement of Communist goals in China. On the contrary, because they are indispensable for the future development of China, experts cannot be allowed to "deviate." See Joseph R. Levenson, *Confucian China and Its Modern Fate: A Trilogy,* Vol. III: *The Problem of Historical Significance* (Berkeley: University of California Press, 1968), p. 81.

17 See the comments of H. Franke in Ho and Tsou (eds.), *China in Crisis,* Vol. I, pp. 41—50; and Joseph Needham, "The Past in China's Present," *The Centennial Review,* Vol.IV (1960), pp. 145—78, 281—308.

18 Jerome Ch'en (ed.), *Mao* (New Jersey: Prentice-Hall, 1969), p. 37.

19 "The Russians, particularly under Stalin, appear never to have understood the need for a basic transformation of the spiritual identities of individuals in organization, or if they did, they could not devise methods for bringing about such a transformation." Schurmann, *Ideology and Organization...*, p. 34.

20 Maurice Meisner, "Utopian Goals and Ascetic Values in Chinese Communist Ideology," *Journal of Asian Studies,* Vol. XXVII, No. 1 (November, 1968), pp. 103—04.

21 This is a familiar theme in Mao's thought. For example: "The country's economic conditions being what they are, the technical transformation will take somewhat longer than the social." Quoted by Schram, *Political Thought of Mao...* p. 346.

22 Mao Tse-tung, "On the Ten Great Relationships," April, 1956, published in Ch'en (ed.), *Mao,* pp. 78—80.

23 See Boyd Compton, *Mao's China: Party Reform Documents 1942—1944* (Seattle: University of Washington Press, 1967). On traditional elements in the Cheng-Feng movement, see: David S. Nivison, "Communist Ethics and Chinese Tradition," *Journal of Asian Studies,* Vol. XVI, No. 1 (November, 1956), pp. 61—68.

24 Robert J. Lifton, *Thought Reform and the Psychology of Totalism* (Harmondsworth: Penguin, 1961), Ch. 20.

25 David S. Nivison, "Communist Ethics...," pp. 55—56; and "The Problem of

'Knowledge' and 'Action' in Chinese Thought since Wang Yang-ming," in A.F. Wright (ed.), *Studies in Chinese Thought . . .,* pp. 112—45.

26 Schwartz, *Communism and China. . .,* p. 21.

27 See note 15.

28 See for example: Mark Gayn, "Mao Tse-tung Reassessed," in F. Schurmann & Orville Schell (eds.), *Communist China* (New York: Vintage, 1967), pp. 92—108; Robert J. Lifton, *Revolutionary Immortality, Mao Tse-tung and the Chinese Cultural Revolution* (New York: Random House, 1968), pp. XV, 32.

29 Rhoads Murphey, "Man and Nature in China," *Modern Asian Studies,* Vol. I, No. 4 (1967), p. 319. "The idea of 'war against nature' is a favorite one of Mao's, and can be traced back at least as far as 1938." Schram, *Political Thought of Mao. . .,* p. 90. See also pp. 391—393. For the application of this idea to reality, see for example: "Battling with Nature," *Peking Review,* Vol. II, No. 49 (Dec. 8, 1959), p. 3.

30 Mao Tse-tung, *Selected Works* (Peking: Foreign Languages Press, 1965), Vol. I, p. 283; Vol. II, p. 152.

31 Stuart Schram, "The Chinese and Leninist Components in the Personality of Mao Tse-tung," *Asian Survey,* Vol. III, No. 6 (June, 1963), pp. 263—68.

32 Harold Zvi Schiffrin, "The 'Great Leap' Image in Early Chinese Nationalism," *Asian and African Studies* (Jerusalem), Vol. III (1967), pp. 101—19.

33 Maurice Meisner, *Li Ta-chao and the Origins of Chinese Marxism* (Cambridge, Mass.: Harvard University Press, 1967), Ch. VI.

34 Shlomo Avineri, *The Social and Political Thought of Karl Marx* (Cambridge: Cambridge University Press, 1970), pp. 65—70.

35 See Dona Torr, *Marx on China 1853—1860* (London: Lawrence and Wishart, 1951); Karl A. Wittfogel, "The Marxist View of China," *The China Quarterly,* No. 11 (July — September, 1962), pp. 1—20 and No. 12 (October — December, 1962), pp. 154—69; Maurice Meisner, "The Despotism of Concepts: Wittfogel and Marx on China," *The China Quarterly,* No. 16 (October — December, 1963), pp. 99—111. Also Donald M. Lowe, *The Function of 'China' in Marx, Lenin, and Mao* (Berkeley: University of California Press, 1966); George Lichtheim, "Marx and the Asiatic Mode of Production," *St. Anthony's Papers,* No. 14 (London: 1963), pp. 86—112.

36 Murphey, "Man and Nature. . .," pp. 324, 333.

37 E. Balazs, "Tradition and Revolution in China," in *Chinese Civilization and Bureaucracy* (New Haven: Yale University Press, 1967), p. 153.

38 Meisner, *Li Ta-chao . . .,* pp. 80—89; 234—56.

39 For example: "It was the class struggle of the peasants, the peasant uprisings and peasant wars, that constituted the real motive force of historical development in Chinese feudal society." Mao Tse-tung, *Selected Works,* Vol. II, p. 308. See also James P. Harrison, "Communist Interpretations of the Chinese Peasant Wars," *The China Quarterly,* No. 24 (October — December, 1965), pp. 92—118.

40 Chalmers A. Johnson, *Peasant Nationalism and Communist Power* (Stanford: Stanford University Press, 1962). See also Donald G. Gillin's Review article,

" 'Peasant Nationalism' in the History of Chinese Communism," *Journal of Asian Studies,* Vol. XXIII, No. 2 (February, 1964), pp. 269—89.

41 Stuart Schram and Helene Carrere d'Encausse (eds.), *Marxism and Asia* (London: Allen Lane—The Penguin Press, 1969), pp. 13—15, 122—23.

42 Maurice Meisner, "Leninism and Maoism: Some Populist Perspectives on Marxism-Leninism in China," *The China Quarterly,* No. 45 (January — March, 1971), pp. 2—36.

43 Meaning, of course, the petty bourgeoisie and the national bourgeoisie and not the "compradores." For the differences see Mao Tse-tung, "Analysis of the Classes in Chinese Society" (1926), *Selected Works,* Vol. I, pp. 13—21. Also Schram, *Political Thought of Mao . . .,* pp. 241—46.

44 Mao, "On the People's Democratic Dictatorship" (1949), *Selected Works,* Vol. IV, pp. 411—24. See also Schram and d'Encausse (eds.), *Marxism and Asia . . .,* pp. 66—67; Schram, *Political Thought of Mao . . .,* pp. 76—78.

45 Schram and d'Encausse (eds.), *Marxism and Asia. . .,* pp. 14—15, 121—22.

46 Schram, *Political Thought of Mao . . .,* p. 42.

47 Schram and d'Encausse (eds.); *Marxism and Asia,* pp. 27—30, 149—203.

48 Mao himself used this term referring to future Communist society: see "On the People's Democratic Dictatorship," *Selected Works,* Vol. IV, pp. 412, 414, and 423, n. 1.

TRADITIONALISM AND SOCIALISM IN BURMA'S POLITICAL DEVELOPMENT

MARTIN RUDNER

Socialism in Burma represents the outcome of an historical sequence of political actions involving selection among rival traditional and modern conceptions of political life. This selection process arose out of political power relationships among competing elites holding differing expectations of the existing situation and varying attitudes toward change. At times these selections reflected politically-determined value preferences; at other times they expressed forced responses to pressures from an external situation, or even historical accident.

Nor did socialism derive from a linear and cumulative sequence of political selection, beginning with a traditional state and culminating in a modern solution. Rather the equilibrium and content of traditionalism and modernism fluctuated over time, according to the balance and composition of political forces wielding dominant authority. As each selection crystallized through authority, the stage was set for subsequent political action.

The process of selection has operated on two analytically distinct levels, that of political philosophy and that of political structure. Since the emergence of a tradition-bound socialist ideology in Burma has been aptly treated elsewhere,[1] this shall be included in the following discussion as a given variable, while the focus will be instead on the political-structural phase of the selection process. Among the points to be stressed are the social organization of political power; the connection between ecclesiastical and temporal political authority; the pattern of economic control and its association with political power; and the relationship between the authority center and societal groups on the periphery, between ruler and ruled.[2] Traditional versus modern variations in political structure, in tandem with their ideological expressions of political culture, have constituted the leading issues of political development in modern Burma.

It is no doubt significant to note that Burma's path to socialism diverged from the rules of the Marxian dialectic. Burma had neither the requisite industrial base nor the proletarian vanguard. Neither was this a Leninist stratagem, since the spearhead of Burmese socialism was not the Communist Party. Rather, Marxian socialism had been integrated into the nascent nationalist movement through an inner process of political selection, conditioned by the pressures of colonial rule and the legacy of classical Burma. It is to this historical sequence of political selection that we now turn.

THE CLASSICAL TRADITION

Burmese political tradition derived from the ideal of a sacralized kingship. Royal authority flowed through the precepts of Buddhism, which set out the goals and norms of political power.[3] Theravada Buddhism not only provided an ecclesiastical basis for monarchical authority, but it further forged an ideological link between the rulers of the political center and the ruled in the rural periphery.[4] Here the welfare state system established in India by Ashoka (c. 300 BCE) came to be regarded as the archetype for political Buddhism. This synthesis of royal despotism[5] with an imperative social ethic underlay the classical Burmese tradition of a "political Ashokan Buddhism."[6]

Political organization, according to this classical tradition, concentrated legitimate authority at the center, i.e., the king. By tradition the king was endowed with ultimate political power. Moreover, official status in this classical tradition derived from designation by the king, who thereby controlled entry into the political elite. Since legitimate politics remained the exclusive prerogative of the appointed officials composing the Royal Court, it was the king who in effect described the boundaries of participation in the political process. In the classical tradition of Burmese monarchy only the Sangha, the order of Buddhist monks, could act as an independent influence upon the politics of the Royal Court.[7]

Political roles in the classical tradition may be described in terms of four tiers, or circles, of relationship to political authority. At the center of political authority stood the king, the supreme patron of Buddhism as well as the ultimate arbiter of political life. Included within the boundaries of the center were the Sangha and the official Court, the former the ecclesiastical underpinning and the latter the executive extension of royal power. Beyond the Royal Court in the third tier were the Burman Buddhist commoners. Although excluded from direct participation in politics, most commoners traditionally owed personal fealty to the king for which they were rewarded by royal grants of land and government services. This traditional social contractual relationship produced a sense of identity between Burman Buddhist commoners and the sacralized monarchy.*[8] Others, not belonging to the Burman or Buddhist fold, were entitled to no claims whatever on the classical political system. Despite the ostensibly universalistic outlook of 'Buddhism, the political criteria for involvement in politics in the classical tradition laid particularistic stress on Burman Buddhist ethnicity and, at the center, royal designation.

Economic life was closely dependent upon the operations of the political process. Since in classical times Burman society was located in the Irrawady Valley of Upper Burma, the agricultural economy required a well-organized administration of water control. This agricultural dependency on irrigation and drainage coincided with the centralized power of the classical Burman Kingdom, which accordingly assumed responsibility for rice production in the riverine economy. The monarchy also assumed management of the country's forests and mines, the main non-agricultural industries, and monopolized foreign trade in these products.[9] Even if these undertakings were rented out to private merchants, as they often were, the state still retained its residual administrative control. Contrary to the widespread misconception of Buddhism's disregard for material well-being, the Burman Buddhist Kingdom took upon itself overall ownership and control of economic enterprise in classical Burma.[10]

The economic involvement of the classical Burmese Kingdom extended beyond concern with production to the management of distribution. In accordance with its Buddhist ethic, the monarchy was obliged to achieve a satisfactory redistribution of economic welfare. Kings of the classical period implemented this ideal by introducing a progressive system of taxation, including a tax on wealth, while providing through the means of transfer payments free food and loans to ensure a minimum level of income.[11] It is significant to note in this context that no social group of any economic position outside the circle of the Royal Court was permitted to exercise claims on the political process.[12] Nor did non-Burman, non-Buddhist groups share

---

* Most Burman Buddhist commoners belonged to the hereditary Ahmudan class. At this point it is convenient to distinguish between Burmans, the dominant ethnic group of Burma, and the legal term "Burmese" which indicates citizenship in the Union of Burma. Where the occasion so warrants, the two will be differentiated in this paper.

in redistribution. Rather the classical concept of the Royal "Welfare State" was one of strict monarchical absolutism, imbued with Buddhist social ethic and therefore restricted to those linked ascriptively to both crown and altar. In this classical ideal, the welfare state was a rational economic prerequisite for the Theravada Buddhist path of salvation.[13] Economic policy therefore became but an instrument of the political cultural goals of the classical Burman state.

The leitmotiv of the Burman state, in the classical tradition, was its Buddhist ethic. Through the fusion of the ecclesiastical establishment with political authority a symbiotic relationship resulted whereby Buddhism conferred religious legitimacy upon royalty in exchange for the structured form accorded the faith by the state.[14] Buddhism was more than merely a religion in Burma, for it permeated broad cultural values, ethical precepts, social attitudes, political expectations, and state symbols.[15] Since both Buddhism and political life focused upon the king, the capacity of the political center to change the world by political action was virtually limitless. Yet this ultimate power of politics was geared, by its linkage to religious ethic, to the realization of Buddhism's cosmic ideal.[16] Burma, according to the classical tradition, was distinctly a sacralized state committed to a political purpose in pursuit of its Buddhist essence.[17]

If Buddhism prescribed the highest of ideals. it is not surprising that the historical gap between the ethic and the political reality was frequently great — and occasionally terrible. Certain of the Burmese kings did subscribe, to be sure, to the achievement of Buddhist ethical goals, but many honored the ideal more in the breach than the observance. Indeed several of the Burmese kings became infamous for the cruelty and terror of their reigns.[18] However, the classical precepts of politics lived on in Burma, as elsewhere, through historical myth. Myth contributed a certain Messianic element to the classical tradition, whereby political action toward the Buddhist Nirvana henceforward attended upon the advent of the Just Ruler.

THE IMPACT OF COLONIAL RULE

Burma finally succumbed to British conquest following three wars lasting over a period of sixty years. What began as a series of skirmishes on the Indian-Burmese frontier had led, by 1826, to Britain's capture of the Arakan and Tenasserim coasts. In 1852 Lower Burma was seized. And after 1886 came the final annexation of Upper Burma.[19] As a result of formal absorption under British rule into the

Indian Empire radical changes were introduced into traditional Burma, particularly into its traditional concept of government, its social stratification, and its economic structure. Burma's passing under European Imperial control meant, in effect, its alienation from its classical political tradition.

The final destruction of the Upper Burmese Kingdom and its replacement by a British colonial administration brought in its wake a revolutionary departure from the Buddhist ethos of government. Imperial rule established a secular regime antithetical to the sacralized classical conception of political order and ends.[20] Probably the most telling description of the political-cultural shock wrought upon Burma by British conquest comes from the pen of Manuel Sarkisyanz:

> The Palace of Mandalay, which had been venerated as the pivot of the cosmic and at the same time moral order became converted into a British club, the 'Upper Burma Club.' And on the place which alone was to stand immovably, even when the whole earth would shake and tremble, British officers and merchants were now drinking whiskey. The state ceased being the symbol of a world order. It was no longer an expression of a system of proprieties in human and superhuman relations. Burma's government had departed from its cosmic prototype.[21]

Following the collapse of the throne of Burma, the state had lost its cosmic purpose. Not only was Buddhism formally disestablished, but the colonial government now allowed Christian missionary activity and secular schooling to threaten Buddhism's residual position in society. And, adding insult to injury, colonial Burma was annexed and governed as a backward province of Imperial India, not meriting separate administrative identity until 1936.

The process of colonialization also engendered a substantial disruption of Burma's traditional social order, bringing about a displacement of Burmans from their past predominance. Native allies of the British, notably the Karens, very early adopted Christianity and played a key role as pawns of the colonial conquest. They were rewarded in turn by a favorable dispensation of offices in the colonial administration.[22] At the same time annexation to India resulted in a fairly large influx into Burma of Indian bankers, merchants, clerks, professionals, and even laborers. To these newcomers accrued most of the economic advantages of colonial rule,[23] so much so that during the first third of the present century Rangoon, the colonial capital, took on the appearance of an essentially Indian town.[24]

Whereas the geographic center of classical Burman civilization was in Upper Burma, the colonial administrative and economic systems centered on Lower Burma, the Irrawady Delta, and Rangoon in partic-

ular. Along with this shift in axis there occurred a southward migra-
tion of Burmans from the old center to the new. Uprooted from their
traditional ties and village bonds, these migrants were to find themselves confined to the margin of the modern colonial center.[25] For
while the country grew increasingly prosperous as an adjunct of the
West, ruled by the British with intermediaries consisting of Anglicized indigenous minorities and Indian newcomers, the Burmans
found themselves quite incapable of coping with the vast forces of
modernization shaping colonial Burma.[26] Unable to participate in the
early process of social modernization, the Burmans found themselves
in a reversal of the social roles of the classical period: in the modern
center established by colonial rule, it was they who now occupied the
periphery.

The economic transformation of Burma between the British conquest and the First World War yielded a distribution of incomes that
reinforced the new pattern of social and ethnic stratification. Especially after the opening of the Suez Canal, Burma, along with other
Asian colonial territories, experienced a rapid economic development.
Export-induced growth led in particular to a considerable increase in
the rice-growing acreage of Lower Burma, which multiplied fifteen-
fold between 1830 and 1940. Most of the required investment came
from private British and Indian sources, amounting to probably the
greatest inflow of agricultural capital in Southern Asian history.[27]
These investments succeeded in transforming Burma from a subsistence agriculture to a cash-crop export economy.[28] As a result of this
development, prosperity had come to Burma, but in the form of a
narrow enclave economy.[29]

Although indigenous Burmans were increasingly redeployed into
the agricultural export sector, the colonial economic system failed to
ensure a parallel spread of development gains to rural rice cultivators.[30] Migrant Burman peasants who opened new rice lands in
Lower Burma increasingly found themselves dispossessed.[31] The age-
old evils of peasant credit relationships, coupled to wide fluctuations
in rice prices and unfamiliar and unstable land tenure laws, transferred,
in effect, most of the development gains from Burman cultivators to
alien rentiers.[32] Whereas in 1901/02 only 17 per cent of the culti-
vated land of Lower Burma was owned by absentee landlords, by
1930/31 the figure exceeded 30 per cent and by 1940 more than
two-thirds was rentier owned.[33] Most of this rentier ownership was
concentrated in the hands of Indian Chettyar moneylenders. On the
rice marketing side as well, cultivators were again subject to the

familiar inequities of middleman (Chettyar) relationships, as well as the monopolistic practices of British rice mills and trading companies.[34] It is hardly surprising in these circumstances that the real incomes of rice cultivators in Lower Burma appear to have fallen by at least a fifth, and probably even more, over the period of British colonial rule.[35] The introduction of a Western colonial economy removed Burman peasants from membership in their traditional welfare system — however imperfect — into a new situation of relative deprivation, both real and growing.

Neither did the colonial government concern itself with the amelioration of the economic well-being of the Burman peasantry. Shortly after the conquest the British administration abolished the state enterprises hitherto maintained by the traditional monarchy, discontinuing as well its welfare policies. Instead the British pursued a liberal laissez-faire approach to the Burmese economy. Under the guise of laissez-faire more was spent by the colonial government on police than on education, more on prisons than on public health and agricultural services combined.[36] Evidently the operational goals of the British administration were directed more at ensuring continual custody over the colony than at promoting widespread gains in economic well-being, either through rural development or income redistribution.[37] Traditional notions of the welfare state had clearly given way to the imperatives of the colonial economic system.

Colonial rule accordingly served effectively to undermine the main political-cultural, social, and economic pillars of traditional Burman statehood.[38] The initial reaction of Burmans took the form of almost endemic turbulence as traditional social controls broke down. The social unrest became politically tinged through simmering guerrilla warfare, violent outbreaks, and occasional race riots.[39] Then, during the 1920's and 1930's, this discontent crystallized into political programs aimed at ending the British colonialist administration and restoring Burmese nationhood.

THE NATIONALIST RESURGENCE

Indeed, Burman political response to the British conquest had not been long in taking nationalist shape. Though influenced by the National Congress of India, to which Burma had been annexed, and given inspiration by the activities of Sun Yat-sen in China as well as by Japan, the resurgent Burman nationalist movement was very much an autochthonous development. Its legitimacy was rooted in the political tradition of Burman statehood, while its several strands articulated needs and aspirations prompted by the colonial situation. Burman nationalism rose to a crescendo during the years between the world wars, reaching a climax in 1943 when, under Japanese occupation, Burma was accorded nominal "independence."[40] Having crossed the threshold of national being, neither the disappointment of continuing Japanese neo-colonialism nor the subsequent return of the British could long delay Burma's transition to genuine independence in 1948.

Perhaps more than its contemporaries elsewhere, the Burmese nationalist movement had to undertake very early in its development a selection between traditional and modern solutions to the fundamental issues of political structure and political culture. Traditionalist sentiments toward political life still proved strong in a society where the cosmic Buddhist formula for statehood remained a central feature of the popular system of beliefs.[41] Moreover, abiding memories of the last Burman Kingdom loomed large, and this psychological legacy provided an emotionally-appealing alternative to the cultural, economic, and social dislocation wrought by Western colonial rule. And yet it was quite apparent, especially to the nascent Western-educated Burman intelligentsia, that a nationalist Burma would have to come to terms with modern political forms. The process of political selection through which Burmese nationalism accordingly passed required choosing among painful alternatives, between deep-rooted traditional formulae and appealing modern concepts of statehood.

Divisions between traditionalists and modernizers in the Burmese national movement related both to the composition and structure of political authority as well as to its dominant goals. These divisions may be treated, for analytical purposes, in terms of set combinations of political-structural and political-cultural aspirations. Accordingly, groups advocating restoration of a sacralized Buddhist society based upon the traditional structure of society can be described as "Buddhist-traditionalists." Conversely, strict "Westernizers" adhered to modern, mainly Anglicized, political institutions and a secular political culture. Between these extremes remains a spectrum of reconciliation among alternative combinations of modern and traditional forms of political structure and political culture. The "Buddhist-modernist" formula accepted modern innovations in political organization though in the continuing context of a sacred society. A "traditional-syncretic" concept of statehood retained certain Buddhist structural or cultural elements, without, however, necessarily aiming at a completely sacralized society.[42] All these divisions have at one time or another served to determine the character and direction of nationalist political activity.

These divisions in the ideological motivation and political goals of Burmese nationalists should be regarded as analytical categories rather than as fixed groupings. Certainly in the real world boundaries between them were imprecise and overlapped. Burmese classified in any one way sometimes re-emerged in another grouping at different times or situations. Rather than being rigid, these divisions reflect the ebb and flow of alternative group selections between the forces of traditionalism and modernization in Burmese political life. Indeed, it will be seen that these divisional groupings are not determined solely by the Burmese themselves, but frequently represent the response of Burmese nationalists to the changing colonial political environment.

The history of Burmese nationalism emphasizes the role of changes in the colonial setting as a determinant of nationalist politics. To be sure, several factors affected the evolution of the Burmese nationalist movement, and it is difficult to ascertain incremental changes over brief periods of time. Nevertheless, a broader time perspective provides evidence of meaningful clusters of changes in the composition and goals of Burmese nationalism. Three main clusters suggest themselves, each demarcated by politically significant shifts in the colonial setting. The first marked the annexation of Burma to India and introduction of direct colonial rule, which lasted from the British conquest until 1937; there followed a period of restored separate identity and limited constitutional self-government, up to 1945;[43] it was succeeded by the transition to independence and nationalist rule. By observing the changes in nationalist groupings from one period to the next we can gain insight into the process of selection which determined the Buddhist-traditionalist-socialist-Westernist complexion of politics in independent Burma.

The period of annexation and direct colonial rule marked the formative phase of Burman nationalism. Probably its most distinctive consequence was its confirmation of Buddhist religious symbols as the hallmark of Burman national identity. Buddhism not only served as a central point of differentiation from India — the immediate threat to Burma's identity — but also offered a widely-accepted counter to the intrusion of Western values and colonial practices. Buddhism as a politico-religious doctrine furthermore offered emotional respite, if not political promise, from the grievous cultural, economic, and social shocks of Western rule.[44]

Compared to the appeals of Buddhism, Westernization suffered a political handicap through blatant association with India and the

Indians, and with British colonial rule and its Anglicized minority supporters in Burma. Westernization thereafter came to be popularly identified with the very sources of Burma's ills. It is hardly surprising, therefore, that the earliest Burman nationalists rejected a strictly Western solution, aiming instead at the regeneration of traditional political values.

It was under the leadership of groups infused with Buddhist aspirations that Burman nationalism first received constitutional expression and became a popular movement. Characteristically the British-educated Burman elite, destined to the civil service and legal professions, initially articulated nationalist demands through the Young Men's Buddhist Association and the "Shoe Question" of 1916-17.[45] Though their campaign was ostensibly based on religious appeal, the Western-educated elite pressed first for constitutional reforms, then for separation from India. Since they tended to focus very largely on constitutional procedures, particularly elections to and proceedings in a narrow-franchise colonial Legislative Council, the Western elite shortly found themselves outflanked by a populist, anti-Western (and also anti-Indian) Buddhist-traditionalist movement.

Organized around the General Council of Buddhist Associations (after 1921 known as the General Council of Burmese Associations) and led by militant Anglophobic *pongyis* (Buddhist monks), among them the radical U Ottama, the Buddhist-traditionalist movement boycotted colonial political institutions while cultivating traditional Burman beliefs and forms of authority. [46] Sporadic violence on the part of these groups, energized by deteriorating rural social and economic conditions, culminated in 1930 in the Saya San rebellion. Here the traditional Burman concept of statehood was blatantly manipulated to galvanize wide-scale support against the colonial authorities. [47] Though the British finally suppressed the rebellion, after slightly more than a year, Burman nationalism clearly had become a popular movement. Coupled to continued pressure by the British-educated elite through the legitimate organs of colonial government, this transformation by 1935 impelled Britain to grant Burma a new Constitution invoking both separation from India and limited responsible parliamentary rule.

These changes in the colonial setting impelled the nationalist movement to adjust its tactics to the new Constitutional situation. Burman nationalism was now clearly in the ascent against its Westernized opponents, including immigrant Indians, Anglicized minorities, and British businessmen. Burma's separate identity was no longer at issue;

its government was set on a course toward self-rule by stages. However, the changed colonial setting also exposed some of the glaring political weaknesses of the then-leading nationalist groupings.

The British-educated elite which had hitherto been closely associated with reform of the colonial legislature had by now forgone much of their radicalism, and in any case neglected to extend their political constituency to rural Burma. Conversely, the rural-oriented, militant Buddhist-traditionalist movement had suffered grievous defeat in the Saya San venture, while its obscurantism tended to alienate the more modernized, urban nationalists. Attempts by the leading nationalist personalities of the day, Dr. Ba Maw and U Saw, to bridge this gap in the Burman political community through the parliamentary mechanism foundered over the incompatibility of urban/rural, Buddhist-modernist/Buddhist-traditionalist expectations.[48]

Taking advantage of Burma's conquest during the Pacific War, Dr. Ba Maw agreed to collaborate with the Japanese in the proclamation in 1943 of an "independent" regime. Though structured along modern, characteristically fascist lines, this wartime regime also adopted the symbolic appurtenances of traditional Buddhist statehood.[49] In a short time Dr. Ba Maw's Buddhist-modernist experiment compromised itself as a puppet of Japanese Imperialism, so that initiative in the Burman nationalist movement passed into the militant hands of young student radicals.

The radical student group that emerged at the fore of the nationalist movement by the end of the Constitutional period grew out of the interplay of social and political forces during the 1920's and 1930's. Drawn from the traditional village environment of Lower Burma, these students were educated locally in English-language schools often up to university level,[50] as compared to an earlier generation of Burmans educated in Britain itself. They accordingly represented a closer synthesis of Western and Burman values. Moreover a certain segment of students, notably from Rangoon University, had chosen in effect to forsake the promise of careers as docile civil servants in favor of militant nationalist action.[51] Significantly, the efforts of these politicized students were aimed primarily at groups similarly on the margin between Western and Burman cultural influence. First they directed their efforts toward the English school students themselves, then toward the recently-urbanized laborers. Finally – and initially without marked success – they proselytized migrant peasants.[52]

The political programs formulated by the politicized students over

the course of their militant demonstrations and later parliamentary
activities reflected the cultural marginalism of their appeal. Organized
after 1930 in the *Dobama Asiayone* (We Burman Society), the politicized students aimed at obtaining political equality between Burmans,
said to have been humbled by a "slave mentality," and their British
colonial masters. [53] This goal, to be sure, implied the modernization of
Burman society to meet the West on its own terms. Yet while the
main thrust of the politicized students was modernist, their acceptance of Western forms was inhibited by its association with colonial
rule and its economic, social, and cultural ills.

During the 1930's, however, politicized students were presented
with a potent new Western and anti-colonial ideology, Marxism. Marxism especially impressed Rangoon student circles as much for its stress
on equality, militancy, and progress as for its apparent adaptability to
traditional notions of a welfare state. This ideological congruency was
to be reinforced on the terminological level by the use of Buddhist
philosophical language, the only available medium for mass political
communications, for expounding Marxian concepts. [54] Since at the
time of Marxism's introduction Rangoon intellectuals had been duly
inspired by feedback from the ill-fated Saya San rebellion, particularly
the nexus between Burman nationalism and traditional concepts of
Burman-Buddhist statehood, [55] Marxism thereafter came to be blend-
ed by politicized student groups into a revolutionary nationalist
Buddhist-syncretic program for political action.

This Buddhist-syncretic political program of the *Dobama Asiayone*,
or "Thakins," gradually garnered political support from similarly
culturally marginal groups. [56] In the 1936 General Elections under the
new Constitution the Thakins Party managed to obtain only minor
parliamentary representation. Nevertheless they maintained stead-
fastly their anti-colonial virtue while other parties maneuvered for
power in concert with the colonial authorities, not even hesitating to
use this power to suppress dissident nationalist manifestations. Indeed
this served only to further radicalize the Thakins and their
supporters. [57]

THE ANTI-FASCIST PEOPLES' FREEDOM LEAGUE

Impelled by their radical anti-colonialism the Thakins succumbed to
Japan's "Asia for the Asians" propaganda. They assisted the Japanese
invasion and lent support to the subsequent "independent" Burmese
regime. When the fictitiousness of Burma's independence became

clear, the Thakins reacted by forming the Anti-Fascist Peoples Freedom League (AFPFL) and launched a guerrilla campaign against the Japanese, eventually even gaining British military support. By war's end the AFPFL had emerged to leadership in the Burman nationalist movement. Despite initial machinations at resistance by the returning British, agreement was finally reached with the AFPFL, which won an overwhelming mandate in the Constitutional Assembly elections of April 1947. Independence was thereafter assured, to be actually realized on January 4, 1948, under an AFPFL government. [58] What had catapulted the politicized ex-students of the AFPFL to the nationalist vanguard was their constant adherence to anti-colonialism, even in the face of the temptations of dyarchy, coupled to an appealingly radical Buddhist-syncretic political program and suitably charismatic leadership.

The spectrum of ideological commitment within the AFPFL leadership covered the full range of Buddhist-Marxist syncretism. While these intra-party differences were carefully sublimated during the period of nationalist struggle, they emerged to the surface with divisive impact once independence seemed assured. This infighting was the more embittered by the belief that, given the tremendous postwar authority of the AFPFL, the ideological formula actually selected would effectively shape the political destiny of a reborn Burma.

Emerging triumphantly from its wartime experiences, the AFPFL found itself deeply split between its Communist faction and its largely non-Communist, Buddhist-syncretic leadership. Parading their Marxist-Leninist affinity literally under a hammer-and-sickle banner, the Communists vigorously proclaimed their goal of a "modern" Nirbana — a Sovietized Burma. [59] Buddhism's role in this Communist schema, in its welfare state aspects, was merely as precedent for the introduction of revolutionary forms on the contemporary Soviet model. [60]

If this Soviet blueprint had limited appeal among the more modernized segments of Burma's labor force and peasantry, it could only alienate the mass of more traditional Burmans and put up the non-revolutionary leadership's guard. For a time the principal Communists adhered to an increasingly uneasy alignment with the AFPFL, despite a breakaway into insurgency by the extremist "Red Flags." Later the official "White Flag" Communists joined the insurrection, ostensibly as a violent reaction to the 1947 independence treaty with the United Kingdom. By then the Communists had been maneuvered into a seemingly anti-nationalist stand, so that from their confrontation at the threshold of independence the AFPFL came out as the custodian of nationalism.

Within the mainstream of the AFPFL the predominant Buddhist-syncretic ideology was further differentiated between leaders who emphasized its modern, socialist aspects and those of a more traditionalist bent. During the early postwar period of nationalist drive the political theme of the mainstream AFPFL was set by its popular, dynamic leader and political architect, Aung San. Aung San articulated an essentially social democratic political program, restricting Buddhism to the sphere of private belief and public ethics. In his image of a modern Burma both doctrinaire socialism and religion were conceded only marginal roles, if any, with emphasis instead on emergence of a secular, nationalist, social democracy:

> Even if we may be eager to build socialism in Burma, conditions are not ready for it. . . . We cannot do without capitalism and private enterprise yet, but we must see that they do not exploit the people but serve their welfare instead. For the peasants we must pursue the policy of land to the tiller. . . . Previously, because we were under foreign rule, many positions in the government service were not open to Burmans. Soon we shall be free, and Burmans will find opportunity to serve the country in *all* positions.
>
> The national minorities must enjoy their rights to the full. The people must also be able to exercise their power effectively . . . and to make the government machinery more responsive to their wishes.[61]

This was to be a highly pragmatic and nationalistic socialism, respectful of parliamentary procedure and minority rights and aiming at limited nationalization, land reforms, and the Burmanization of the public service.[62] Buddhism was to be relegated to a mere cultural position separate from political life:

> Some say that politics is religion. That also is not true. . . . Religion is a matter of individual conscience, while politics is social science. . . . We must draw a clear line between politics and religion, because the two are not one and the same thing. If we mix religion with politics, then we offend the spirit of religion itself. Politics is pure secular science.[63]

Buddhism would, however, play a role in remaking Burma's Western-style Constitution into something "essentially Burmese in ideology and purport."[64] In July 1947, this political blueprint came to sudden grief upon the assassination of Aung San, at the time Chief Minister of Burma, together with other leading members of his pre-independence

Cabinet by henchmen of the politician U Saw. To fill the resulting vacuum the British Governor called upon U Nu, vice-president of the AFPFL and president of the Constituent Assembly, to form the new government that was to lead Burma to independence.

The ascendancy of a syncretic Buddhist-socialist regime in independent Burma marked the outcome of a dual process of ongoing political selection. One process involved the recruitment of a nationalist political leadership from among the rival groupings of Burman society. Related to this was a process of ideological selection between traditional and modern conceptions of statehood which took place within the leadership elite and which will be considered below. Political recruitment, as has been seen, operated through the mechanism of nationalist competition and was tested upon occasion in the crucible of dramatic events. The resolution of the Party, its capacity to mobilize politically-significant backing, and its commitment to the nationalist cause, underwent trial under the Constitutional instrument of 1935 and the ordeal of Japanese conquest. From this acid test the AFPFL emerged to gain nationalist leadership. Yet in the last analysis, the political recruitment of the AFPFL leadership, destined to govern the character of independent Burma, depended on historical accident. In the event it was the sudden assassination of Aung San that brought to power a man, U Nu, for whom − more than most others in the AFPFL leadership − modern forms were comprehensible only in a familiar Buddhist context.

BUDDHISM AND SOCIALISM IN THE POLITICS OF INDEPENDENT BURMA

The fact of independence, devolving political control onto the nationalist leadership, obliged the introduction of policy content into the complex belief system that had hitherto provided them a comforting sense of direction and purpose. The urgency of nationalist movement had to make way for the more mundane need to establish criteria and guidelines for national policy. Here again a process of political selection among alternative traditional and modern goals of development was involved. Periodic changes in the goals actually pursued after independence reflect political upheavals altering the social composition of the ruling elite, or less dramatic but no less meaningful evolution of the existing elite's own perception of the ideal.

Since Burma's independence, its political life has been dominated for most intents and purposes by two elites − the AFPFL Party leadership and the Army Officers Corps.[65] Interestingly enough, the Buddhist Sangha, who had given Buddhist leadership and sanction to the early nationalist resurgence, after independence remained aloof from institutional involvement in political controversy.[66] Out-groups operating through violent insurrection — including ethnic-regional separatists as well as White Flag and Red Flag Communists — were contained, if not actually suppressed, during the 1950's by the AFPFL and Army working together. However, within the leadership of the AFPFL itself, and certainly between the Party and the Army, there remained distinct conceptual differences regarding the traditional-modern equilibrium in national strategy. These differences prompted the 1958 split in the AFPFL between its "Clean" and "Stable" factions and were instrumental in the Army's rising against the Party to take power in 1962.

By way of contrast with the orthodox Communists, the AFPFL leadership integrated Marxist ideological concepts into an essentially Buddhistic, though still syncretic, value order. Marxism for them reiterated Buddhism's familiar emphasis on social equality and distributive justice, i.e., the welfare state. Conversely they rejected the orthodox Communist insistence on class struggle and dialectic materialism as incompatible with Buddhism, stressing instead the reunion of hitherto antagonistic social groups around a Buddhist ethical base. Burman Buddhist nationalism accordingly provided an ethical background for the promulgation of "socialist" policies aimed at a *Lokha Nirbana*[67] — the Earthly Nirbana. In the popular view, and for most politicians as well, *Lokha Nirbana* came to be associated with a welfare-type state.[68] Others, more religiously inclined, regarded the *Lokha Nirbana* as but a worldly stepping stone to the ultimate, Buddhist Nirbana. Whereas such differences in nuance were later to generate political consequences, the central point remains that under initial AFPFL inspiration Buddhism had become the ethical mainspring, and socialism its policy expression for a syncretic national ideology.[69]

It might be noted, parenthetically, that the main political and social impact of Buddhism has never been as purely religious theory, but as an integrated belief system.[70] Buddhist states have historically merged their Buddhism with other cults into a more or less syncretic ideology, in which Buddhist ethics enjoyed pride of place. This legacy of ideological syncretism on social and political issues facilitated Buddhism's later accommodation with Marxian socialism in independent Burma.

Whereas Buddhism and socialism singly and together served as threads of ideological continuity for the nationalist movement, the mixture and balance of ideological syncretism was hardly consistent for all segments of the AFPFL. True to its nationalist appeal, the AFPFL included in its political constituency both the modern and traditional elements of Burmese society. It was precisely this dichotomy, reflected in personal rivalries, ideological differences, and divergent social interests, that was to divide the AFPFL between "two distinct classes" — the so-called "Educated" or "College" Socialists and the "Uneducated" or "Pongyikyaung" (Monastery School) Socialists.[71] The "Educated" group, led by U Kyaw Nyein and U Ba Swe, represented the urban labor and technocratic classes and were concerned with the more modern sectors of the economy. Though socialists, they utilized Buddhist religious symbols within the framework of their secular, modern objective of a socialist welfare state.[72]

In contrast, the "Uneducated" segment of AFPFL leadership was rooted in the peasantry and inclined toward a more traditional Buddhistic conception of socialism. This entailed, in effect, a gradual shift to a Buddhist-modernist ideological stand, in which socialism was intended as a political instrument for the realization of an essentially Buddhist cultural goal.[73] As the early unity of the Party wore thin over time, these many divisions — personal, social, ideological — crystallized in 1958 into an actual split between the Educated group, which became known as the AFPFL-Stable on the one hand, and the Pongyikyaung Socialist group, the AFPFL-Clean, later termed the Union Party, on the other. By virtue of "natural" electoral preponderance, shown in 1951, 1956, and again in 1960, this rural-oriented, Buddhist-modernist socialist faction, led by U Nu, succeeded in dominating political life during Burma's periods of parliamentary rule, 1948-58 and 1960-62.[74]

U Nu's successful leadership style combined an appealing political program with Messianic thrust and charismatic personality.[75] For U Nu, socialism was an instrument of political structure rooted in traditional Buddhism and aiming at the achievement of a *Lokha Nirbana.* Socialism thereby constituted an essential stage toward realization of *Matria Buddha,* the advent of the Buddha in whose imminent coming most Burmans believe.[76] This Buddhist-socialist blueprint for Messianic political action found support in the traditional Burman Buddhist conception of leadership, as one aware of the sources of human suffering and able to provide relief through policy means. Inheriting the mantle of power and benefiting from identification with both nationalist socialism and traditional Buddhism U Nu's political formula transformed him in the eyes of many into "a Buddha in the coming."[77] The sense of Messianic political purpose ascribed to U Nu typified the Weberian notion of a charismatic leader serving to bridge the cultural hiatus between traditional and modern value orders.

U Nu's Buddhist inspiration obtained policy expression through his government's steps toward the re-sacralization of the state as well as its treatment of social and economic issues. Independent Burma was conceived as a nominally secular democracy, yet Buddhism always occupied a special place in the state's politics.[78] Government support was extended to Buddhist religious institutions.[79] At one point U Nu even personally encouraged civil servants to practice meditation during working hours.[80] For the occasion of the 2500th anniversary of the Buddha's birth, U Nu's government convened in Rangoon a grandiose World Buddhist Council that went on from 1954 to 1956. Two years later U Nu, with the assent of his Cabinet, denounced Marxism as Communism and rejected both as antithetical to Buddhism.[81] By 1961 Buddhism had been officially proclaimed the religion of state, with due assurances given minority faiths.

Indeed it was in this sphere of relations with ethnic minorities that U Nu's Buddhist conception of politics underwent its severest test. Burma's 1947 Constitution had defined the new state as a federal union, albeit with highly centripetal features. However, the failure to accord federal status to certain ethnic minorities, notably the Karen and Mon, prompted these groups to respond by insurrection.[82] While the Union government managed, sometimes with difficulty, to contain the rebels militarily, a political solution to the minorities issue came up against divided opinion within the Cabinet itself. On the one hand U Nu held out for the original precept of union, which in effect meant subordination of ethnic minorities to dominant Burman nationalism and coincided with the traditional social hierarchy of the Burman Buddhist kingdom. His Buddhism, on the other hand, moved U Nu to seek accommodation with the insurgent minorities on the basis of tolerance. It nevertheless required more than a decade of intermittent civil war before even the principle of a restructured federal relationship was finally adopted into policy by U Nu's post-1960 Government.[83] Until then, the paradox of Buddhism as a traditional *Burman nationalist* force evidently outweighed its pacifist and tolerant spirit.

Regarding economic policy, the socialist principles[84] articulated in independent Burma's Constitution appear to owe as much to the classical Burman ideal as to the Marxian prescription. Significantly, in terms of the traditional legacy, Burma's new Constitution provided for the ultimate ownership of all lands by the state; the operation of all public utilities and the exploitation of natural resources by public or cooperative corporations; and the undertaking of national planning "with the aim of increasing the public wealth, of improving the material conditions of the people and raising the cultural level." Private enterprise was to be subject to and conditional upon public need. However the Constitution indicated none of the sense of urgency usually identified with European declarations of socialist intent. Rather it treated economic policy and planning as but stepping stones toward the realization of higher cultural values.[85]

Economic policies implemented by U Nu's government accordingly aimed at achieving an appropriate level and distribution of economic well-being so as to permit attainment of transcendental Buddhist goals. The keynote of this economic strategy was struck in 1954 with the adoption of the *Pyidawtha* ("Pleasant Royal Country") program.[86] Until that time, a two-year postwar reconstruction program had been undertaken, together with measures to rectify land tenure conditions. As a result of the Land Nationalization Act of 1948 property of absentee landlords, mainly Indian Chettyars, were expropriated with compensation, and the lands transferred to peasants.[87] The *Pyidawtha* program undertook to follow up the land reform with increased public investment in land reclamation and rehabilitation and agricultural services. Measures were introduced to alleviate the age-old exploitation of peasants through the provision of adequate low-cost agricultural credit and the reorganization of marketing cooperatives.[88] In the non-agricultural sphere, the Plan called for moderate industrial expansion and improvements to economic infrastructure and public utilities.[89] Social investment, particularly in rural public health and vocational and technical education, had a leading role to play in this Plan.[90]

The *Pyidawtha* program was anything but a radical social scheme for income redistribution and forced growth. The road to a "welfare state" was conceived instead in terms of social values and benefits: "good education," and "good health," "cultural values," "good character," and "good fellowship," as well as "good economic position."[91]

Political participation in policy formulation in U Nu's Burma involved both formal parliamentary procedures and extra-constitutional means. In accordance with the 1947 Constitution mass participation in politics operated through the parliamentary mechanism to give rise to an elected, British-style cabinet government. Three comparatively free and competitive general elections were actually held, in 1951, 1956, and 1960, resulting in clear-cut parliamentary majorities for U Nu's Party each time. Elections notwithstanding, Burma's party system nevertheless remained an essentially urban elitist device, extending its constituency to the countryside only at election time. While the mass of the peasantry were therefore able ultimately to decide the character and composition of government by their votes, effectively the responsibility for policy determination devolved more specifically upon those urbanized elites dominating the party system.[92]

Parliamentary control over government was only partial since there was an unclear demarcation of authority between elected politicians and the professional bureaucracy. Based originally on the Indian Civil Service, Burma's bureaucratic establishment enjoyed a legacy of power and control in colonial political affairs. Indeed, at the time of independence, there existed considerable suspicion between the nationalist Party leaders and the Burmese civil servants who had lately "served" the British. This suspicion reinforced conflicts over status and role between the politicians, who had made sacrifices on behalf of the nationalist struggle, and the educated, experienced ex-colonial civil service.[93] To be sure, senior bureaucrats continued to serve their respective cabinet ministers, even attending cabinet sessions when their subjects were deliberated, and managed the machinery of their specialized departments. Yet this Westernized professional bureaucracy never really won the complete confidence of the autochthonous, Buddhist-modernist political leadership. In face of the influence and persuasive power of bureaucratic expertise — whose modernism was firmly backed by a vibrant English-language press and the University of Rangoon — a doubting AFPFL government preferred to institute certain extra-constitutional arrangements designed to bring countervailing influences into national policy formulation.

The two-year reconstruction plan was the product of a cotery of senior Burmese civil servants comprising the Economic Planning Board of the new state. However, the Burmese government turned as well to foreign consultants, mainly American. In 1951 and 1952 an American combined economics-engineering team undertook a comprehensive study of Burma's economic and social development on behalf of the Burmese government.[94] Their policy recommendations were to form the technical underpinnings of the AFPFL's subsequent development program. Despite the seeming paradox of a newly-independent socialist Burma deciding its development objectives in collaboration with American advisers, the participation of United States' expertise apparently assisted the novice political leadership considerably in overcoming its initial insecurity in matters of policy administration.

A second device for mobilizing countervailing political influence in favor of the political leadership was the government's convocation, in August 1952, of the *Pyidawtha* Conference. Organized outside the framework of the Union Parliament, the Conference gathered together more than a thousand delegates representing the socio-economic groupings of Burmese society. By way of contrast with the urban-elitist party composition of the elected Parliament, the *Pyidawtha* Conference accorded due representation to rural and peasant organizations.[95] Cabinet ministers presented to the Conference policy guidelines with a strong rural-populist orientation.[96] In seeking a primary political mandate from the *Pyidawtha* Conference, the still not quite self-confident U Nu leadership aimed at mobilizing mass support for its *Pyidawtha* development strategy. Only after the Conference did the government turn to Parliament to seek legal-institutional ratification of its program.

Over the years of independence, as the nativist, Buddhist culture of the predominantly peasant society seeped through the Western-style political process, U Nu's government took on an increasingly *Buddhist* socialist cast. Then in 1962, just when this Buddhist socialism had begun actually to crystallize in policy form, the Army stepped in to seize power.[97] In most respects General Ne Win's coup d'etat represented a radical departure from the elected government's Buddhist bent. This was a return toward the more modernist Buddhist-syncretic outlook of the original *Dobama Asiayone*.[98] Here the distinctively *Burman* elements of traditional Buddhist statehood became, with the disestablishment once again of religious Buddhism, the temporal expression of a regained national identity. By blending traditional national symbols into a modern organization, bound to ultimate national goals, the military manifested itself as the conscience of the nation.[99]

Ne Win's post-1962 regime was rooted in Burma's most modern, most cohesive societal organization, the Army. Support for the military regime came from Red Socialist politicians sharing its syncretic, urban, radical outlook.[100] While the bureaucracy had to be indoctrinated in socialism through lectures and subjected to military supervision of their performance for a time after the coup, the military at least enjoyed the bureaucrats' tacit support. If the Army retained for itself the reins of power, it nevertheless articulated as well the aspirations of the more modernized, Western-educated, urbanized groups in society. Opponents of the regime, including AFPFL politicians of both factions, regional separatists, communists, and even dissident colonels, students, editors, and socialists, were firmly dealt with.[101]

The direction of military politics since 1962 may be expressed in the regime's own terms, as "The Burmese Way to Socialism."[102] This political strategy emphasized the military regime's strictly secular socialism, which claimed to represent "democratic" humanism and was intended to restore purely national values.[103] Both secular socialism and democracy were, however, to be given a peculiar operational twist in "the Burmese Way." Nevertheless, the political-cultural aspirations of the military "Revolutionary Council" remained distinctly modern.

As for its political configuration, the Ne Win regime concentrated political power on the very center of military authority, the Revolutionary Council. This was a highly centralized, hierarchical political structure. To mediate between the Revolutionary Council and other critical groups in the political community, the military regime set up a number of new organizations. Special organizations were created to provide the center with a political communications link, the Burma Socialist Program Party for the modern, non-military elite as well as other organs for urban workers and peasants.[104] In practice, however, these organizations served to channel the transmissions of military directives, political exhortations, and ideological indoctrination to civilian society with but a minimal feedback function.[105] If this was the military's notion of democracy,[106] it was a highly disciplined democracy indeed.

This disciplined, centralized democracy organized by its Revolutionary Council implied a final rejection of transplanted Western standards of parliamentarianism. In its place the military created their own distinctly Burmese institutions of political organization. Neither did the Revolutionary Council hesitate to include traditional institutions in its political arrangements, in order to reinforce centralized control.[107] Indeed, there appears to be a structural congruency between the centralized political organization of the military Revolutionary Council and the traditional "oriental despotism" described by Wittfogel.

Like its civilian predecessor, the military spent considerable energies on expressions of ideology. Actually, there was a remarkable and sub-

stantial intensification of ideological indoctrination through the
Revolutionary Council's refurbished political communications apparatus. Its lack of genuine ideologues notwithstanding, the military
aimed at achieving a syncretic National Ideology containing elements
of socialism, traditional values, and democracy. An elaborate ideological statement, "The System of Correlation of Man and His Environment," offered a curious compound of Buddhist welfare state-ism and
Western socialism, but was anything but a blueprint for political
action.[108] Nonetheless, the military regime undertook strenuous
propaganda efforts through its own party, the Burmese Socialist Program Party (BSPP), the controlled media, the schools, and through
specially created indoctrination organs to convey this National
Ideology to the civilian population. These intensive indoctrination
flows largely dominated the Revolutionary Council's network of
political communications.[109]

Despite the domination of political communications by the military
center of authority, the Revolutionary Council has proved singularly
devoid of charismatic leadership. No "cult of personality" has evolved,
nor did the military leadership create for itself an aura of charismatic
appeal. In U Nu's government the Prime Minister's charisma had
served to bridge the cultural gap between a modern political center
and a traditional rural periphery,[110] while Ne Win's regime has tried
to manipulate its political communications apparatus to the same
effect.

It was through its economic strategy that the Revolutionary
Council gave policy expression to its much-vaunted National Ideology.
In doing so the military regime dispensed with much of its liberal-
constitutional baggage. No longer was the government to be bound by
the polite moderation of Western-style politics. Rather the military
regime sought to define The Burmese Way to Socialism operationally
into a centralized, indigenous socialist policy program.[111] Going
ahead with nationalization measures, the military regime in 1964 proceeded to take over the approximately 40 per cent of manufacturing,
commercial service, and financial enterprises[112] that had remained in
private hands. The military thereby became the country's dominant
economic entrepreneurs, adding direct controls to its already radical
utilization of the more usual instruments of fiscal and monetary
policy.[113]

Significantly, the Revolutionary Council did not see fit to resort to
comprehensive central development planning in pursuit of its economic strategy. With the abrogation of the civilian government's

Second Four-Year Plan (fiscal 1961/62 to 1964/65) and the disbandment of its planning apparatus, centralized direction of economic
policy proceeded henceforward on a short-term, pragmatic, ad-hoc
basis. [114] The Revolutionary Council evidently preferred central control, pure and simple, to the complex administrative requirements of
national planning.

The Burmese Way to Socialism was translated into practice in two
policy directions at the same time. One aimed at social redistribution,
the other at growth of national income. In the event it was the former
that has been pursued with the more vigor and effect. Nationalization
of enterprises during 1964-65, already referred to, transferred the
larger part of the manufacturing, commercial, and financial sectors
into state hands. [115] Land reform proceeded more slowly, [116] but
measures were taken to reduce or abolish land rents, encourage
collective cultivation, and facilitate agricultural credit, supply, and
marketing. [117] At about the same time as these redistributive policies
were being introduced, the Revolutionary Council also embarked on
an expanded program of public capital investment, financed almost
exclusively by the government's own resources, without external aid.
Here the accent was on creating new economic infrastructures,
notably electric generating capacity and roads, expanded manufacturing industry, and improved agricultural inputs. [118] Against this, public
expenditure on social services such as education declined somewhat, [119] while general consumption standards fell to drastic
austerity.

Because of the drainage of valuable resources into expanded
counter-insurgency campaigns and the flight of skilled minorities
abroad — both consequences of the regime's political strategy —
coupled with administrative bottlenecks, the Revolutionary Council
failed to reach its growth objective. Burma's per capita gross domestic
product grew scarcely at all during the late 1960's, and ranked as one
of the lowest in all Asia. [120] Rather, the main economic consequence
of The Burmese Way to Socialism has been the wholesale displacement
of minority ethnic groups from their entrepreneurial position in
Burma's economy by a redistributive economic nationalism.

Burma's military socialism effectively excluded hitherto privileged
ethnic minorities from its political boundaries. This ethnic (instead of
strictly class) basis of social redistribution meant the sequestering of
considerable resources from "foreign" hands to Burman; the majority
of sufferers were Indian, but Chinese, Eurasian, Karen, Shan, Kachin,
and other minority groups were also affected. [121] To the extent that

these ethnic minorities comprised a substantial portion of Burma's human capital stock — entrepreneurs, administrators, professionals, and skilled laborers — The Burmese Way to Socialism deprived itself of much of its economic growth potential, at least until these human resources are replaced. [122] Burma's exercise in socialist redistribution accordingly proved dysfunctional to short- and even medium-term growth prospects. Yet in revealing its true policy preferences, redistribution over growth, the military regime proceeded to eliminate the remaining socio-economic vestige of the colonial period from "revolutionary" Burma.

If the Revolutionary Council bears striking resemblance to traditional "oriental despotism," this was more a similarity of style than of content. In line with the traditional style of governance, the military regime secured the absolute political authority of the center, while promoting a welfare state for, and asserting the domination of, ethnic Burmans. Nevertheless the content of its political ideology and political structure was emphatically modern, secular, and socialist. Where traditional elements were maintained, these were but structural appurtenances intended to express the continuity of temporal, national symbols.

Ne Win's Revolutionary Council is an essentially modern, intensely nationalist, and secular socialist alternative to U Nu's more traditional Buddhist conception of statehood. That the military's conquest has hardly been total or complete is evidenced by persistent reports of Burman insurrectionary movements, prompted by deep-rooted traditional Buddhist political aspirations among the peasantry in particular. Certainly the gap between the centers of "Revolutionary" authority and the traditional Buddhist countryside still remains to be effectively bridged.

NOTES

1 See in particular, Manuel Sarkisyanz, *Buddhist Backgrounds of the Burmese Revolution* (The Hague: Martinus Nijhoff, 1965); Fred von der Mehden, "The Changing Pattern of Religion and Politics in Burma," *Studies on Asia* (Lincoln: University of Nebraska Press, 1961); Winston L. King, "Buddhism and Political Power in Burma," *Studies on Asia* (1961).

2 Harry J. Benda, "The Structure of Southeast Asian History," in R.O. Tilman (ed.), *Man, State and Society in Contemporary Southeast Asia* (London: Pall Mall, 1969), p. 25; Robert Redfield, *Peasant Society and Culture* (Chicago: University of Chicago Press, 1956), p. 70 ff.

3 Sarkisyanz, *Buddhist Backgrounds* . . ., pp. 14—15; Thaung, "Burmese Kingship in Theory and Practice During the Reign of Mindon," *Journal of the Burma Research Society* (1959), p. 176. See also Robert von Heine-Geldern, *Conceptions of State and Kingship in Southeast Asia,* Cornell University, Southeast Asia Program Data Paper No. 18.

4 Benda, "The Structure of Southeast Asian History . . .," pp. 30—31.

5 For a discussion of the application of Karl Wittfogel's "Oriental Despotism" to mainland Southeast Asia see Benda, "The Structure of Southeast Asian History," p. 25; also Karl A. Wittfogel, *Oriental Despotism: A Comparative Study of Total Power* (New Haven, Conn.: Yale University Press, 1957).

6 Sarkisyanz, *Buddhist Backgrounds* . . ., p. 36.

7 On the political structure of the classical Burmese monarchy see L.W. Pye, *Politics, Personality and Nation Building; Burma's Search for Identity* (New Haven, Conn.: Yale University Press, 1962), pp. 67—68; J.F. Cady, *A History of Modern Burma* (Ithaca, N.Y.: Cornell University Press, 1958), p. 4.

8 Pye, *Politics, Personality and Nation Building* . . ., p. 73.

9 Sarkisyanz, *Buddhist Backgrounds* . . ., p. 54; G.H. Luce, "Economic Life of the Early Burmese," in Burma Research Society, *Fiftieth Anniversary Publications,* No. 2 (Rangoon, 1960), p. 326.

10 Cf. Manuel Sarkisyanz, "The Social Ethics of Buddhism and the Socio-Economic Development of Southeast Asia," in M. Rudner (ed.), *Society and Development in Asia,* Asian and African Studies, Vol. 6 (Jerusalem: Israel Oriental Society, 1970), pp. 7—21.

11 Sarkisyanz, *Buddhist Backgrounds* . . ., pp. 54—56.

12 Pye, *Politics, Personality and Nation Building* . . ., p. 68.

13 Sarkisyanz, *Buddhist Backgrounds* . . ., p. 56. In saying this, Sarkisyanz denies Max Weber's contention that the Buddhist ethic of the welfare state was motivated solely by a religious goal, to the exclusion of national considerations of economics. Max Weber, *Gesamelte Aufsatze Zur Religionssoziologie* (Tubingen: JC. B. Mohr, 1920/21), Vol. 2, p. 262.

14 Pye, *Politics, Personality and Nation Building* . . ., pp. 75—76.

15 Von der Mehden, "The Changing Pattern of Religion . . .," p. 66.

16 Pye, *Politics, Personality and Nation Building* . . ., p. 71; Sarkisyanz,

Buddhist Backgrounds..., Ch. 6–7; J.F. Cady, *Thailand, Burma, Laos and Cambodia* (Englewood Cliffs, N.J.: Prentice-Hall, 1963), p. 57.

17   Winston L. King, "Buddhism and Political Power . . .," p. 12. See also J.F. Cady, *A History of Modern Burma . . .,* pp. 8–9.

18   For a history of Burma to the British conquest see G.E. Harvey, *History of Burma* (London: Longmans, Green & Co., 1925); J.F. Cady, *Southeast Asia: Its Historical Development* (New York: McGraw-Hill, 1964), Ch. 6.

19   See J.F. Cady, *A History of Modern Burma . . .,* Ch. 3–4; and Frank N. Trager, *Burma: From Kingdom to Republic* (New York: Praeger, 1966), Ch. 2, for historical accounts of the British conquest of Burma.

20   British rule formally disestablished Buddhism, terminated government support of the Sangha, and subjected ecclesiastical personnel to the jurisdiction of civil law. J.F. Cady, *A History of Modern Burma . . .,* p. 169; O.H. Mootham, *Burmese Buddhist Law* (London: Oxford University Press, 1939), pp. 123–27.

21   Sarkisyanz, *Buddhist Backgrounds . . .,* pp. 106–07.

22   Cady, *A History of Modern Burma . . .,* pp. 138–41.

23   R. Hatley, "The Overseas Indian in Southeast Asia: Burma, Malaysia and Singapore," in R.O. Tilman (ed.), *Man, State and Society in Contemporary Southeast Asia . . .,* pp. 454–55.

24   Sarkisyanz, *Buddhist Backgrounds . . .,* pp. 138–39.

25   Cady, *A History of Modern Burma . . .,* pp. 156, 174–75.

26   Cady, *A History of Modern Burma . . .,* p. 156.

27   Pye, *Politics, Personality and Nation Building . . .,* pp. 85–87.

28   Cady, *A History of Modern Burma . . .,* p. 155.

29   Cf. W.W. Rostow, *The Stages of Economic Growth* (New York: Cambridge University Press, 1961), pp. 44–45.

30   John S. Furnivall, *Colonial Policy and Practice* (New York: New York University Press, 1948), pp. 2–7.

31   On economic conditions on Burma's agricultural frontier see Cady, *A History of Modern Burma . . .,* pp. 158–63; and Sarkisyanz, *Buddhist Backgrounds . . .,* pp. 144–45.

32   For an account of some of the usurious practices of British and Chettyar rentiers, see Cady, *A History of Modern Burma . . .,* p. 304.

33   J. Russell Andrus, *Burmese Economic Life* (Stanford: Stanford University Press, 1947), pp. 77 ff; *Government of Burma: Report on the Administration of Burma for the Year 1930/31* (Rangoon: 1932), p. 16; Sarkisyanz, *Buddhist Backgrounds . . .,* pp. 143–44.

34   During the 1920's four British firms exercised monopolistic (or more properly, monopsonistic) control over the rice export trade and used this power to keep down the purchase price of rice. Cf. Peter Ady, "Economic Basis of Unrest in Burma," *Foreign Affairs* (1951), p. 477; Cady, *A History of Modern Burma . . .,* p. 179. Collusive buying by member firms of the so-called "Bullinger Pool" depressed prices and therefore impoverished Chettyar middlemen and rice cultivators alike, but the latter, being weaker, suffered more.

35   John S. Furnivall, in *An Introduction to the Political Economy of Burma* (Rangoon: Peoples Literature Committee and House, 1957), p. 77, maintains that real agricultural wages in Lower Burma declined by 20 per cent between 1870-1931. V.D. Wickizer and M.K. Bennett in *The Rice Economy of Monsoon Asia* (Stanford: Stanford University Press, 1941), on p. 216, further point out that the Burman's own consumptional rice was reduced by about a quarter during the last decades of British rule, to 1941. This would appear to indicate a fall in real peasant agricultural incomes by 20-25 per cent over the period.

36   G.E. Harvey, *British Rule in Burma 1824-1942* (London: Faber and Faber, 1946), pp. 38, 58.

37   On political organizations and their operational goals, custodial or developmental, see G.D. Ness, *Bureaucracy and Rural Development in Malaysia* (Berkeley: University of California Press, 1967), Ch. 1. For an account of the refusal of the British administration to adopt developmental or redistributive policies, see Cady, *Southeast Asia: . . .*, p. 400.

38   Cady, *A History of Modern Burma . . .*, pp. 173–78.

39   In response to the British conquest a Burman rebellion broke out and lasted five years, having "assumed the proportions of a national rising" (Cady, *Southeast Asia: . . .*, p. 393). Subsequently Burma was wracked with lawlessness and civil disorder which continued unabated throughout the period of colonial rule and afterwards. Violent crime was so rampant that in 1927 one district of Lower Burma had as many murders as Al Capone's Chicago, while two districts had as many as all Britain. G.E. Harvey, *British Rule in Burma 1824-1942*, pp. 38, 58, maintains that not only did crime increase under British rule, "it is even arguable that it was caused by British rule." Then in 1830-32 there occurred the Saya San Rebellion (cf. Sarkisyanz, *Buddhist Backgrounds . . .*, Ch. 22), followed by anti-Indian riots of varying severity down through the 1930's.

40   On the emergence of Burman nationalism, its development in the interwar period, and the creation of an "independent" Burma under wartime Japanese auspices, see Cady, *A History of Modern Burma . . .*, p. 185 and *passim*; Trager, *Burma: From Kingdom to Republic . . .*, pp. 43–67; and Sarkisyanz, *Buddhist Backgrounds . . .*, pp. 128–91.

41   Observers note that Buddhism is more than simply a religion in Burma: it permeates cultural values, political precepts, and social attitudes. This, according to F. von der Mehden, has made Burma Buddhist in a way that Western theologians have wished Europe to be Christian. Cf. "The Changing Pattern of Religion . . .," *Studies on Asia* (1961), p. 66 and *passim*. See also Manning Nash, "Burmese Buddhism in Everyday Life," in R.O. Tilman (ed.), *Man, State and Society in Contemporary Southeast Asia . . .*, pp. 103–14.

42   This includes the possibility of combining a Buddhist-traditional political structure with a secular political culture. While to some this may seem to be a virtual contradiction in terms, such a solution appeared to recommend itself to certain cultural innovators among the nationalist intelligentsia of the 1930's,

resulting in a Buddhist-Marxist syncretism. Cf. Sarkisyanz, *Buddhist Backgrounds . . .*, Ch. 23.

43 Both the Constitution of 1935 (actually implemented only in 1937) and the "independence" of 1943 under Japanese auspices involved only limited powers of self-determination for the Burmese, who remained effectively under the tutelage of their British and subsequently Japanese conquerors. For a history of the nationalist period see Cady, *A History of Modern Burma . . .*, Part III and Cady, *Southeast Asia: . . .*, Ch. 17 and 22.

44 Cady, *A History of Modern Burma . . .*, p. 190. On the role of the religion in the formative phase of nationalism generally, see Rupert Emerson, "Paradoxes of Asian Nationalism," reprinted in R.O. Tilman (ed.), *Man, State and Society in Contemporary Southeast Asia . . .*, p. 250, and *From Empire to Nation* (Cambridge, Mass.: Beacon Press, 1960).

45 Burman sensitivies over Westerners wearing shoes while visiting pagodas was taken up by a politically-minded faction in the Anglo-educated, elitist YMBA to become Burma's first nationalist "cause." Cf. Cady, *A History of Modern Burma . . .*, pp. 189–90.

46 Cf. Cady, *Southeast Asia: . . .*, pp. 508–15; Cady, *A History of Modern Burma . . .*, p. 231 and *passim.*

47 Saya San, the ex-pongyi leader of the rebellion that bore his name, actually proclaimed the restoration of the Burman Kingdom with himself as king. While the Saya San affair was far from a mass rising, it did invoke considerable admiration even among urban educated groups otherwise unsympathetic to its obscurantism. For an historical account of the causes, proceedings and effects of the rebellion see Cady, *A History of Modern Burma . . .*, p. 309–20; on its ideological implications see Sarkisyanz, *Buddhist Backgrounds . . .*, Ch. 22.

48 Dr. Ba Maw was a European-educated nationalist who generally reflected the urban, Buddhist-modernist perspective. Although his *Sinyetha* (Poor Man's) Party program of agrarian reforms seemed to bridge the urban-rural gap for the 1936 General Elections, they were eventually discarded as casualties of Dr. Ba Maw's coalition government. U Saw, on the other hand, was a populist politician who appealed to feelings of nationalism and religion among peasants and recently urbanized migrants. During his brief tenure as Prime Minister in 1940-41, U Saw cancelled the unpopular capital and household taxes, which fell heavily on the peasantry, pressed to Burmanize the civil service, and proposed to found a Buddhist university. For an account of Burman nationalist politics during the constitutional period see Cady, *Southeast Asia: . . .*, pp. 516–37 and *A History of Modern Burma . . .*, Ch. 12.

49 Cady, *Southeast Asia: . . .*, pp. 576–77; *A History of Modern Burma . . .*, Ch. 14. Styling himself *Adipati* (derived from the Pali-Sanskrit term for Head of State), Dr. Ba Maw appealed for "one party, one blood, one voice, one command" while introducing into his regime the rituals and symbolism of the traditional Burman Royal Court.

50 The University of Rangoon was established by the colonial government of Burma in 1921.

51 Cf. Pye, *Politics, Personality and Nation Building* . . ..

52 The first university strike took place in 1920 only three days after the scheduled opening of Rangoon University, and its waves were soon felt throughout Lower Burma. Student unrest was to reach a climax during the half-decade 1932-1937 with another major strike at the university. Cf. Cady, *A History of Modern Burma* . . ., pp. 217–21; 373–83.

53 Sarkisyanz, *Buddhist Backgrounds* . . ., p. 167, ascribes this concern with "slave" versus "master" mentality to the influence of Nietzsche. It is interesting to note that members of the Dobama Asiayone adopted the title "Thakin," or "Master," as a sign of equality with European colonials. The Dobama Asiayone is therefore sometimes referred to as the "Thakins Society."

54 Sarkisyanz, *Buddhist Backgrounds* . . ., p. 168. Sarkisyanz appears to feel that this terminological usage was important in adapting Marxism to the Buddhist cultural environment of Burma.

55 Cady, *Southeast Asia:* . . ., p. 516. See also Mi Mi Khaing, *The Burmese Family* (Bombay: 1946), p. 94, on the impact of the rebellion upon the Burman educated elite's national awareness, despite their general rejection of Saya San's obscurantism.

56 Cf. J.S. Thomson, "Marxism in Burma," in Frank N. Trager (ed.), *Marxism in Southeast Asia* (Stanford: Stanford University Press, 1959), p. 26.

57 Cf. Sarkisyanz, *Buddhist Backgrounds* . . ., p. 180–81. Maung Maung Pye, *Burma in the Crucible* (Rangoon: 1951), p. 41, describes how Burman governments collaborating with the colonial dyarchy shot down monks and student demonstrators in Mandalay (February 1936) and proceeded to systematically arrest radical nationalists, and particularly Thakins. Cited in *ibid.*, p. 181.

58 For an account of the Thakins' wartime activities and the AFPFL rise to power in independent Burma, see Cady, *A History of Modern Burma* . . ., pp. 417–577.

59 U Tan Pe, *Sun Over Burma* (Rangoon: 1949), p. 36, *passim.*

60 For a survey of postwar Communist programs in Burma, see Cady, *A History of Modern Burma* . . ., pp. 519–20; Thomson, "Marxism in Burma . . .,"; and V. Thomson, "Burma's Communists," *Far Eastern Survey* (1948), pp. 103–04.

61 "Foundations of Burma's Democracy," from Aung San's speech to the AFPFL Convention for drafting the Burmese Constitution, May 23, 1947, reprinted in Maung Maung (ed.), *Aung San of Burma*, (The Hague: Martinus Nijhoff, 1962), p. 130.

62 Cf. Union of Burma, Economic Planning Board, *Two Year Plan for Economic Development for Burma* (Rangoon: 1948). Preparation of this Plan was begun before the assassination of Aung San and Thakin Mya, the economic minister-designate.

63 Aung San, "Religion, the Sangha and Politics," from the inaugural address at

the AFPFL Convention, January 1946, reprinted in Maung, *Aung San of Burma,* pp. 126–27.

64 Aung San, cited in Sarkisyanz, *Buddhist Backgrounds . . .,* p. 192.

65 Although the AFPFL was to split in 1958 into the AFPFL-Clean of U Ba Swe-U Kyaw Nyein and AFPFL-Stable of U Nu, in their leaderships and even in their organizations the two represented a political legacy of the AFPFL institution. For a political history of Burma since independence see Trager, *Burma: From Kingdom to Republic . . ..*

66 While the *Sangha* as an institution generally desisted from political debate, individual monks and Buddhist lay thinkers occasionally made their contributions to the intellectual controversy between Buddhist idealism and modern materialism. Cf. Sarkisyanz, *Buddhist Backgrounds . . .,* pp. 202–03.

67 On the Buddhist-Marxist ideological formulations of the AFPFL leadership see Sarkisyanz, *Buddhist Backgrounds . . .,* p. 198ff.

68 The notion of *Lokha Nirbana,* which came to mean Perfect Society, apparently originated in the secularizing trend of the Buddhist-modernists during the 1920's. Cf. Sarkisyanz, *Buddhist Backgrounds . . .,* pp. 199–200.

69 Manuel Sarkisyanz explains this syncretism as the outcome of the traditionalist-modernism dichotomy in the nationalist acculturalization process. "The Social Ethics of Buddhism and the Socio-Economic Development of Southeast Asia," in M. Rudner (ed.), *Society and Development in Asia . . .,* p. 17.

70 See Heinz Bechert, "Theravada Buddhist Sangha: Some General Observations and Political Factors in its Development," *Journal of Asian Studies* (August 1970), p. 775, on this point.

71 Sein Win, *The Split Story, An Account of Recent Political Upheaval in Burma with Emphasis on the AFPFL,* pp. 14–15. See also Richard Butwell, *U Nu of Burma* (Stanford: Stanford University Press, 1963), pp. 151–66.

72 Kyaw Nyein, the group's leading theoretician, affirmed that ideological commitment to classic European Marxism, rejecting only its Soviet Communist deviation. The place of Buddhism in this scheme of things was to be essentially symbolic and legitimate, similar to "Christian" Socialism in the West. Cf. Sarkisyanz, *Buddhist Backgrounds . . .,* p. 225.

73 F. von der Mehden, "The Changing Pattern of Religion . . .," p. 71.

74 Although Ba Swe, of the "Educated" faction took over briefly as Prime Minister in 1955-56, this was only an interim measure devised to enable the popular Prime Minister, U Nu, to conduct the AFPFL general election campaign unencumbered by the burdens of office. This interregnum did not signify any change in the AFPFL constellation of power, or policy. In 1958 General Ne Win was invited by U Nu to take over power owing to severe internal crises, but this was essentially a caretaker regime that left quite alone the existing development strategy. For a consideration of the politico-economic approach of the military caretaker government of 1958-60 see L.W. Pye, "The Army in Burmese Politics," in J.J. Johnson (ed.), *The Role of the Military in Underdeveloped Countries*

(Princeton: Princeton University Press, 1962), p. 245—49. Such was the electoral success of U Nu's party that the leaders of the rival AFPFL-Stable, U Ba Swe and U Kyaw Nyein, were each defeated in his own constituency by Union Party candidates in 1960.

75 For a political biography of U Nu, see Butwell's *U Nu of Burma.*

76 Cf. Sarkisyanz, *Buddhist Backgrounds,* pp. 222—25, and King, "Buddhism and Political Power . . .," p. 17. See also Sarkisyanz, "On the Place of U Nu's Buddhist Socialism in Burma's History of Ideas," *Studies on Asia* (1961).

77 F. von der Mehden, "The Changing Pattern of Religion . . .," p. 71.

78 *Constitution of the Union of Burma,* 1947, Section 21. Buddhism was accorded a "special" position as the faith of the majority of citizens.

79 This included laws improving the position of the Buddhist clergy, restoring the traditional authority of Ecclesiastical Courts, establishing a Pali University, creation of a Ministry of Religious Affairs and granting financial appropriations to religious institutions. Cf. Trager, *Burma: From Kingdom to Republic . . .,* pp. 128—29 and Sarkisyanz, *Buddhist Backgrounds . . .,* pp. 229—32.

80 Cf. Trager, *Burma: From Kingdom to Republic . . .,* pp. 197—98; Sarkisyanz, *Buddhist Backgrounds . . .,* pp. 229—32.

81 U Nu, *Towards a Socialist State* (Rangoon: 1958). Here "socialism" was by implication distinct from Marxism or Communism and compatible, instrumentally, with Buddhism.

82 For a history of Burma's ethnic problem and the post-independence insurrections see Cady, *A History of Modern Burma . . .,* pp. 544—54, 589—99; and Trager, *Burma: From Kingdom to Republic . . .,* Ch. 5.

83 Thus after the 1960 election, the party conference rejected negotiations with "rebels," but conceded the claim to statehood of the Mon and Arakan minorities. A Karen (Kawthooly) State was only conceded by the Ne Win military regime in 1964. Cf. Trager, *Burma: From Kingdom to Republic . . .,* Ch. 9.

84 M. Lissak, "The Military in Burma: Innovations and Frustrations," *Asian and African Studies* (1969), pp. 134—35.

85 Louis J. Walinsky, "Burma," in E.E. Hagen, *Planning Economic Development* (Homewood, Ill.: Richard A. Irwin Co., 1963), pp. 27—28.

86 On the Pyidawtha program and Burmese economic policy during the 1950's see *ibid.,* and Louis J. Walinsky, *Economic Development in Burma, 1951-1960* (New York: Twentieth Century Fund, 1961); E.E. Hagen, *The Economic Development of Burma* (Washington: National Planning Association, 1956); and Frank N. Trager, *Building A Welfare State in Burma, 1948-1956* (New York: Institute of Pacific Relations, 1958). Note the terminological association of the new welfare state program with the traditionalist notion of a "Pleasant Royal Country."

87 According to the *Economic Survey of Burma, 1957* (Rangoon: 1958), the land nationalization had affected 1122 village tracts, including 900,051 acres redistributed to over 105,000 families, by 1955-56.

88 Cf. Trager, *Building a Welfare State in Burma . . .,* pp. 35—51.

89   Trager, *Building a Welfare State in Burma* . . ., pp. 57—65. The minor role assigned to industry in the postwar Burmese economy is indicated by its inclusion under the classification "other" in official government statistics.

90   Trager, *Building a Welfare State in Burma* . . ., pp. 80—88.

91   U Nu, *Towards a Welfare State* (Rangoon: 1952), p. 2.

92   The dominant party elite's hold on political power was further augmented by authoritarian imperatives of the counter-insurgency campaign of the early 1950's. On the composition and role of the political party elite see Trager, *Burma: From Kingdom to Republic* . . ., pp. 131—32.

93   For an analysis of the post-independence clash between politicians and bureaucrats, see Pye, *Politics, Personality and Nation-Building* . . ., pp. 115—17.

94   Walinsky, "Burma . . .," pp. 28—29.

95   Walinsky, "Burma . . .," p. 29.

96   During the 14 days of the Conference, ten substantive resolutions were presented by the Cabinet for approval. These included: 1) decentralization of decision-making powers to local authorities; 2) democratization of local authorities to make them representative and responsible for local welfare; 3) agricultural development; 4) investment in economic infrastructure; 5) land nationalization; 6) development of hill and frontier areas; 7) an expanded housing plan; 8) improved transport and communications; 9) expanded educational services; 10) expanded health services. Throughout the emphasis was on devolution of powers to local authorities, coupled to development of the rural areas. Cf. *Pyidawtha: The New Burma* (Rangoon: 1954); and Trager, *Building a Welfare State in Burma* . . ., pp. 20—21.

97   Interpretations regarding the motivation of the 1962 coup d'etat vary widely. Trager, *Burma: From Kingdom to Republic* . . ., and William C. Johnstone, *Burma's Foreign Policy: A Study in Neutralism* (Cambridge, Mass.: Harvard University Press, 1963), point to the Army's rejection of U Nu's indicated compromise with regional ethnic minorities over a proposed federal union. John H. Badgley, "Two Styles of Military Rule: Thailand and Burma," *Government and Opposition* (1969), p. 101, argues that the military combined with peasant interests to "exorcise" colonial influences and return the country to "pure Burmeseness." This line of argument would appear to neglect, however, U Nu's own transition from his original Western style to an essentially Buddhist-modernist political stand. Sarkisyanz, *Buddhist Backgrounds* . . ., maintains that the military coup represented the ascendancy of an "efficient," albeit Buddhist, organization over muddling politicians. See also Richard Butwell, "The Four Failures of U Nu's Second Premiership," *Asian Survey* (1962), p. 74. However, if we examine the goals of the military regime the differences in political strategy between it and its civilian predecessor help explain the origins of the Army's political actions. Cf. M. Lissak, "The Military in Burma," pp. 148, *passim.*

98   Cf. Sarkisyanz, *Buddhist Backgrounds* . . ., Ch. 28.

99   Cf. P.J. Vatikiotis, *The Egyptian Army in Politics: Pattern for New Countries* (Bloomington, Indiana: Indiana University Press, 1961), p. 15.

100 Badgley, "Two Styles of Military Rule," p. 107. The "Red Socialists" were the former Burma Workers and Peasants Party, an urban-based organization led by "educated" socialists of the Buddhist-syncretic socialist variety.

101 Badgley, "Two Styles of Military Rule," p. 104. Army suppression of those groups who shared its political values, notably university students and secular socialists-politicians, reflected the officers' conviction that they understood better what socialism is or is not than such sloganizing politicians. Cf. Richard Butwell, "Civilians and Soldiers in Burma," *Studies on Asia* (1961), p. 77.

102 *The Burmese Way to Socialism, Policy Declaration Issued by the Revolutionary Council of the Union of Burma on April 30, 1962,* reprinted in *New Times* (Moscow), 16 May 1962, and cited in Gunnar Myrdal, *Asian Drama* (New York: Pantheon, 1965), Vol. 2, pp. 836–37.

103 Myrdal, *Asian Drama,* Vol. 1, p. 374; Lissak, "The Military in Burma . . .," pp. 137–41.

104 Lissak, "The Military in Burma . . .," pp. 153–55. These included the Burman Socialist Program Party; the Security and Administrative Committees; the peasant councils and Burmese Way to Socialism Workers Units.

105 On the structure of power in post-1962 Burma see James F. Guyot, "Political Involution in Burma," *Journal of Comparative Administration* (1970), pp. 299–321.

106 "The Burmese Way to Socialism" proclamation of the Revolutionary Council is cited in W.C. Johnstone, *Burma's Foreign Policy . . .,* Appendix IV, pp. 315–16. On the Revolutionary Council's retreat from Western parliamentary democracy see also Trager, *Burma: From Kingdom to Republic . . .,* p. 200 *et passim.*

107 Badgley, "Two Styles of Military Rule," p. 105; Maung, *Cultural Value and Economic Change in Burma . . .,* pp. 533–34.

108 On the philosophy of the Burmese Socialist Program Party: *The System of Correlation Between Man and His Environment* (Rangoon: 1963). See also Lissak, "The Military in Burma . . ., p. 157.

109 Cf. Lissak, "The Military in Burma . . .," pp. 153–60 and Badgley, "Two Styles of Military Rule . . .," pp. 112–13.

110 Pye, *Politics, Personality and Nation-Building in Burma . . .,* p. 29. On this function of charisma see also G. McT. Kahin, Guy J. Pauker and L.W. Pye, "Comparative Politics in Non-Western Countries," *American Political Science Review* (1955), p. 1025.

111 Mya Maung, "Cultural Values and Economic Change in Burma," *Asian Survey* (1964), pp. 63–64.

112 L.J. Walinsky, "The Role of the Military in Development Planning in Burma," in R.O. Tilman (ed.), *Man, State and Society in Contemporary Southeast Asia,* p. 347. According to Howard Cayden, "Country Profiles," Vol. II of *Higher Education and Development in Southeast Asia,* UNESCO and the International Association of Universities (Paris: 1967), p. 31, the sweeping nationalization

measures of 1964 encompassed enterprises accounting for some 60 per cent of total production, the remainder still remaining in private hands.

113 Walinsky, "The Role of the Military in Development Planning in Burma," p. 347, *passim*. Monetary measures in particular were utilized to expropriate Burma's Indian minority. See also L.D. Stifel, "Economics of the Burmese Way to Socialism," *Asian Survey* (1971), pp. 803–817; and "Burmese Socialism: Economic Problems of its First Decade," *Pacific Affairs* (1972), pp. 60–74.

114 Howard Cayden, *Higher Education and Development . . .,* Vol. II, p. 29. The "pragmatic" quality reflected the extensive reliance of military policy-makers on economic surveys of both problems and the impact of recommended policy changes.

115 Myrdal, *Asian Drama . . .,* Vol. I, p. 374.

116 *Ibid.,* Vol. 2, p. 837.

117 Cayden, *Higher Education and Development . . .,* p. 31.

118 *Ibid.,* pp. 31–32.

119 Between 1957/58 and 1962/63 public expenditure on education declined almost a full percentage point from 2.9 to 2.0 per cent of national income. Cf. Cayden, *Higher Education and Development . . .,* pp. 90–91.

120 R.O. Tilman (ed.), *Man, State and Society in Contemporary Southeast Asia,* Appendix Tables 14 and 15.

121 Ruth M. Pfanner, "Burma," in Frank H. Golay et al., *Underdevelopment and Economic Nationalism in Southeast Asia* (Ithaca, N.Y.: Cornell University Press, 1969). See also Badgley, "Two Styles of Military Rule . . .," p. 101.

122 Burma's Indian community was not only despoiled of its wealth but was also forcibly driven from the country. Myrdal, *Asian Drama . . .,* p. 374; Walinsky, "The Role of the Military in Development Planning in Burma . . .," p. 347.

MYTHS AND REALITIES IN AFRICAN SOCIALISM

NAOMI CHAZAN

I

"African Socialism" constitutes an amalgam of European socialist thought and African ideas and forms which has come primarily as a response to a situation of change that created basic challenges common to most African countries. The late 1960's and the early part of this decade saw the overthrow of some regimes, as well as rapid political shifts in Africa. This situation will undoubtedly continue. Thus the utility and viability of the concept "African Socialism" must be re-evaluated in terms of these recent changes. First, an attempt will be made to delineate the basic theoretical premises of African Socialism, in order to better comprehend its European and African sources. Second, the primary challenges facing African countries and the causes for the turn by some leaders to socialism as a means of responding to these challenges will be analyzed. Third, some of the practical implications of African Socialism will be examined. Finally, African Socialism will be evaluated in terms of the selection from European and African sources, the challenges facing African countries, and the practical utility of the concept.

Ideology in the new nations operates on three levels and, consequently, has three functions: 1) the philosophical-symbolic level, whose function is to legitimize and justify given policies and situations; 2) the identity level, which aims at expounding and providing a focus for national identity;[1] 3) the practical level, which attempts to define and tackle the concrete goals of the society. Each stage of this analysis will rely on and, simultaneously, attempt to elucidate the applicability of these three levels of ideology and their functions.

II

The pre-independence roots of African Socialism provide an important setting for a discussion of this concept. Historically, socialism in its various modern forms was introduced to Africa by two diverging branches of the anti-colonialist movements, Pan-Africanist and specific nationalist movements.[2]

The Pan-African movement was initially an import to Africa, a movement initiated by blacks in the United States and the East Indies. Three central figures are associated with the founding of an early pan-Africanism: Marcus Garvey, W.E.B. du Bois, and George Padmore. Garvey's thought, as an historical antecedent of African Socialism, is of less importance than that of du Bois and Padmore. W.E.B. du Bois's importance lies in his emphasis on the racial issue as the key problem of twentieth-century life. Indeed, by disregarding class as a divider and replacing class divisions with color distinctions, du Bois assessed the basic societal confrontation in terms that are both recognizable and fitting in the African context.[3] Personally, du Bois himself was attracted to socialism only at a much later stage of his life; even then his conception of Marxist ideology was clouded by his unwillingness to reconcile the question of class struggle with that of race conflict. An extremely active member of the Pan-African movement since its inception, du Bois undoubtedly influenced not only actual events in Africa, but also specifically two levels of ideological thought. By emphasizing the centrality of racial struggles, he raised points of great theoretical significance and simultaneously provided a focus for psychological identity.

George Padmore, unlike du Bois, was in his early life an active member of the Communist Party. After a period of disenchantment Padmore finally withdrew from the Party in 1934, convinced that Marxism was insufficiently relevant to the colonial situation.[4] By bringing his strong ideological background to bear on anti-colonial activities, Padmore did influence events. But more importantly, he acted as intellectual mentor to future African leaders, especially Kwame Nkrumah.

Both Padmore and du Bois influenced the direction of Pan-Africanism from outside Africa. Thus, their influence was primarily intellectual. The Pan-African conference held in Manchester in 1945 marked a turning point in the movement, as it was here that the leadership was assumed by African leaders, specifically Kwame Nkrumah and Jomo Kenyatta. At this conference, nationalism, political democracy, and socialism were accepted as the main themes of the Pan-African movement. Thus the Pan-African movement, under the intellectual aegis of Padmore and du Bois, introduced the notion of the centrality of socialism as the ideology of African protest. The early Pan-African movement was essentially theoretical in nature, i.e., it did not imply a realistic and practical action program. Such programs were ultimately the legacy of specific anti-colonial struggles in respective African countries.

The conception of socialism as a platform for pragmatic protest was introduced to the African nationalist movements by British and French communist and socialist circles. In the French-speaking African territories, the *groupes d'etudes communistes* provided a most acceptable framework for the penetration of socialist and, specifically, Marxist-Leninist thought. After World War II, formal connections were established between the Communist Party in France and the *Rassemblement Democratique Africaine* (RDA) in French West Africa. Similar affiliations were developed between Leopold Senghor's *Bloc Democratique Senegalaise* (BDS) and the French Socialist Party. The affiliation of the RDA with the French Communists was severed in 1950 after much internal dissension among RDA leaders. Felix Houphouet-Boigny, who saw the affiliation as a tactical one, was eager to cut these ties when they no longer proved profitable. Sekou-Touré of Guinea and Modibo Keita were more attracted to the theoretical aspects of the Communist connections, and consequently more unwilling to break away from this affiliation.[5] Thus, when Marxist ideology was introduced into African life in the late colonial period, its essential impact was on a minute proportion of the local population. However, it was these few individuals who were to assume leadership roles in the new Africa and at the same time to do so in the name of African Socialism.

The ties between the British Communist Party and the specific African nationalist parties were much less institutionalized. No formal connections existed, although both Communist and Fabian groups directly influenced such major African leaders as Nyerere, Obote, Kaunda, Nkrumah, and Awolowo of Nigeria.

Two concepts which developed in the colonial period were to have great importance for the development of African Socialism in the later stages of national independence. The concept of *negritude,* which first appeared in Parisian African circles connected with the journal *Presence Africaine* and was especially championed by Senghor, referred to the beauty and basic dignity of the African past. This concept was usually expressed in artistic and literary forms. The concept of an African personality was a parallel idea developed within the English context and referred to the singularity and centrality of the African being on the international scene.[6] Both of these concepts mark a trend toward a search for those aspects of African culture and history which were common to African societies as a whole. This search was seen as a means to the creation of a unifying and shared African tradition. The universality of Pan-Africanism implied in this trend was, however, ultimately to clash with the innate localism and specificity which is integrally a part of African Socialism. Thus, while African Socialism has certain generalizable and trans-African sources, it is nevertheless inextricably rooted in specifically-determined geographical and cultural situations of Black Africa, often defined by technological and economic conditions.[7]

III

The introduction of socialism to Africa included a process of adaption and revision which included both a filtration of certain purely European aspects as well as the addition of particularly African elements. This dual process of selection and adaptation has resulted in different emphases and tendencies in African Socialism.

What have African socialist leaders accepted from the language and thought of European socialism? First, they have adopted certain of the critical and anti-capitalist elements of Marxism, transforming them into justifications for anti-colonial and anti-neocolonial tendencies. Second, they have found in the concept "dialectical materialism" a key and a convenient tool for debate and analysis. Third, they have copied crucial aspects of the Marxist personal and social ethic and social theory. Finally, they have adopted socialism as a comprehensive political, social, and economic strategy and program for action to meet the major challenges they face.[8]

What aspects of European socialism were rejected by African socialists? First, African leaders could not forget the historical fact that European socialists, specifically Marx, ignored Africa, its people, and its problems. In a sense, Lenin via his work on imperialism was much closer, and consequently more relevant, to African realities than Marx. Second, the precise nature of Marxist humanism differs greatly from that humanism implied by African leaders. Third, the notion and role of the state in European and African socialism is widely divergent. The

African notion is primarily one of democratic centralism and pluralism; the Marxist notion is totalitarian in essence.[9]

The concrete differences between European and African Socialism
result from differing conceptions of respective realities. In Europe,
socialism has always been connected with the working class. In Africa,
on the other hand, socialism has been seen as the ideology of the
entire population, who have been exploited by foreign forces. In
Europe, socialism has emphasized industrial growth; African socialists
appeared more interested in the expansion and development of the
agricultural sector. Most European socialists have emphasized the
notion of atheism. However this concept was and is totally unaccept-
able and unadaptable to the African emphasis on religion and its centrality in human existence.[10] In Europe, socialism has taken on certain universal and international connotations. In Africa, it is precisely
socialism which was in many cases specific and particularistic, whereas
nationalism and the anti-colonialist struggles carried more universal
overtones.[11]

A closer examination of the process of selection assists in the elucidation of these differences between European and African Socialism
on the one hand and between different theories of African Socialism
on the other. The selection of elements of socialism revolved around
three major issues: humanism and the dignity of man; identity and
questions of orientation-change; and economic development.

"To be a socialist, for an African, is above all to recognize the great
dignity of man, of all men engaged in a single destiny: existence in the
world."[12] Socialism provided the African with a place in the world, as
well as granting him a humanitarian aura. This emphasis on the importance of the individual is especially evident in Tanzania, Uganda,
and Senegal. In Tanzania, the Arusha Declaration placed primary importance on the humanitarian and human aspect of socialism. Obote's
"Charter of the Common Man" emphasized almost exclusively the
utilization of socialism as the ideology concerned with the improvement of individual well-being. Similarly, Senghor's "African Road to
Socialism" stems from a keen evaluation of the humanitarian and
egalitarian notions implied in European socialism.

The selection of certain humanitarian aspects of socialism enabled
the formation of a trans-African international identity, as well as
specific national identities. The possibility of the common man's participation in socialism on an equal basis provides him with an identity
and a focus for identification — hence the emphasis in African Social-

ism on the humanitarian aspects of the future. The true meaning of African Socialism, in this view, is "to remold African society in the socialist direction; to reconsider African society in such a manner that the humanism of traditional African life reasserts itself in a modern technical community."[13] The selection of humanitarian and utopian aspects of socialism lies mainly in the theoretical plane. While these elements may provide guidelines for future policy, they do not, in themselves, have practical ramifications.

The second aspect of the selective process of African Socialism revolved around the theme of changing orientations. Socialism was seen in this sense as a focal ideology for changing attitudes. Indeed, the utilization of socialism in this context may have implied a decolonization of spirit. As a channel for changing orientations, socialism legitimized the denunciation of certain old and unproductive habits, such as sacrifices, the giving of presents, and nepotism.[14] Psychologically, socialism similarly provided new reference points, particularly notions of efficiency, programming, and hard work. Practically, socialism implied concrete means for the achievement of these goals. Hence socialism in Africa has been used as a justification for necessary critical reviews and reforms, and re-interpretations of reality. This function of ideology is not uncommon. "Political ideology becomes an incantation which genuinely transforms reality, even if nothing else, by changing man's view of it."[15]

The practical dogmas of African Socialism relied on choices of economic aspects of European socialism. Socialism, as a framework for economic change and development, provided an alternative to the familiar Western capitalist mode. It also pointed to a pattern of rapid acceleration, as in the cases of some Eastern European and Asian countries.

The selective acceptance of certain economic aspects of socialism varied from situation to situation in Africa. First, some African socialists emphasize aspects of socialist economic production as opposed to distribution. This position was justified in terms of the notion that increased production implies more goods, and therefore larger benefits for greater segments of the population. Emphasis on the productive elements of economic change has brought about differing African views on questions of method. Nkrumah and Sekou-Touré have viewed the adoption of socialism as a means for justifying rapid industrialization. Other African socialists have viewed socialism as a means of inducing the rapid development and diversification of the agricultural sector, as well as a method of introducing small agri-

culturally-connected industries. The strong emphasis on economic production in African socialist thought pointed to a change in the role of
trade unions. These organizations, in this framework, cease to be con-
sumptionist units and become more and more productive units.[16]

Second, African socialists have placed different emphases on the
rational/practical aspects of European socialism. Consequently, these
leaders chose planning and economic centralization as guidelines,
enabling the creation of state-owned enterprises and the nationalization of expatriate firms. The extent of government involvement in
ownership of the means of production has varied from country to
country. There appears, however, to be little difference between
socialist and non-socialist African countries on questions of rational
planning and government-directed and -owned industries. These ideas
were integrally related to the economic development process as a
whole and have become elementary parts of development thought.

The basic themes of the selection process from European socialism
contain social implications which help explain some trends in African
Socialism. First, the acceptance of socialism as a guiding ideology has
assisted African rulers in emphasizing the importance of the obligation
to work. Second, socialism in its European context has implied the
existence of a class society. Although most African leaders have rejected the notion of class struggle, .some, including Modibo Keita and
Sekou-Touré, have accepted this concept and transposed it to Africa.
Third, the acceptance of socialism has encouraged the development of
focal institutional tendencies and emphasized the centrality and
primacy of the government in economic development schemes.[17]

It is possible, in summary, to outline schematically those aspects of
European socialist ideology which were accepted or rejected by
African Socialism in terms of the three ideological levels. On the theoretical level African Socialism adopted the following aspects of European socialism: 1) the dialectic notion; 2) the concept of disalienation;
3) the idea of internationalism; 4) historical determinism. On the
other hand, African Socialism is inconsistent with European socialism
in its rejection of atheism, and in some cases of materialism; in its
avoidance of the notion of class struggle; and its rejection of the
principle of universality. Thus it can be seen that on the theoretical
level African socialists were extremely selective in their choice of
aspects of European socialism, and were quite willing to revise and
reject certain aspects when these clashed with basic elements of African realities.

On the psychological level, African socialists have accepted the notion of a new ethic. However, the socialist-collectivist ideal when transferred to Africa has taken on more communal connotations. Besides retaining the two basic psychological elements of European socialism, African socialists have used their ideology on this level to initiate new identities and reinforce existing orientations.

It is on the third level, the practical plane, that one finds the greatest discrepancies between European and African forms of socialism. European socialists reject the possibility of alliance with capital; not so most African socialists, who have often seen such an alliance as necessary in their present economic situation. The European notion of a one-party dictatorship or a workers' democracy was totally revised by African socialists. They accept the importance of a single party structure, but view it in terms of democratic centralism. African Socialism rejects the essentiality of nationalization of industries. Thus it was on the practical level that African socialists have rejected or revised most of the concepts which they have borrowed from non-African socialism, and have differed most greatly among themselves.[18]

It is thus possible to see that the selection of aspects of European socialism has been uneven. Unquestionably, most African socialists have been attracted more by the theoretical and psychological aspects of socialist thought, and less by its practical implications. There existed, consequently, an imbalance in the process of transfer which had important implications for the uses and utility of African Socialism.

IV

The Africanization of socialism was a necessity dictated by historical and psychological realities. In Europe, socialism was to some extent a reaction to the first stages of modernity. In Africa, socialism was adapted by the new "modern" elite, the first modernizers. As leaders in the anti-colonial struggle, the first African socialists were unwilling and unable to accept totally all aspects of European socialism precisely because of its source. Secondly, the Africanization of socialism was a reaction to the overwhelming technical and ideological superiority of the West.[19] Finally, the Africanization of socialism was a reaction to certain nihilistic aspects of Western culture. While reacting to aspects of European culture, African socialists were nevertheless concerned with making their socialism meaningful to the greatest number of Africans. This purpose could be achieved only by bringing socialism more in line with aspects of Africa's past and present. It is clear, then, that socialism had to be made compatible with African myths and realities in order to gain widespread acceptance and applicability.

Prior to examining in depth those aspects of African tradition which were borrowed by African socialists, it is necessary to take a closer look at the concept "tradition" in the African context. Tradition in Africa has been used to describe two separate phenomena. First, tradition has been used to refer to the many aspects of Africa's pre-colonial past. Second, tradition has been utilized in regard to existing customs and institutions which relate to similar customs of the past.

It has already been noted that pre-colonial Africa lacked a unifying great tradition. Nevertheless, certain customs were, and are, widespread. The return, on the part of many African leaders, to the African pre-colonial history has been expressed by a form of idealization which does not always converge with the findings of historians and anthropologists. Tradition, in its historical sense, has been distorted by African socialists and widely taken out of context. Nkrumah once stated that African Socialism "united us in the recognition that the restoration of African humanist and egalitarian principles of society call for socialism."[20] Similarly, Senghor has utilized pre-colonial African traditions in order to promote socialism. Tradition, in its first meaning, points to an interesting effort by some African leaders to reconstruct common African roots. But the return to African history, its mystification, distortion, and idealization, touches only one aspect of tradition in Africa.

Tradition in Africa may also refer to aspects of present-day reality which are related to the past. In this sense, it is preferable to utilize the term traditionalism. African leaders have necessarily had to contend with existing traditionalist structures and institutions, including the tribal and chieftancy institutions. They have also had to deal with traditionalist values and tendencies. However, while actively reconstructing African traditions — and constructing them anew, in a different way — these leaders have viewed African traditionalism, as an impediment to modernization and the implementation of socialism in Africa.[21] This distinction between tradition and traditionalism is crucial to the understanding of the African elements of African Socialism.

In terms of African tradition, the heart of the issue was: What aspects of the African past were malleable to the theoretical framework of socialist ideology? A primary notion of African tradition in this context was the idea of communalism. This concept was deeply rooted in the solidarity and unity of the traditional kinship group. Nkrumah pointed to the importance of communalism in African traditions when he wrote that "Socialism stands to communalism as capitalism stands to slavery."[22] African socialists, then, were concerned with an attempt to universalize the concept of communalism, and to transfer it to the national and trans-national levels. However, this concern was greatly complicated and frustrated by the sociological fact that the notions of communalism implicit in African tradition are much less applicable on these national and trans-national levels than to the tribal, expanded family, and service group level. Communalism as a functional concept has thus been distorted by some African socialists because it has been removed from its sociological context. As a more universal concept, communalism has taken on mystical overtones, which leave the definition of the concept in its socialist context unclear.

The utilization of the communalistic concept by African socialists has led them to emphasize allied notions which are either substantiated by African history, or by certain African leaders' view of this history. First, traditional/symbolic African notions of consensus, collectivism, group orientations are emphasized by African socialists.[23] Second, African socialists have found or created traditional roots for ideas of communal landownership, coupled with the safeguarding of individual rights. Finally, African socialists have sought substantiation for their rejection of the notion of class struggle by pointing to and, simultaneously, mystifying the essentially unstratified nature of traditional African societies. The discovery or invention of basic socialist values in the pre-colonial past has led African leaders to claim that African societies were built on notions of traditional African Socialism. The notion of a traditional African Socialism provided an excellent base for the reconstruction of socialism in a modern African setting.

The African socialist leaders' withdrawal into the African past and emergence with a series of observations which bear little relationship to known facts constitutes a form of social mythology-building prevalent in a situation of social flux.[24] Not only are these concepts out of touch with known facts of African history, they are also Western in terms of tools of analysis and uses of language. This idealization of African pre-colonial life is, therefore, problematic on two counts. First, it ignores the concrete realities of the organization of specific African social groups. Second, it is removed from Africa because it utilizes Western terminology and approaches. On the other hand, this

idealization of Africa's past is utilitarian in the sense that it provides
the groundwork, on a theoretical level, for the creation of a common
great tradition in Africa.

Not only history but also religion has provided a malleable source
for African socialists: a source with traditionalist and traditional overtones. Indigenous African religions vary from place to place. They
include not only religious and spiritual precepts, but also socio-
economic and political guidelines. Traditional African religions are
dynamic because they have not, in most cases, been codified, and
therefore they are subject to constant change. African socialists have
found the variability of traditional religions useful in their attempt to
single out African bases of socialism. Thus traditional African religions
underwent a process of idealization and mystification in the hands of
African leaders, similar in many respects to these leaders handling of
aspects of African history. The leaders adopted and adapted those
elements which were useful to the legitimization of socialism and
ignored those aspects which were not utilitarian.

Islam, the second major religion of Africa, also provided a source of
selection for African elements of socialism. Islam in the past has provided Africa with some semblance of a unifying great tradition. The
underlying unity of Islam did not prevent the development of specific
characteristics in each place, thus modifying and expressing itself in
slightly differing forms in different African environments. It is therefore necessary to look at African Islam in a number of ways: as a
religion, as a way of life, as a means to achieving certain goals, and as
an environment.

Islam as a religion and a way of life has expressed itself in a restrain-
ing fashion in Africa. The most outstanding examples are Northern
Nigeria, Senegal, and Mauritania. In these areas Islam has acted as a
check on modernization, as a safeguard against the destruction of
existing patterns of life. In Mali and Guinea, Islam has provided a
comfortable background for the development of socialism. This may
be a result of the fact that Islam in these contexts acted as a "milieu,"
a backdrop, for certain developments, and not necessarily as a framework for all social and political activities.[25] In those cases where Islam
was compatible with basic concepts of socialism, the religion could be
used as a means of bringing together and unifying different populations. Islam in these cases also strengthened the idea of the creation of
a great ideological tradition in Africa. Christianity, the third major
religion of Africa, is not only an import to Africa, but also a modernizing force in itself.[26] As an important channel for the transference of

Western values and norms, Christianity obviously cannot serve as a purely African source of socialist theory.

The choice of elements of African tradition in African Socialism operated on two levels, the spiritual and the pragmatic. The general trend has been for African socialists to revive certain traditions of the pre-colonial African past, but to question or destroy traditionalist structures and institutions. "Thus, what socialist thought in Africa must recapture is not the *structure* of 'the traditional African Society' but its *spirit,* for the spirit of communalism is crystallized in its humanism and in its reconciliation of individual achievement with group welfare."[27] This emphasis on the ideal, as opposed to the concrete, tended to remove the choice process in African Socialism even further from the reality of African existence. Furthermore, it raised African Socialism more and more into the purely intellectual realm. This aloofness of African Socialism from the realities of African traditionalism tended to foster certain doubts as to its credibility and relevance to present-day Africa.

V

The delineation of the challenges facing most African countries at the time of independence assists in elucidating the causes for the turn by some African leaders to socialism, and the practical tasks expected of this ideology. These challenges were largely defined by the nature of the situation of African countries and the changes they were undergoing. African countries achieved independence as a result of a political, economic, and social struggle against the colonial regimes. The political struggle has implied a change in political attitudes and mass mobilization for political and economic advance. It has also implied the continued independence and persistence of these political systems. The economic struggle is one which has required the creation of African solutions to long-existing problems through the development of existing human and natural resources. The social struggle's main aim has been ethnic integration and the prevention of the increasing stratification of these societies.

These struggles have implied, above all, the existence of a revolutionary situation, i.e., the rejection of many existing institutions and the creation of new, independent, and specifically African ones. In Africa, however, the socio-economic and political revolution is conceived of as evolutionary rather than violent.[28] In this situation of social flux, the flexibility implied by socialism was attractive to

African leaders. The use of socialism as a slogan implied a certain universalism, while also allowing a type of particularism specifically acceptable to some African leaders. This flexibility produced an ideology which is easily adaptable to specific African countries and situations.

African Socialism is, then, to a large extent one type of response to specific situations of social, economic, and political flux. It cannot be understood except within the context of certain basic challenges facing African countries in the period of independence. In this sense, socialism in African countries came as a tool to answer some pressing and unique problems of African states.

One of the first and essential challenges facing almost all African countries was the issue of the definition of national existence, i.e., the process of construction of a nation from divergent ethnic and social groups. At the heart of this challenge was the problem of the creation of a national identity and the issue of national integration. Such integration is dependent on the creation of a value system which may serve as a focus or source of cohesion for disparate people.[29] The development of a national orientation may, of course, be realized negatively, as a result of common protest to foreign influence, "to make a manifestly evolutionary situation and to pretend that it is revolutionary."[30] The struggle for national definition implied not only integration but also mobilization. It was not sufficient to simply bring about a conception of national identity. It was also crucial to mobilize the participation of the largest possible number of people for the tasks of nation-building and economic development. Thus, both mobilization and integration implied a radical change in orientations. The third aspect of the challenge of national definition revolved around the theme of unity and unification. As a result of the influence of the Pan-African movement, it is possible to discern, even among the least Pan-African leaders, a trend toward a confrontation with local problems in terms of Africa as a whole. The sharing of challenges implied a sense of unity in both the national and the continental spheres.[31]

The challenge of national definition assists in understanding some further attractions of socialism. First, it was especially convenient to espouse socialism at a time when capitalism was associated with the very Western and colonialist powers which only recently had been expelled. Second, socialism had become fashionable in the newly-independent countries of Asia, and this "fashionableness" was transferred also to the African situation. Socialism, as the ideology of protest in the struggle for independence, was accepted, acceptable, and, theoretically, a common means of declaring ideological independence. Third, socialism was relevant because it had come to be regarded, at least by some leaders of the third world, as the ideology and means of salvation of the oppressed countries, a commendation attained partially because it was a convenient justification and legitimizer for many of the policy procedures and decisions of certain African countries. In short, "socialism has always been the creed of the have-nots. Its intellectual appeal has been its offer to eliminate the distinction between the haves and the have-nots, to create a system of equality by devising political and economic mechanisms to raise the standards of the have-nots."[32] Fourth, the humanitarian aspects of socialism were also especially appealing to African leaders. The egalitarian socialist ethos assisted leaders of African countries in defining their position in relation to each other and to the outside world. Socialism brought an aura of humanity and humaneness to a situation of rapid change.

The second series of challenges centered around the issue of economic development. An aspect of this issue implies a reaction to and a protest against the economic state of African countries. The challenge of economic development can be viewed as a struggle between the haves and the have-nots, an attempt by the African states to free themselves from economic domination by the developed countries.[33] The challenge of economic development also necessitated a search for tools, methods, frameworks for rapid growth, and thus implied a choice between industrial or agricultural development, the transformation of the traditional economic group into a productive unit, and the transmission of new economic orientations.[34] The challenge of economic development was also integrally related to the question of identity. Many would see economic growth as the true test of Africa's emergence to full-blown membership in the world of nations.

Again, the definition of this challenge elucidates some further reasons for the attractiveness of socialism. First, socialism was "regarded as essentially rational as opposed to haphazard, and as planned and controlled as opposed to arbitrary; for these reasons it gives the best hope of rapid economic transformation."[35] In fact, socialism was regarded as a viable tool or slogan for economic development. Second, socialism was seen as a useful tool in changing basic orientations and refocusing them in such a way that they could become an aid to economic growth. Socialism was thus viewed by some African leaders as the ideology of modernization and modernity. Finally, socialism was considered as a viable economic alternative to both the Western capitalist and Eastern communist models.

The two foregoing challenges imply a third challenge. The challenges of national definition and economic growth require means through which they can be achieved. New problems require new approaches, and hence the final challenge: the creation of viable frameworks through the construction of new institutions or the revisions of existing ones to meet the major challenges facing the society. In this sense, socialism as a visionary and idealistic, even utopian, ideology was relevant for countries concerned with the construction of new and better societies and ways of life. That is, the apocalyptic aspects of socialist ideology were especially attractive in terms of this last challenge.

This discussion of the reasons behind socialism's appeal to some African leaders also indicates the tasks which socialism in Africa was expected to implement. The first task of African Socialism was seen as the reform and replacement of given structures and institutions with new or revised ones. Second, socialism in Africa implied the development of indigenous industries, thus bringing a harmonious solution to the dilemma of agricultural vs. industrial development. Third, African Socialism was to provide a tool for agrarian reform through the nationalization of lands, introduction of new techniques, and the establishment of cooperative ventures and resettlement schemes. Fourth, African Socialism was expected to foster the establishment of community institutions for political, social, and economic advancement. Fifth, African Socialism was meant to encourage reliance on the human factor and human investment through various institutions which engender national service. Finally, socialism was seen as a means of combating various social injustices through attempting to raise general standards of living.[36]

Socialism has been viewed as a malleable ideology in face of the challenges facing African countries. Its attractiveness has been seen in terms of these challenges. Unquestionably, however, socialism was not the only viable framework for action in independent Africa, and the acceptance of an ideology of African Socialism was largely a result of a previous disposition and awareness of its European forms. Where such an awareness did not exist, most countries sought other paths for the solution of these pressing problems.

VI

The previous sections have been concerned with the analysis of the process of the formation of African Socialism both in terms of the process of selection from European socialist and traditional roots and modifications of these sources and in terms of the problems and challenges which it came to solve. It is now possible to focus on some of the economic, political, and social manifestations of the particularly African forms of socialism.

The first practical implications of African Socialism were reflected in the economic sphere. The first significant manifestation of African Socialism on the economic level was a clear movement toward state ownership of industry. This trend implies two separate processes in terms of African economic conditions. First, the centralization of means of production in the hands of the state implies the construction of new, state-owned industries. This is clearly seen by the fact that most African countries, both socialist and non-socialist, have established new industries under governmental control. Second, this process implies the nationalization of foreign-owned enterprises. Although there are some non-socialist countries in Africa which have state-owned corporations, their policy toward foreign enterprises, which is basically non-regulatory, acts as a key to the absence of African Socialism.[37] It is, of course, true that this trend toward nationalization or control of foreign enterprises in socialist African countries proceeded at different rates. Guinea found it advisable, indeed necessary, to nationalize very quickly. Recently, the government of Guinea has been loosening regulations concerning foreign economic activity in the country. In Ghana, on the other hand, although Nkrumah's theoretical outlook was as close to orthodox Marxism-Leninism as can be found anywhere in Africa, the regulatory onslaught against expatriate firms was extremely gradual.[38] In most African socialist countries, the pace of nationalization was slow. As a first step, usually, the scope of the activities of foreign firms was curtailed and jealously controlled. This control was expressed primarily on questions of repatriation of earnings and re-investment. As a second step, vital heavy industries, banks, and insurance corporations were nationalized.[39] In most cases, total nationalization of all foreign firms has not been achieved.

This tendency toward nationalization and control means Africanization of the major industries. Indeed, the goal of Africanization has served as a basic motive for the various regulatory measures undertaken by African socialists. The approach of African socialists toward nationalization of major corporations has been exceptionally pragmatic. Nationalization procedures have been tempered by the problem of mobilization. Economic means have been used to increase the mobilization and utilization of human resources for developmental purposes. If nationalization and control of expatriate enterprises assisted in this mobilization process, then they were, in the eyes of African socialists, acceptable additions to the governmental programs.[40]

These two trends toward state ownership of industry, establishment of government-owned industries and nationalization of foreign enterprises, were further heightened by the nature of foreign aid to Africa. Foreign assistance has placed large capital grants for development purposes in the hands of African governments, thus minimizing to some extent the role of the private sector.

The widespread trend toward centralization of economic growth and government control and intervention of industry raises a dilemma for the student of African Socialism. The question remains whether increased government control is a phenomenon of economic development in Africa as a whole. The Ivory Coast, a specifically and avowedly non-socialist African country, has preferred rapid economic development through lax control of foreign enterprises. Ghana under Busia, although having inherited many state-owned corporations from the Nkrumah era, showed its anti-socialist reaction precisely by an openness for foreign capital investment. The Busia government attempted control of small (under $500,000 annual turnover) foreign enterprises by transferring them to the hands of private Ghanaian businessmen, and not by nationalization.[41] Tanzania, on the other hand, has nationalized all vital industries. New industries have been placed under state control. The same holds true for Guinea, Mali under Modibo Keita, Zambia, Uganda under Obote, and Senegal. The process of increased governmental control is thus much more in evidence in so-called socialist African countries than it is in non-socialist states.

The second major economic manifestation of African Socialism has been the concern with the promotion of efficiency through central planning. In the African context, efficiency refers mainly to the production of goods and services, and not necessarily to distribution. Planning has been viewed as a basic means of improving and directing production. The three-, five-, or seven-year plans of Tanzania, Ghana, Guinea, Senegal, Mali, Kenya, Uganda, and Zambia are prime examples of the use of planning as a key to socialist development in

Africa. In these countries, the purpose of central planning was two-fold. The plan heralded a new economic era, i.e., the commencement of an economic revolution. Its impact was seen not only on the practical but also on the psychological level. Through socialist manifestos published in conjunction with the development plans, such as the "Work and Happiness Program" in Ghana, the "Arusha Declaration" in Tanzania, the "Charter of the Common Man" in Uganda, planning was viewed in new terms, development was ensconced in a new language, and new approaches were presented. The publication of manifestos and development plans is not the sole province of socialist countries in Africa. Here again, the idea of central planning is an integral part of economic policy in developing countries. However, in socialist African countries the plan has been used not only as a practical economic tool, but also as a tool for changing orientations. In this respect, planning in African socialist and non-socialist countries differs.

The first two economic trends, nationalization and planning, operate on the national level. African Socialism has also manifested itself in economic activities on the local level. First, some socialist leaders have encouraged the intertwining of planning and control with the communal humanitarian base of African Socialism[42] This has been achieved through the initiation, notably in Senegal and Mali, of new programs of *animation* and *investissement humain.* In other countries this approach has resulted in the establishment of national service and youth movements, such as the Workers Brigade and the Young Pioneers in Ghana, the Tanzanian National Service Corps, and the Kenya National Youth Service. The purpose of these movements in socialist countries has been, first, to develop and raise the standard of living in the rural areas; and, second, to inculcate the youth with basic precepts of the national ideology. These youth programs are not unique to socialist countries in Africa: Malawi's Young Pioneers and the Ivory Coast's Service Civique Ivoirien are cases in point.[43] Thus, the structures which have been established to deal with problems of economic growth on the local level are fairly similar throughout Africa, and, although similar to structures in socialist countries elsewhere, they are in no way a manifestation of socialist regimes alone.

A second manifestation of the implementation of socialism on the local level involved the revival and/or encouragement of certain existing local structures. The central government intervened and stimulated the establishment of cooperatives and state farms to promote economic growth and agricultural diversification. When stemming from indigenous patterns, these cooperatives were easily assimilated into the local institutions and became viable structures, as in the case of Tanzania. Cooperatives and state farms lose their viability when they are imposed artificially from above. The failure of the state farms scheme in Nkrumah's Ghana is a case in point. The unsuccessful transplant of cooperatives and state farms was discontinued after the overthrow of Nkrumah.

The injection, by socialist leaders in Africa, of new methods of approaching economic development, through government control, nationalization, and the construction of institutions to deal with local growth in the rural areas has taken on overtones of protest against existing modes of thought and work. African traditionalist economic structures have often encouraged the development of a certain type of parasitism which has had negative implications for national economic growth. African socialist leaders, including primarily Nkrumah and Nyerere, have constantly spoken out against this phenomenon, and preached the moral obligation to work. Nyerere has said: *"mgeni siku mbili, siku ya tatu mpe jembe"* (a guest is a guest for two days, on the third day give him a hoe).[44] This preaching is often a tool, a means of mystifying and idealizing an obligation which does not necessarily exist.

Although in favor of the implementation of the three main measures of economic socialism, African socialists have disagreed widely on the optimal means of achieving economic growth. The more scientific socialists, under the leadership of Nkrumah, advocated placing major emphasis on industrialization. The more pragmatic socialists, on the other hand, have claimed that such an approach is untenable, and have, albeit sometimes reluctantly, viewed agriculture as the core of economic development in their countries. Those who see agriculture as the main factor in development have emphasized measures for the modernization of agricultural methods, land reforms, and the diversification of crops.[45]

In the past few pages, some major economic trends of African Socialism, as viewed by African socialist leaders, have been observed in broad outline. Not one of these three major economic trends is sufficient, in itself, to constitute a practical manifestation of socialism in Africa. If it were, countries such as Ethiopia and Gabon would have to be included, in a certain sense, in the socialist camp. Obviously, such a conclusion is unrealistic. Thus, although certain practical trends in the economic sphere are not unique to African socialist countries, what is unique is the use of socialism as a slogan which legitimizes and sanctions the employment of new methods in economic development.

Socialism itself thus has become another constituent factor in economic development in these countries, not so much in terms of its practical manifestations as for its psychological implications vis-a-vis the development process.

A second category of practical manifestations of African Socialism has been in the political sphere. The most salient political institution in the post-colonial period has been the single, dominant party. The importance of the party as the main focal-institution of African society has been emphasized elsewhere at great length.[46] The understanding of the connection between the single party structure and African Socialism is a valuable key to evaluating both the political relevance of socialism in African countries, and the concept of one-party states in general.

How did political parties establish their institutional pre-eminence in the post-colonial period in Africa? The exact reasons are multiple and, at times, vary significantly from one country to another. It is possible to correlate a composite list of the more notable reasons.[47] First, late colonial policies were an important contributing factor. Both the British and the French encouraged a clear majority by one party prior to the granting of independence. Second, a party, once having achieved power in Africa tended to turn itself into a political machine in order to maintain this power. Third, in a period of transition and decolonization, the party was often the only institution able to provide the needed aura of stability and continuity. Independence brought about changes in the roles of existing institutions. The major party provided a semblance of stability in a period of flux. Fourth, because of the party's role as the core of anti-colonialist protest, it provided a focus for integration and mobilization in the new era of independence. Fifth, the party assumed certain duties which heretofore had been the role of the extended family and the tribal group. Essentially these functions entailed providing a psychological security, a feeling of identity with a group, material benefits, and social security. Sixth, it appeared that the party received a great deal of mass support, at least in the early period of independence, although this is not necessarily substantiated in all cases.[48]

To the above general causes may be added another group of more specific significant factors. Undoubtedly, the personal ambitions of the leaders of the party played an important part in the development of single-party dominance. At times, the numerical strength and dominating tendencies of given ethnic groups were important. Control of economic resources and the distribution of these resources by the party provided an additional factor. Finally, single parties often became prominent on the political scene precisely because other sources of power and opposition were systematically eliminated.[49]

The causes for the rise of one-party states in Africa are integrally related to the leaders' visions of the structure and functions of the party. The myth of the single-party state greatly emphasized the mobilizing and integrative functions of the party in a society in transition. There are, however, major differences of opinion among African leaders and former leaders on this question. Sekou-Touré has viewed his party, the *Parti Democratique de Guinee* (PDG) as a mobilizing and integrating force. Nkrumah, on the other hand, saw the Convention Peoples Party (CPP) as an elitist vanguard whose role was to show the masses the proper way to achieve the declared goals of the state.

The single-party systems of Africa may be viewed as similar to Weber's patrimonial type – within the party structure, the relationship between those at the top and their subordinates was often based on personal loyalties.[50] Nevertheless, especially in the early years, it appears that the party was an open institution operating as an integrator in two senses. Internally, the party brought together people of diverse backgrounds and provided them with security within an organized setting, controlling access to offices, goods, and services. Externally, the party as a whole initially worked to provide a psychologically dynamic force for national advancement. Within this context, the single party – an evolution of development of the national needs of African states – had as one of its main functions the harmonization of political and economic behavior.[51]

The so-called one-party states of Ghana, Mali, Tanzania, Guinea, Senegal have often been cited as the classic embodiments of African Socialism in action. Such a characterization is problematic in several senses. Chronologically, it is not clear whether the single-party preceded or antedated the development of the concept of African Socialism. A closer analysis indicates that the major party had achieved dominance prior to the widespread introduction of the idea of African Socialism. It appears, then, that socialism may have been used as a malleable tool to justify certain actions and certain institutions already in existence.

What, in fact, is "socialist" about the concept of a single-party state? The notion of a single, focal, dynamic societal institution is borrowed from experiences in Eastern Europe and contains clear socialist overtones. In the African context, the phenomenon of a single-party state has been connected with international non-alignment and political radicalism. This interpretation, however, disregarded the experience of central and southern African countries such as Malawi and Lesotho, or of West African countries like the Ivory Coast and Gabon. Indeed, the rise of one predominant party is in no way logically connected with the adoption of socialist principles. Rather, it appears to be a result of the situation of flux existent in African countries on the eve of Independence. Furthermore, the importance of the party as the main stable political institution appears to have been over-emphasized, especially in view of the large number of recent military coups in Africa, which point only too convincingly to the extreme vulnerability of the single party as a central, stable, institution of government.

It thus appears, from recent political developments in Africa, that the role of the party has been gravely exaggerated. It is not surprising that the party, as the most salient and obvious political institution, was immediately seen as the focus of analysis and study. But, was it – or is it – really in the center of African political institutions? Other political trends, such as questions of political culture, political socialization to certain norms, problems of mobilization and integration, questions of decision-making, the role of elites and bureaucracies, have not been sufficiently analyzed to enable a clear response to this question.[52] It is, however, quite clear that emphasis on the party has been misleading.[53] In terms of practical manifestations of African Socialism, the role of the party and its actual influence remains nebulous. There are indications that some aspects of socialism not only are not practically manifested in the internal politics of African countries, but actually conflict with basic political values.

The notion of unity implied by the great emphasis placed on the monolithic party structures does have some practical implications among African socialists in a different sphere. Perhaps the most practical expression of these implications lies in the regional and Pan-African levels. On issues of Pan-African unity it is unquestionably the African socialists who have been the groundbreakers. Most African socialists have adhered to some basic concepts of African unity. First, that a common traditional culture should unite African peoples. Second, that common background and history, and consequently similar problems, foster a sense of unity and purpose. Third, that cooperation, definitely in the economic and social spheres and occasionally in the political arena, may lead to strength and progress. Finally, that socialism acts not only as an incentive for the idea of unity, but also as a means for achieving this goal.[54] On the issue of

Pan-African unity the difference between socialist and non-socialist countries has been much more clear-cut. The socialists have acted as strong advocates of continental unity; the non-socialists have been indifferent or at times actively opposed, as in the case of the Ivory Coast, to closer inter-African cooperation.

The third set of practical manifestations of socialism lies in the social-symbolic sphere. Socialism in Africa has been utilized as a symbolic and practical tool for the achievement of a sense of national community. Socialism provided, in this sense, a focus for the initiation of mobilization and integration in a new political framework. At the same time, the African aspects of African Socialism have provided a sense of historical and cultural continuity which must not be discounted. African Socialism, as a means of constructing and coordinating feelings of national unity, has provided an important stability in a situation of institutional destruction, construction, and reconstruction. Stemming from the traditional notion of communality, it has provided psychological continuity and enabled the elimination, or weakening in some cases, of certain traditional institutions without major dislocations.

Indeed, it is useful to note the attitudes of African socialists to two aspects of modern traditionalism: the tribal group and the institution of chieftancy. The institution of chieftancy has posed a major threat, both politically and psychologically, to some African socialists. They have seen traditionalist authorities as dysfunctional to the establishment of socialism. Nyerere in Tanzania and Sekou-Touré in Guinea have waged an outright war against the chiefs and have formally banned the institution of chieftancy. Nevertheless, in most other African countries traditional authorities do exist and continue to provide a focus for political activities on the local and the national levels. Thus, alongside the national political system, there exist, in most African countries, traditional structures and systems which, though separate and dissimilar, interrelate with and influence national leaders.

The dynamics of this interrelationship between the traditionalist leaders and the national leaders has not yet been fully studied.[55] African socialist leaders have attempted, alternatively, either to combat the chiefs or to encourage them to cooperate with the central government. Their approaches to the tribal group has been similar to their approaches to chieftancy. Some, including Nyerere and Sekou-Touré, have attempted to destroy tribal identities. Others have viewed the tribal grouping as a reality which must be accepted, at least temporarily. No African Socialist leader has attempted to construct his notions of socialism upon the existing tribal and chieftancy units. Practically, the utilization of African Socialism as a tool for the creation of a sense of national community has implied practical steps to inculcate socialist thought. This has been achieved, in countries such as Ghana, Guinea, and Tanzania, partially through the creation of special ideological institutes and study groups. The cadres of activists formed in these ideological centers have subsequently been used to spread the basic socialist precepts to rural areas. The educational system, both in its formal and informal setting, has been used as a forum for ideological inculcation, notable in Guinea, Mali, and Tanzania. The common school framework, coupled with creation of national ideological youth and student movements, has been an important channel for the spread of African Socialism, and, consequently, for the creation of a common sense of community and purpose.[56] Although African Socialism has achieved significant results in fostering a sense of community in Africa through various educational means, other ideologies may be able to fulfill similar roles in Africa in the future.

In the social sphere, while African Socialism has acted as a mobilizer and integrator, it has not necessarily been an equalizer. Most African countries, both socialist and non-socialist, have exhibited tendencies toward growing stratification, thus creating privileged groups led by the politicians and holders of office themselves.[57] In this sense, the egalitarian theoretical notions visible in African Socialist thought, with the exception of the Tanzanian example, have not had clear practical manifestations. The three spheres of practical implications of African Socialism, the economic, the political, and the social, point clearly to the grave discrepancies which exist between socialist thought and socialist action in these countries.

VII

Differential selection and implementation of socialism in Africa has resulted in four discernible trends in African Socialism. According to an analysis by Fenner Brockway, these categories of African Socialism are a result of "a clash . . . between the European intellectual sources of socialism and the influence of Africa's social evolution."[58]

The first category of African Socialists may be termed the "Pure-Marxists." Mainly seen in the *Parti Africaine de l'Independence* (PAI) in Senegal and the banned Communist Party in South Africa, the Pure-Marxists agree with the European Marxists both on doctrinal and strategical questions. These Pure-Marxists have failed in Africa because they insisted in following all the stages of revolution, an inflexible demand in view of the African situation.[59]

The second category of African socialists, the "African-Marxists," has included Kwame Nkrumah, Sekou-Touré, and Modibo Keita. These African Marxists differed from the Pure-Marxists in that they were flexible and willing to adapt their ideologies to the specific exigencies of the African situation. On the other hand, the African-Marxists have tended to accept major *doctrinal* aspects of Marxism.[60] And of these three major African-Marxists, Nkrumah and Keita were ousted from power.

The majority of socialists in Africa fall into the third category: that of "Pragmatic-Socialists." These socialists, including Senghor, Nyerere, Obote, and Kaunda, reject outright the notions of class struggle and dictatorship of the proletariat. They see in socialism primarily a tool of economic development and mobilization. They are much more evolutionary in approach. The Pragmatic-Socialists have been more adaptable to African traditions, and, as a result, less attached to the doctrinal aspects of socialism.[61]

The final group of African socialists, the "Democratic Socialists," find few adherents in Africa. The most salient example of democratic socialism in Africa is Kenyatta's Democratic African Socialism as expressed in the 1966 manifesto. The Democratic Socialists have not accepted socialism as a doctrine, but solely as a tool and slogan.[62]

All African socialists have had in common their protest against the colonial situation and recurrent neo-colonial tendencies. They have combined the protest aspects of socialism with the concrete desire to achieve rapid economic growth. Socialism has been seen as a means of relating differing understandings and idealizations of the African past with full comprehension of the present in order to construct frameworks for future actions.

Most African socialists have added a number of concepts to European socialism. They have, first, embraced the belief in God and reaffirmed the importance of various spiritual values. Secondly, they have tied socialism to the notion of a nation, and subsequently to the idea of Pan-Africanism. Finally, African socialists have given a specific and particularistic dimension to socialism by extending it to certain basic African values.[63]

African socialists have, similarly, faced common obstacles to the imposition of socialism in their countries. First, there exists a natural contradiction inherent in the simultaneous peaceful promotion of economic, social, and political progress in most African countries. Second, the noticeable development of individualistic and corruption-oriented tendencies has clashed with the attempted implementation of African Socialism. Third, inertia and disagreement among the various elites has compounded the problem of socialist implementation. Fourth, the lack of strong and efficient bureaucratic infrastructures has placed another obstacle in the face of socialist development in Africa. Finally, the masses – when not successfully mobilized – are disinterested and indifferent to the imposition of new forms of ideology.[64]

Cognizant of the different and common elements of socialism in Africa, as well as the obstacles facing African socialists, we can now reassess the connection between the various aspects of African Socialism analyzed earlier. To what extent is there a connection between the challenges facing African countries, the selection of socialist and traditional elements, and the practical implications thereof?

The first major problem facing African countries was that of economic development. In the selection process, socialist aspects of economic growth were heavily emphasized. Socialism, in its economic definitions, was efficiently used as a slogan for economic progress. Practically, however, African Socialism has not pointed to new or revolutionary approaches to African economic problems. Thus, there has existed a gap between African socialist theory and practice in the economic sphere.

The second problem mentioned was that of national definition: acquiring an identity through the achievement of mobilization and integration. Here protest aspects of socialist choice combined with the idealization of pre-colonial Africa to provide a framework for common identity. Once again, when reduced to the level of implementation, it is difficult to find specific political achievements in this field. Mobilization and integration goals have also determined other aspects of selection and implementation. Problems of mobilization have placed heavy emphasis on the selection of humanitarian aspects of socialism. Integration has determined the choice of socialism as a focus for changing orientations. These two goals have consequently guided the symbolic utilization of traditional notions of unity and consensus. Practically, notable measures have been taken to achieve these goals through the utilization of African Socialism as a means of achieving a common sense of community.

The final challenge mentioned above was the challenge of unity, on both the national and continental levels. The selection of aspects of a common ideology has tended to foster such unity, and a common cultural and historical experience has strengthened this trend. African socialists have been, practically speaking, strong advocates of African cooperation.

The precarious connections between challenges, theory, and action are more easily understood in terms of three ideological levels, the theoretical, the psychological, and the practical. Theoretically, although African Socialism may be thought-provoking, it is in places inconsistent, at times contradictory. By attempting to embrace too much, to provide intellectual responses for all people, to expand its theoretical scope, African Socialism has tended to be logically unclear and theoretically untidy. The fuzziness of African socialist thought has been most evident on the practical level. There has been a considerable gap between theoretical assumptions and practical achievements. As a result, on the level which affects the largest number of people, the effects of the African socialist experience has been negative. Since the ideology was designed to embody and give impetus to modernization and change, this lack of practical results reveals, to a large degree, its failure. Only on the psychological level, as a focus of common identities and orientations, has African Socialism appeared to have some potential. It is, however, precisely these issues of attitudes and conceptions which are most difficult to measure immediately.

The concept, African Socialism, is obviously inextricably linked to the development of African society; however this link is more complex and problematic than often assumed. African Socialism in many instances is more properly used as a convenient slogan and unifying phrase of the thrust toward total independence in contemporary African society, rather than as a descriptive and operative political, economic, and social program. African Socialism is important as an expression of the frustrations and hopes of African societies today; it is less valuable as a statement of a practical program for dealing with these frustrations and hopes.

While African Socialism is clearly rooted in European socialist ideology, it nevertheless undergoes a significant metamorphosis in terms of its African setting. That is, the African form of socialism is distinctively shaped, amended, and, in some instances, totally changed when transported into its local context. Consequently, any truly relevant attempt to understand this concept can only be effected by careful confrontation with and analysis of it within its particular manifestation. Such a confrontation does indeed reveal that the real heart of African Socialism belongs to its given rather than its family name. In other words — it is far more African than Socialist, and can be best understood as a uniquely African attempt to create an ideology and consequent practice to meet the demands of contemporary African existence.

NOTES

1 Ruth Schachter-Morgenthau, "African Socialism: Declaration of Ideological Independence," *Africa Report,* VIII, 5 (May 1963), p. 3.

2 On this specific point see Thomas Hodgkin, *Nationalism in Colonial Africa* (New York: New York University Press, 1957), pp. 169—184, and "A Note on the Language of African Nationalism," in William Hanna (ed.), *Independent Black Africa* (Chicago: University of Chicago Press, 1964), pp. 235—252.

3 See Dorothy Nelkin, "Socialist Sources of Pan-African Ideology," in William H. Friedland and Carl G. Rosberg (eds.), *African Socialism* (Stanford: Stanford University Press, 1964), pp. 63—89, for an excellent summary of this issue.

4 See George Padmore, *Pan-Africanism or Communism: The Coming Struggle for Africa* (London: Dobson, 1958).

5 Cf. Ruth Schachter-Morgenthau, *Political Parties in French-Speaking West Africa* (London: Oxford University Press, 1964), pp. 22—27.

6 A.A. Mazrui, *Towards a Pax Africana* (Chicago: University of Chicago Press, 1967), p. 65.

7 L.V. Thomas, *Le Socialisme et L'Afrique, Vol. II: L'Ideologie Socialiste et les Voies Africanines de Développement* (Paris: Le Livre Africain, 1966), p. 235.

8 This and following examples and comparisons are based on L.V. Thomas, *Le Socialisme et L'Afrique, Vol. I: Essai sur le socialisme Africaine* (Paris: Le Livre Africaine, 1966), pp. 20—32 and 59—70.

9 See *ibid.,* pp. 62—73.

10 *Ibid.,* pp. 29—30.

11 Mazrui, *op. cit.,* p. 102.

12 Thomas, *op. cit.,* Vol. I, p. 107.

13 Kwame Nkrumah, "African Socialism Revisited," *African Forum,* I, 3 (Winter, 1966), p. 3.

14 Thomas, *op. cit.,* Vol. I, pp. 152—153.

15 Aristide R. Zolberg, *Creating Political Order: The Party States of West Africa* (New York: Rand McNally, 1966), p. 65.

16 Margaret Roberts, "A Socialist Looks at African Socialism" in Friedland and Rosberg, *op. cit.,* pp. 89—90.

17 For explanation of this term and other sociological concepts of Africal Socialism, see William H. Friedland, "Basic Social Trends," in Friedland and Rosberg, *op. cit.,* pp. 15—34.

18 This analysis is based on the elementary chart presented in Brockway, *op. cit.,* pp. 23—24. It is useful to note some of the main African sources on these subjects: Mamadou Dia, "African Socialism," in Friedland and Rosberg, *op. cit.,* pp. 248—249; Kenneth D. Kaunda, *A Humanist in Africa* (London: Longmans, 1966); Madeira Keita, "Le Mali et la Recherche d'un Socialisme Africaine," (Washington, D.C.: Embassy of the Republic of Mali, no date); Tom Mboya, "African Socialism," *Transition* I, 8 (March 1963), pp. 17—19; Kwame Nkrumah, *Towards Colonial Freedom* (London: Heinemann, 1962); Kwame Nkrumah,

Consciencism (London: Heinemann, 1964); Julius K. Nyerere, "The Arusha Declaration and Tanu's Policy on Socialism and Self-Reliance" (Dar es Salaam: Tanu, 1967); Julius K. Nyerere, *Freedom and Socialism* (Dar es Salaam: Oxford University Press, 1968); Sekou-Touré, *Experience Guinéene et Unité Africaine* (Paris: Presence Africaine, 1961); Leopold S. Senghor, *Nationhood and the African Road to Socialism* (New York: Praeger, 1963).

19 Paul E. Sigmund, *The Ideologies of the Developing Nations* (New York: Praeger, 1963), p. 32.

20 Nkrumah, "African Socialism Revisited," *op. cit.*, p. 3.

21 Aristide R. Zolberg, "The Dakar Colloquium: The Search for a Doctrine," in Friedland and Rosberg, *op. cit.*, p. 122.

22 Nkrumah, "African Socialism Revisited," *op. cit.*, p. 8.

23 Charles F. Andrain, "Patterns of African Socialist Thought," *African Forum*, I (Winter, 1966), p. 42.

24 For a similar viewpoint, cf. Igor Kopytoff, "Socialism and Traditional African Societies," in Friedland and Rosberg, *op. cit.*, pp. 53–62.

25 For a similar argument see Thomas, *op. cit.*, Vol. I, pp. 92–97.

26 On the modernizing effect of Christianity, see Thomas Hopkins, "Christianity and Socio-Political Change in Sub-Saharan Africa," *Social Forces*, XLIV, 4 (June 1966), pp. 555–562.

27 Nkrumah, "African Socialism Revisited," *op. cit.*, p. 5.

28 Roberts, *op. cit.*, p. 92.

29 Zolberg, *Creating Political Order, op. cit.*, p. 93.

30 Ayi Kwei Armah, "African Socialism: Utopian or Scientific?" *Presence Africaine*, 64 (Winter, 1967), p. 28.

31 Kwame Nkrumah, *Africa Must Unite* (London: Mercury Books, 1963), *passim*.

32 Margaret Roberts, Anthony Crosland, Ernest Gellner, Paul Mbayi, and Robert Serugama, "Talking Aloud on African Socialism," *Transition*, V, 24 (1966), p. 46.

33 Fenner Brockway, *African Socialism: A Background Book* (Chester Springs, Pa.: Dufour Editions, 1963), p. 14.

34 See Chandler Morse, "The Economics of African Socialism" in Friedland and Rosberg, *op. cit.*, pp. 35–52.

35 *Ibid.*, p. 84. A definition of African Socialism has not been attempted in this paper, because there is no clear-cut definition available. On this general problem of defining African Socialism see A.H.K. Jumba-Masagazi, *African Socialism: A Bibliography* (Nairobi: The East African Academy, 1970), p. 8.

36 Thomas, *op. cit.*, Vol. I, pp. 174–195 for further clarification.

37 Edward Marcus and Mildred Marcus, "African Socialism and International Financial Flows," *African Forum*, I, 3 (Winter, 1966), p. 39.

38 Martin Kilson, "The Politics of African Socialism," *African Forum*, I, 3 (Winter, 1966), p. 19.

39 Morse, *op. cit.*, pp. 39–40.

40 See Roberts, *op. cit.*, for elucidation of this question.

41 The Ghanaian Business Promotions Act, 1970.

42   Roberts, *op. cit.,* pp. 84—85

43   See *Youth and Development in Africa* (London: Commonwealth Secretariat, 1969).

44   Julius K. Nyerere, "Ujamaa: Speech made at Tanu Conference on Socialism," in Friedland and Rosberg, *op. cit.,* p. 241.

45   Leopold S. Senghor, "The African Road to Socialism," *African Forum,* 1, 3 (Winter, 1966), p. 13.

46   Friedland, *op. cit.,* pp. 31—33.

47   See Martin Kilson, "Authoritarian and Single-Party Tendencies in African Politics," *World Politics,* XV, 2 (January 1963); Gwendolyn Carter, "African One-Party States," in P.J. McEwan and R.B. Sutcliffe, *The Study of Africa* (London: Methuen, 1967), pp. 201—209; Thomas Hodgkin, *Nationalism in Colonial Africa, op. cit.;* Immanuel Wallerstein, "The Decline of the Party in the Single Party State," in La Palombara and Weiner, *Political Parties and Political Development* (Princeton: Princeton University Press, 1967); Ruth Schachter-Morgenthau, "Single-Party Systems in West Africa," *The American Political Science Review,* LV (1961), pp. 294—307; Edward Feit, "Military Coups and Political Development: Some Lessons From Ghana and Nigeria," *World Politics,* XX, 2 (January 1968), pp. 179—193.

48   Carter, *loc. cit.*

49   David E. Apter, "Some Reflections on the Role of a Political Opposition in New Nations," *Comparative Studies in Society and History,* IV (June 1962), p. 158.

50   Zolberg, *Creating Political Order, op. cit.,* p. 141.

51   Kilson, "The Politics of African Socialism," *op. cit.,* p. 22.

52   Only a few empirical studies have been carried out on aspects of political socialization and political culture. The empirical data is insufficient, and many more specific empirical studies are required in this field.

53   See comments by Zolberg and Feit, *op. cit.,* on this question.

54   Thomas, *op. cit.,* Vol. II, p. 232.

55   For a clear exposition on this point, see Zolberg, *Creating Political Order, op. cit.,* and Norman Miller, "The Political Survival of Traditional Leadership in East Africa," *Journal of Modern African Studies,* VI, 2 (August 1968), pp. 183—198.

56   A recent study carried out by this author of political attitudes of members of youth organizations in Ghana substantiates this point.

57   Friedland, *op. cit.,* pp. 31—32.

58   Brockway, *op. cit.,* p. 19. Categories are taken from the classification in this book.

59   *Ibid.,* pp. 19—20.

60   *Ibid.,* p. 21. Also in Thomas, *op. cit.,* Vol. I, pp. 46—48.

61   *Ibid.,* p. 22.

62   *Ibid.,* pp. 22—23.

63   Thomas, *op. cit.,* Vol. I, pp. 73—78.

64   *Ibid.,* pp. 161—166.

NKRUMAISM: GHANA'S EXPERIMENT WITH AFRICAN SOCIALISM

NAOMI CHAZAN

I

To understand Ghana — the early years of independence as well as the Ghana of today — an insight into Kwame Nkrumah and Nkrumaism is indispensable. Some students of Ghana of the 1951-1966 period sought to understand the nature of Ghanaian political, social, and economic life in terms of Nkrumah himself,[1] while others have spotlighted the centrality of Nkrumaist ideology as the key determinant of policy during the Nkrumah era.[2] Thus it is useful, at this stage, to re-examine the importance of political thought in the Ghanaian context and to re-evaluate the role of ideology in Ghanaian life during the early period of independence.

In order to systematically analyze the nature and functions of Nkrumaist ideology, it is first necessary to note those principles and values which were directly selected from Europe. Second, it is important to isolate the indigenous African bases of Nkrumaist thought. Third, it is necessary to delineate the challenges facing Ghana at independence. Fourth, the practical implications and manifestations of Nkrumaism will be studied. Finally, the adaptability of Nkrumaist ideology to basic Ghanaian norms of thought and action will be evaluated.

These five stages in the analysis and evaluation of ideology within the African context will be implemented in terms of three ideological levels, and, subsequently, in terms of three ideological functions. Structurally, ideology in the new nations has a philosophical-symbolic level; an identity or orientation level; and a practical level. Functionally, African ideologies seek to provide legitimacy for the actions of a given regime; to provide a focus for national identities; and to provide a program for specific actions in the political, economic, and social spheres.[3] Each stage of ideological selection and implementation will be analyzed in terms of the three structural levels and the three functional aspects of ideology in the African context, in an attempt to elucidate the importance of political thought in independent Ghana during the Nkrumah regime.

II

The history of decolonization and early independence in Ghana is usually divided into four periods. The first period, from 1947 to 1951, was an era of intense anti-colonial feeling and the rise of the Nkrumaist Convention People's Party (CPP). The second period, 1951-1954, was a period of dyarchy, of cooperation between the CPP and the British government. The third period, from 1954 to 1956, was the period of internal opposition and stress, when the political monopoly of Nkrumah and the CPP was seriously threatened by local groups throughout the country. The fourth period, from 1957 to 1961, after independence was attained, was a period of consolidation of the CPP position and the systematic elimination of the opposition. Officially, the socialist period in Ghana began in 1961.

The post-World War II era in West Africa was one of rapid political awakening, which culminated in increased demands for independence from colonial rule. In the Gold Coast, these anti-colonialist protestations were first actively put forward by the United Gold Coast Convention (UGCC), an amalgam of business and intellectual groups, with some support from various chiefs. Kwame Nkrumah, after serving for a short period as the general-secretary of the UGCC, broke away to form the CPP in 1949. With the assistance of young school-leavers, the CPP launched a period of "positive action." The resulting civil unrest brought about the jailing of Nkrumah in 1950. In 1951, the first elections were held in the Gold Coast; the CPP beat the UGCC handily, gaining 34 of the 38 seats in the Legislative Assembly. Nkrumah was immediately released from prison and appointed Leader of Government Business. Subsequently, he was named Prime Minister.

The 1951 elections marked the culmination of the active anti-colonial period in the Gold Coast and the peak of mass mobilization and participation in this struggle.[4] But during this first period three themes of essential importance to the understanding of later events in Ghana became evident. First, the CPP emerged as a movement of great organizational complexity, capable of attracting support in many peripheral areas. Second, Kwame Nkrumah became not only the leader but also the symbol of the political struggle for independence in

the Gold Coast. As the embodiment of the movement for decolonization, certain superhuman, and at times Messianic, characteristics were
attributed to him.[5] Third, it became clear that Nkrumah was leading
not only a movement against colonialism, but also an inter-
generational conflict: the CPP has been termed "the political
expression of a new social group — the elementary school-
leavers."[6]

The period of dyarchy, which began in 1951, saw the entrenchment
of CPP power. "Once in office, the CPP stayed in, and this may well
have been the happy fate of any successor government during the fat,
harvest years of the first decade of party rule."[7] The creation of the
Cocoa Purchasing Company (CPC) as a CPP-controlled government
body was the first indication that the power position of the Party
could and would be utilized as a source of Party funds, Party patron-
age, purchasing votes, and enriching the Party faithful.[8]

The era of severe internal dissension commenced immediately
following the elections of 1954 with the creation of the National
Liberation Movement (NLM), an Ashanti-based political party supported by the chiefs, the cocoa farmers, and the young men of the
Ashanti. Similar particularistic political groups sprang up in other areas
of the Gold Coast: the Northern People's Party in the Northern
territories, the Togoland Congress in the present Volta Region; the
Muslim Association Party (MAP) in main cities of the south; and the
intellectual-led Ghana Congress Party. Internal strife, violence, and
disagreements marked the immediate pre-independence years, with
Nkrumah and the CPP attempting to combat the centrifugal tendencies of these new opposition parties. In a hard-fought election in 1956,
the CPP gained 57% of the vote and 71 of the 104 seats in parliament.
However, only approximately 30% of the eligible voters participated
in these elections.[9]

The pattern of decolonization in the Gold Coast, which culminated
in the granting of independence to Ghana on March 6, 1957, provided
important clues to later events. First, the centrality of the notion of
protest, and the importance of political action within this context,
became a major theme which carried over to the period of independence. Second, the importance of protest as a theoretical and practical
tool clearly overshadowed economic, educational, and social demands
which were brewing during the ten years of active decolonization.
Third, the roots of discontent were evident in the later opposition
period; the significance of this political awakening in more peripheral
areas cannot be overestimated. Fourth, the monopolistic tendencies

of the CPP foreshadowed the centrality of its role in political mobilization and political coercion in later years.[10] Fifth, Nkrumah's ideological pronouncements indicated the trend of future action."I am a Marxist Socialist and an undenominational Christian. I am not a communist and have never been one. . . . I stand for no discrimination against any race or individual, but I am unilaterally opposed to imperialism in any form."[11] Finally, the legitimation granted the leader of the decolonization struggle, Kwame Nkrumah, created a personality cult which allowed the future personalization and sacralization of authority in independent Ghana.

The early period of Ghanaian independence was one of consolidation, but scarcely of innovation. Between 1957 and 1960, Nkrumah systematically outlawed political opposition and detained or exiled the leaders of these groups. In 1960, Ghana was declared a Republic, and Kwame Nkrumah her first president. The consolidation of CPP national political power papered over the cracks which were beginning to form in other spheres. Economically, ostentatious spending by political leaders, coupled with decreasing cocoa prices on the world market, continuously threatened Ghana's economic stability. Socially, the power monopoly of the young men was resented not only by the older intelligentsia and traditional authorities, but also by farmers in the rural areas. Politically, the CPP itself was beginning to show signs of internal conflict and decay. Nkrumah himself was at the same time the center of decision-making power and the focus of both loyalties and disagreements. At this stage of Ghanaian history Nkrumaist socialism was officially introduced as the ideology of the new Ghana – as the means of achieving national identity, legitimacy for the regime, and practical economic, political, and social goals.

III

The understanding of socialism in Ghana is inextricably tied to Nkrumaism – the body of Nkrumaist thought as expressed in hundreds of speeches and a series of written works.[12] Consequently, a careful analysis of basic themes of Nkrumaist ideology is a valuable and indispensable key to a full comprehension of the first nine years of Ghanaian independence. Theoretically, Nkrumah was influenced by three main sources. First, while studying in the United States and Britain, Nkrumah was greatly influenced by Marxist-Leninist thought, which he came to view as *the* ideology for oppressed Africa.[13] Second, Nkrumah came under the direct influence of the British Communist Party, where he imbibed methods of political organization and agitation which were utilized later in the decolonization struggle. Third, the tradition of the church, not only dogmatically but also symbolically, was to have a major impact on the delineation of Nkrumaist ideology and practice.[14] Conversely, there is no indication that Nkrumah's thought was influenced directly by Ghanaian traditions or history, although he did actively attempt to build a great tradition for the entire continent upon his Ghanaian base.

Socialism, in its purer forms, was undoubtedly the external source of greatest influence for Nkrumah's ideological development. Nkrumah's own definition of socialism provided a key to his selective choice of elements of European socialism: "Socialism is a form of social organization which, guided by the principles underlying communism, adopts procedures and measures made necessary by demographic and technological developments . . . Socialism, therefore, can be and is the defense of the principles of communalism in a modern setting."[15] Nkrumah's understanding of socialism established the theoretical basis for the development of his own political philosophy, "Nkrumaism," which was officially defined as: "The ideology of the New Africa, independent and absolutely free from imperialism, organized on a continental scale, founded upon the conception of one and united Africa, drawing its strength from modern science and technology and from the traditional belief that the free development of each is the condition for the free development of all."[16]

The four main themes of Nkrumaism were closely connected to basic elements of European socialism. The first major theme of Nkrumaism was the notion of protest. Nkrumah saw socialism as the ideology of protest against the colonial situation, and it is precisely these protest aspects of socialism which were most developed in Nkrumaist thought. The preoccupation, both in the pre- and post-independence periods, with the anti-colonial struggle was a function of Nkrumah's perception of the stages of anti-colonialism. The first stage in this struggle was the demand for political freedom, which was paramount in Nkrumaism. The second stage in the anti-colonial struggle involved a revolt against poverty and exploitation, the social ills of the colonial inheritance. The theoretical conception of the stages of protest dictated different practical programs at each stage.

Nkrumah saw the people, the leadership, and a dynamic organization as the key elements of the first struggle, the political contest. The backbone of the anti-colonialist revolt, according to Nkrumah, were the people. Theoretically, he emphasized specifically the role of the workers in this struggle.[17] While this view is conceptually similar to the Marxist view of the proletariat, practically — in his own CPP — Nkrumah relied most heavily on the young men. But the people could not rise without the second element, leadership. Nkrumah saw that the movement would be led in its beginnings by two groups: political extremists; and political moderates and members of the aristocratic classes. Eventually, the leadership would be taken over entirely by the political extremists, so that the second stage, the societal revolution, could eventually be implemented without the interference of neo-colonial elements.[18] In Nkrumaism, mass participation and a radical leadership combined with the centrality of a dynamic organizational party framework were the three main tools which could implement the first stage of the anti-colonialist protest.

While the concrete tools and goals of the political stage of anti-colonialism were always implicit in Nkrumaist thought, this was not the case in relation to the second stage, the societal revolution. The primary tool of effectuation of this period of reconstruction was seen as the Party, which, in Nkrumaism, became the focus of all activities after independence. The Nkrumaist conception of the role of the Party was not always clear. Unquestionably, the Party was viewed as the center and vanguard of any political activity; it was to be open and to be based on Nkrumaism. The purpose of this ideological training given to Party members was to create a Party vanguard which could assist in reconstructing the society.[19] However, the justification for the centrality of the Party in the independence period was given in terms of the protest theme. "A people's parliamentary democracy with a one-party system is better able to express and satisfy the common aspiration of a nation as a whole, than a multi-party parliamentary system, which is in fact only a ruse for perpetuating, and covers up, the inherent struggle between the have's and the have-nots."[20]

The protest themes of Nkrumaism, chronologically associated primarily with the period of decolonization, were superseded in the 1960's by a second strain, the economic theme. Nkrumah saw socialism, initially, as an economic program, and not necessarily as a theoretical base for the protest themes so prominent in his own thinking: "Capitalism is too complicated a system for a newly independent nation. Hence the need for a socialistic society."[21] Socialism thus became an economic tool to assist in the solution of the various economic and social challenges facing Ghana. The main principles of Nkrumaist economic thought may be summarized as follows:[22] 1) The role of the state was central to economic growth. 2) National economic planning was crucial to economic progress. 3) This planning was to be geared to socialism. 4) Foreign aid was to be utilized in a manner which would give full control to the recipient. 5) It was necessary to diversify the sources of foreign assistance. 6) Attitudinal changes should be initiated in the productive sectors of the population. 7) The formation of a new privileged class should be prevented. 8) A new monetary and fiscal system was to be launched. 9) The role of the Party in economic development was paramount. 10) In order to effect these economic steps, it would be necessary to drastically change the administrative system.

Nkrumaist economic thought, with its emphasis on industrialization and increased production, differed in these two respects from most other African socialist ideologies. Nevertheless, as a framework for socialist economic activity Nkrumaism was weak on one crucial point: the type and rate of nationalization of private enterprises. The economic themes in Nkrumaist thought did, however, point to the major economic steps which should be taken to achieve economic growth, and to the main objectives of this development.

The third major theme of Nkrumaism was the notion of changing orientations. Nkrumah viewed his ideology as a means of bringing about basic changes of thought patterns and philosophical norms in order to create, ultimately, a great tradition for all of independent Africa. Initially, the theme of changing orientations relied on the concept of African personality and the creation of an identity around all things African. The concept of African personality aimed at achieving cultural and intellectual equality with non-African countries; later it was transposed into a dynamic concept whose purpose was to project the goals of Africa on the international political level. This specific glorification of the African personality, which Nkrumah himself saw as differing from Senghor's concept of *négritude*,[23] led to a renewed interest in African history as a basis for changing orientations.

The theme of changing orientations was inextricably tied to the concept of African unity, the fourth major theme of Nkrumaism. Nkrumah felt that African unity could not be achieved unless there existed a common intellectual basis. *"Philosophic consciencism* will give the theoretical basis for an ideology whose aim shall be to contain the African experience of the Islamic and Euro-Christian presence as well as the experience of traditional African society, and, by gestation, employ them for the harmonious growth and development of that society."[24] The intellectual base of African unity presupposed, according to Nkrumah, a common framework. "African unity sets the horizon and provides the moving spirit in the teachings of Nkrumaism. In it, his entire philosophy lives, and moves, and has its being."[25]

The four major themes of Nkrumaist thought are interrelated and guided by Nkrumah's desire to achieve and maintain total independence. These themes of protest, economic development, orientation change, and African unity were developed upon a socialist intellectual base. Nkrumah has summarized those basic elements which he selected from socialist thought:

> The socialism of a liberated territory is subject to a number of principles if independence is not to be alienated from the people. When socialism is true to its purpose, it seeks a connection with the equalitarian and humanist past of the people before their social evolution was ravaged by colonialism; it seeks from the results of colonialism those elements (like new methods of industrial production and economic organization) which can be adopted to serve the interest of the people; it seeks to contain and prevent the spread of anomalies and domineering interests created by the capitalist habit of colonialism; it reclaims the psychology of the people, erasing the 'colonial mentality' from it; and it resolutely defends the independence and security of the people. In short, socialism recognizes dialectic, the possibility of creation from forces which are opposed to one another; it recognizes the creativity of struggle, and, indeed, the necessity of the operation of forces to any change. It also embraces materialism and translates this into social terms of equality. Hence philosophical consciencism.[26]

The major themes of Nkrumaism were connected not only with socialism but also with Nkrumah's understanding of and attitudes toward the African past and existing traditionalist institutions. There existed a dichotomy in Nkrumah's thought between his attitudes toward tradition and traditionalism on the symbolic and intellectual level as opposed to the practical and realistic level. Thus, on the one hand, Nkrumah worked, theoretically and practically, for the destruction and elimination of existing traditionalist structures; and on the other hand he effectively utilized the symbolic importance of the notion of the tribe and the authority of the chiefs for mobilizational purposes. Nkrumah's conception of the importance of the African past, the equality and communalism of the pre-colonial setting, and the historical base for independent political growth all pointed to his understanding of the symbolic utility of African traditions. The neglect of existing traditionalist structures pointed, on the other hand, to Nkrumah's inability to accept and utilize tradition and traditionalism for practical purposes.

Nkrumah's view of the African past was not necessarily based on the Ghanaian experience. His search for historical roots consisted of several attempts to mythologize, idealize, and, at times, redefine the *spirit* of the total African past — but not its concomitant *institutions*. This paradoxical approach to African traditions in Nkrumaism was further complicated by Nkrumah's own personal superstitions. Nkrumah, personally, was diligent in the performance of certain rites, primarily the pouring of libations, and he carefully observed certain taboos, regularly consulting his fetish priest before arriving at any major decisions.[27] Again, this dichotomy may best be explained as an illustration of Nkrumah's understanding of the symbolic uses of tradition and customary rites, but not their practical and realistic implications.

In summary, the large body of Nkrumaist thought did not provide a well-balanced ideological framework, both structurally and functionally. On the theoretical level, Nkrumaism was too greatly concerned with legitimizing and glorifying past and present actions; hence the great emphasis on the themes of protest and African unity. On the identity level, while striving to provide a focus for identity and changing orientations, Nkrumaism tended to disregard basic elements of the Ghanaian experience. On the practical level, the concern with the protest aspects of economic development ignored many of the basic economic needs of Ghanaian society, and thus provided only a weak framework for action. Similarly, Nkrumaism was not necessarily in keeping with some basic objective challenges confronting Ghana during the early years of independence. The major part of Nkrumaist thought was geared toward self-induced challenges, and these not always constructively, through the themes of protest, changing orientations and African unity. Nkrumaism dealt only secondarily with the problems of economic development, unquestionably the basic need of Ghana at the time.

Thus, Nkrumaism was primarily an African rather than a Ghanaian ideology. In attempting to satisfy everyone, Nkrumah's ideology was too broad to be practicable, too confused a synthesis to be intellectually rewarding, and too removed from specific realities to be a practical success.

IV

Three major challenges faced Ghana in 1961. The first and most obvious of these challenges was that of economic growth. Popular pressure on the Nkrumah regime demanded the fulfillment of economic promises made during the decolonization period, promises that were contradicted by the austerity measures of the first years of independence. Furthermore, demands were made on the government to provide basic amenities commensurate with rising standards of living. In other words, not only civil servants, workers, and traders but also cocoa farmers and people in the rural areas were demanding the material returns which they considered their due following independence.

This popular demand for economic development was integrally related to local demands for education at all levels: education in Ghana was viewed as the key to initiation into modern economic life and its consequent material benefits. On the other hand, the Nkrumah regime saw economic development as the key to self-reliance and self-assertion in the international sphere, and internally as a means of assuring common support for its rule. The assumption of socialist trappings, of the many possible options, was initially conceived as a radical solution to the severe economic difficulties facing the country.[28] The discrepancies between government and local interests evident in the delineation of the causes for the economic challenges facing Ghana in 1961 provided a clue to future divergences between popular demands and government conceptions of these demands.

The second major challenge facing Ghana in the early 1960's was the challenge of national definition. This challenge, as perceived by the government, implied the integration of the various smaller ethnic groups with the dominant Akan-speaking peoples into the entity known as Ghana. Such integration would provide not only internal stability, but also a common front on the Pan-African and international levels. The challenge of national definition also pointed to the importance of the process of mass mobilization as a means of achieving national identity and economic development. This challenge of national definition was primarily a government dictated challenge, and not one which necessarily resulted from popular desires and pressures.

The third major Ghanaian challenge in 1961, as enunciated by the Nkrumah regime, ·was the challenge of continental unity. The unification of Ghana itself was to act as a first stage in the unification of Africa as a whole. This general outward orientation of the Nkrumah regime was to act as a major guiding force in external and internal policies in the later Nkrumah era. The centrality, to Nkrumah, of the problem of Pan-African unity was also to subsume many internal demands placed on his regime, and to cause him to ignore them.

An alternative conception of the main challenges facing Ghana in the early years of independence was closely connected with differing views of the Ghanaian situation at the time. The challenge of national definition, the challenge of unity, and the causes of the challenge of economic development as assessed by the Ghanaian government were not necessarily in accord with the more material and practical educational demands of large segments of the Ghanaian population. The divergent conceptions of Ghanaian needs and realities affected future policy choices and acceptance or non-acceptance of these policies by some parts of the polity. The Nkrumah regime's delineation and conception of the major challenges acted as a guideline and justification for socialist choice and implementation. This conception of challenges — though often a distortion of objective wants and goals and definitely at odds with the balanced needs dictated by economic, social, and political realities — elucidates the understanding of the inherent weaknesses in the Nkrumah regime.

V

A political ideology must be assessed not only in terms of its theoretical cohesiveness, but also in terms of its practical applicability and its adaptability to specific conditions. It thus becomes necessary to look at and evaluate the practical manifestations of Nkrumaism. Socialism was officially introduced as the guiding ideology of Ghana in late 1961, partly as a result of severe economic difficulties. The practical manifestations of this new period were delineated in two documents: The CPP's Work and Happiness Program and the First Seven-Year Development Plan.[29] These plans constituted an attempt to translate ideological goals into practical provisos in the economic, political, and social spheres.

The first series of practical implications of Nkrumaism were in the economic area. First, the Ghanaian government accepted the notion of central planning. The seven-year development plan (1963-1970) called for more than two hundred specific improvements within a socialist framework; only half of these items had any relevance for practical policy.[30] The basic emphasis of the plan called for a shift from economic infrastructure to productive aspects of an industrial nature. However, in 1965 a full 63% of government expenditure was still being invested in infrastructure.[31] Second, the implementation of the seven-year development plan called for the nationalization of foreign enterprises and the establishment of state-owned companies. The establishment of state enterprises as a means of implementing basic economic aspects of Nkrumaism was not viable economically. Indeed, the 32 government-owned enterprises in existence in 1965 carried an accumulated debt of more than £40 million.[32] Furthermore, the state enterprises were centers of corruption, nepotism, and favoritism, sometimes utilized as a means of repaying political loyalty.[33] Third, the increased governmental intrusion into the economic sphere was unquestionably seen in terms of government expenditure. In the mid-1950's government expenditure stood at £50 million. In the mid-1960's this figure had quadrupled and reached over £200 million. Increased government expenditure bore no relationship to the standard of living and prices of food staples and semi-luxury goods. There are indications that prices rose in the two-year period of 1963-1965 between 45 and 80%.[34] Finally, on the local level, the Nkrumah regime established a network of state farms to serve as pilot schemes for surrounding areas. Also centers of favoritism, the state farms were largely unsuccessful in introducing modern farming techniques and diversifying agricultural production.

At the time of the coup d'état against Nkrumah in 1966, Ghana had dissipated her foreign reserves and had a foreign debt exceeding £200 million. The Nkrumah regime's inability to stem the economic stagnation facing the country was at the base of the discontent which led to the overthrow of the government.[35] Indeed, the Nkrumah regime's attempt to implement socialist industry-oriented ideology in the Ghanaian situation was a monumental failure. The poor implementation of Nkrumaism in the economic sphere pointed not only to the inability of the government to turn policy into practice, but also to the possible incompatibility of this policy with basic Ghanaian norms.

The second series of practical manifestations of Nkrumaism were in the political sphere. The first practical political implication was in the area of Party structure and functions. The monolithic Party structure which emerged during the first few years of independence was achieved by the forced elimination of the opposition and by the systematic absorption of voluntary and professional associations into the CPP. The supra-political machine of the CPP had some logical drawbacks. First, membership in the CPP soared, and, consequently, it was apparent that this organization was slowly becoming an unwieldy and ineffective political tool. Second, the absorption of various opposing interest groups under the Party banner only succeeded in internalizing dissension and creating rival factions within the Party.

The Party did have, initially, certain positive functions however. The CPP could mobilize some sections of the population, although there is some evidence that it was incapable of educating an aware and action-oriented polity.[36] The CPP, as the leader of a generational revolt, did succeed, to some extent, in fostering common national identities and integrating toward common national norms. Despite the lack of effective success of certain functional aspects of the monolithic Party, the CPP still held two tools. First, it could, and did, develop a cult around the political leader. Second, it could utilize force to achieve certain goals unattainable by normal methods. The CPP created a Party police force and a wide network of secret informants, while utilizing two Party youth organizations, the Workers Brigade and the Young Pioneers, as showcases and "rowdy boys" for purposes of political coercion.[37]

The second practical political manifestation of Nkrumaism revolved around the political personality of Nkrumah himself. The personalization of authority and the deification of Kwame Nkrumah during the latter part of his regime was not necessarily discordant with the traditional homage paid Akan chiefs. Indeed, the efficiency of charisma in the Ghanaian context may partially be explained by the fact that it fulfilled some of the functional requisites of traditional leadership in the past.[38] These neo-traditional, Messianic symbols[39] with which Nkrumah cloaked himself, and the cult which developed around him, were not, however, compatible with any of the ideological themes of Nkrumaism. They were, on the other hand, largely dysfunctional to the creation of a stable and routinized political regime. In the short run, the personalization of authority under Nkrumah served, temporarily, to maintain the continuity of the regime. Conversely, however, it removed Nkrumah from the people and severely blocked lines of communication to the grass roots. After several attempts on his life, Nkrumah surrounded himself with foreign advisors, jailed trusted Ghanaian lieutenants, disassociated himself from the mainstream of Ghanaian life, and directed his political efforts beyond Ghana. The ideological incompatibility inherent in the deification of Kwame Nkrumah had major implications in terms of the practical political success of Nkrumaism.

The third political implication of Nkrumaism lay in the field of ideological indoctrination. Sincere attempts were made to familiarize people with the basic tenets of Nkrumaist thought. The Kwame

Nkrumah Ideological Institute established at Winneba was staffed primarily by foreign instructors whose sole task was to teach the basic texts of Nkrumaism. The radical CPP journal, *The Spark,* became a vehicle for further ideological indoctrination. The CPP's newspaper, *The Evening News,* showed the daily ideological perceptions of the regime. Nkrumaism was also taught in schools and in various CPP-affiliated organizations. However, the attempts at indoctrination often had only superficial success; they did not always penetrate to the grass-roots level.

Major national political developments in Ghana under the Nkrumah regime did not always agree with the basic themes of Nkrumaist thought. In this sphere, ideology appeared to serve as a legitimizing tool for existing policies, rather than as a pragmatic framework for future political action. The centrality of the Party in Nkrumaist protest thought did not adhere to the basic political balance. The construction of a personality cult was also ideologically incompatible with Nkrumaism. Forced ideological indoctrination was necessary for the creation of ideologically-steeped vanguards oriented toward the central government, but the lack of penetration provided only partial ideological consensus.

The final set of practical manifestations of Nkrumaism were in the Pan-African and international spheres. A staunch supporter and initiator of the concept of African unity, Nkrumah acted as host to numerous Pan-African conferences, the last in Accra in 1965. Within Ghana he trained foreign "freedom fighters" in order to combat what he viewed as colonial and neo-colonial infiltration.[40] There is no question that on the continental level Nkrumaism was being spread and, at times, implemented, and that Nkrumah considered himself, and was considered by many, to be a great African leader.[41]

VI

Nkrumaism was designed as the ideology of the new Ghana, and, increasingly, as the ideology of the new Africa. The effectiveness of Nkrumaist ideology in Ghana may be judged not only in terms of its theoretical cohesiveness and practical applications, but also in terms of its adaptability and compatibility with basic Ghanaian political norms. Political culture in Ghana relies on two major traditions: basic orientations passed on from the pre-colonial era from generation to generation; and newly-acquired orientations provided by colonial contact with a small elite, through the transference of British educational institutions to the Ghanaian setting. Thus the dominant political culture of independent Ghana was integrally related to the history of the area as a whole, as well as to individual attitudes.[42]

The basic unit of traditional Ghanaian societies was the extended family. Nkrumaism sought traditional legitimacy by comparing its institutional forms to those implicit in the communalism of the tribe and the clan. "Afrocracy is the extension of communalism to the national political sphere. That is why our national legislature is composed of only one party. The parliamentarians are the equivalent of the clan heads; the constituencies are the clan groups. The king, of course, is the head of state. The same checks and balances, duties and liberties that operate at the tribal level are expressed nationally."[43] This attempt at legitimizing Nkrumaism in traditional terms was largely ineffective because it ignored the basic attitudes behind the communalism of Ghanaian societies. First, the traditional method of decision-making — discussion followed by, usually, unanimous agreement — was deeply imbedded into Ghanaian society. Agreement did not, however, imply unanimity of thought. Rather, it proved to be serious intellectual activity, providing possibilities of persuasion, and, finally, of consensus. Thus the notions of a political party, elections, authoritarian decision-making were largely foreign to traditional decision-making patterns.[44]

Second, Ghanaians traditionally have been reluctant to criticize political leaders openly, although mechanisms did exist by which discontent could be expressed. Indeed some Ghanaian languages do not have words by which a young man may openly disagree with an elder.[45] The rise of the CPP was often associated with the disaffection of young men with traditional authority.[46] It was difficult, and perhaps impossible, for the CPP to demand consensus and respect due to traditional authority on the one hand, and to attempt to destroy these traditional institutions on the other.

The colonial period in the Gold Coast introduced Western orientations and aspirations which combined into basic demands. First, education in the Western pattern was, and is, viewed as a primary goal. The emergent class divisions in Ghanaian society, on the basis of educational achievements, are indicative of the direction of social change. Second, the spread of education gave an impetus to rising economic expectations. The government, as the controller of economic activity, was seen as the central organ capable of implementing this basic quest for education and rising standards of living. Nkrumaism was largely incompatible with the traditionally rooted political attitudes and Western-influenced demands. Theoretically, "Modern Socialism has no popular roots in Ghanaian society. Its present influence is not primarily a response to needs felt by the masses of workers and peasants; it is the result of a deliberate choice of policy by Nkrumah and an elite in the CPP."[47] On a practical level, "Consciencism was no substitute for cassava, nor Nkrumaism, or democratic centralism, for a pair of cheap hard-working boots."[48]

The discordance between Nkrumaist thought and common values and aspirations could have possibly been overcome, if Nkrumah had not introduced practices that were unquestionably in opposition to these values. First, the careful and intense grooming of elitist vanguards — specifically the nucleus of the National Association of Socialist Students' Organizations (NASSO) and the Party Vanguard Activists (PVA's) — was not compatible with the easy-going pace of Ghanaian life. Second, constant spying and insecurity created an atmosphere of mutual suspicion and general lack of trust. Thus, not only was Nkrumaism without roots in Ghanaian traditions and values, but, in some cases, it was in direct contradiction to existing life patterns.

VII

Although Nkrumaism and socialism in Ghana were basically intertwined with an understanding of Nkrumah himself, it is nevertheless possible to analyze and evaluate Nkrumaist ideology in terms of levels and functions of ideology within the Ghanaian context. First, on the philosophical level, Nkrumaism came largely to legitimize rather than to initiate. Only the themes of economic identity were fully relevant to the basic challenges facing Ghana at independence. The main themes of protest and African unity were not necessarily compatible with or relevant to these challenges. In its practical manifestations, these themes of protest and African unity were the goals of many actions of the Nkrumah regime. This overemphasis on the legitimizing aspects of Nkrumaism, however, created an ideological imbalance incompatible with basic norms.

Second, on the practical level, the economic themes of Nkrumaism, while in accord with basic challenges and political values, were mostly unsuccessful. The function of this practical level of ideology was to provide a viable framework for action and to respond to basic economic demands. In this sphere, Nkrumaism's lack of success was due primarily to inefficiency, nepotism, and corruption.

Third, on the identity level, Nkrumaism was relevant to the challenge of national definition. However, in Ghanaian conditions, Nkrumaism attempted to provide a common focus for identity which was based on principles not acceptable to large segments of the population. Thus the programmatic functions of ideology were not operable at almost all levels in Nkrumaism. The identity-creating and innovative functions of this ideology were not in line with basic societal aspirations. Only the legitimizing functions of Nkrumaism left any important impact, but in this case mostly outside Ghana.

The overthrow of Nkrumah pointed to the decline of Nkrumaism in the Ghanaian context, but not to the overall failure of this ideology on the continental scale. As a legitimizing framework for the anti-colonial struggle, Nkrumaism stands out as the major African ideology of protest to date, and in this respect it was deeply influenced by the socialist example. As a legitimator of African unity, and as a philosophical framework for the creation of a great, common tradition for all Africa, Nkrumaism was an innovative ideology which stressed common African goals and traditions. But as a Ghanaian ideology geared to the exigencies of the Ghanaian situation, Nkrumaism was out-of-touch — both theoretically and practically — with its basic sources; it had no long-lasting influence in Ghanaian life. Nkrumaism, though stemming from Ghana, developed into an African ideology of protest and unity, with a basic socialist orientation. Nkrumaism, thus, can best be understood as a socialist African ideology, rather than as the socialist ideology of Ghana.

NOTES

1 See, for example, Colin Legum, "Socialism in Ghana: A Political Interpretation," in W. Friedland and C. Rosberg, *African Socialism* (Stanford: Stanford University Press, 1964); H.T. Alexander, *African Tightrope* (New York: Praeger, 1966); Timothy Bankole, *Kwame Nkrumah: His Rise to Power* (Evanston: Northwestern University Press, 1963); and Henry L. Bretton, *The Rise and Fall of Kwame Nkrumah* (London: Pall Mall Press, 1966).

2 Cf. David Apter, "Ghana" in J. Coleman and C. Rosberg, *Political Parties and National Integration in Tropical Africa* (Berkeley: University of California Press, 1966); Ali Mazrui, "Nkrumah: The Leninist Czar," *Transition*, VI, 1 (1966); Bob Fitch and Mary Oppenheimer, *Ghana: End of an Illusion* (New York: Monthly Review Press, 1966); T. Peter Omari, *Kwame Nkrumah: The Anatomy of an African Dictatorship* (Accra: Moxon Paperbacks, 1970); and Bretton, *op. cit.*

3 See the theoretical framework established in the previous chapter, "Myths and Realities in African Socialism."

4 Fitch and Oppenheimer, *op. cit.*, p. 73.

5 David Apter, "Political Religion in the New Nations," in Clifford Geertz (ed.), *Old Societies and New States* (London: Collier and Macmillan, 1963), pp. 57–105.

6 Dennis Austin, "Opposition in Ghana: 1947-1967," *Government and Opposition*, II (1967), p. 554. Also see, on this subject, Roger Genoud, *Nationalism and Economic Development in Ghana* (New York: Praeger, 1969), pp. 48–49.

7 Dennis Austin, *Politics in Ghana, 1946-1960* (London: Oxford University Press, 1964), p. 181.

8 Fitch and Oppenheimer, *op. cit.*, pp. 49–50.

9 See Austin's definitive work, *Politics in Ghana*, for complete details on the 1956 elections.

10 Apter, "Ghana," p. 285.

11 Quoted in Timothy Bankole, *op. cit.*, p. 104.

12 There are indications that Nkrumah was not the author of most of his published works, although he did sanction their publication in his name.

13 Bretton, *op. cit.*, p. 30.

14 Apter, "Political Religion in the New Nations," *passim.*

15 Kwame Nkrumah, *Consciencism: Philosophy and Ideology for Decolonization and Development* (New York: Monthly Review Press, 1964), p. 73. Also see, the Editors of *Spark*, *Some Essential Features of Nkrumaism* (Accra: Spark Publications, 1964), p. 108.

16 As quoted in Donald G. MacRae, "Nkrumahism: Past and Future of an Ideology," *Government and Opposition*, I, 4 (1966), p. 536.

17 The Editiors of *Spark*, *op. cit.*, p. 25.

18 *Ibid.*, 3–5.

19 For a further exposition, see Kwame Nkrumah, *Africa Must Unite* (London: Heinemann, 1963), *passim.*

20 Nkrumah, *Consciencism,* pp. 100–101.

21 Kwame Nkrumah, *Ghana: The Autobiography of Kwame Nkrumah* (Edinburgh: Thomas Nelson and Sons, Ltd., 1959), p. viii.

22 The following summary is based on the Editors of *Spark, op. cit.,* pp. 55–68.

23 Kwame Nkrumah, "The African Genius," speech delivered at the opening of the Institute of African Studies of the University of Ghana, Legon, October 25, 1963.

24 Nkrumah, *Consciencism,* p. 70.

25 The Editors of *Spark, op. cit.,* p. 70.

26 Nkrumah, *Consciencism,* p. 106.

27 Omari, *op. cit.,* p. 143 and elsewhere, delves deeply into the personal superstitions of Nkrumah and their effect on overall policy.

28 Fitch and Oppenheimer, *op. cit.,* p. 91 and *passim.*

29 Legum, *op. cit.,* p. 142.

30 Reginald H. Green, "Four African Development Plans: Ghana, Kenya, Nigeria and Tanzania," *Journal of Modern African Studies,* III, 2 (1965), p. 253.

31 Douglas Rimmer, "The Crisis in the Ghana Economy," *Journal of Modern African Studies,* IV, 1 (1966), p. 21.

32 *Ibid.,* p. 25.

33 Various commissions to examine individual and company assets, established during the National Liberation Council era, substantiate the great amount of graft and corruption in the state enterprises. Also see Bretton, *op. cit.,* p. 65, on this point.

34 See conflicting figures in Rimmer, *op. cit.,* p. 26, and J. Kirk Sale, "And Now Nkrumah: The Generals and the Future of Africa," in W.C. McWilliams, *Garrisons and Government* (San Francisco: Chandler Publishing Co., 1967), p. 289.

35 Omari, *op. cit.,* and Fitch and Oppenheimer, *op. cit.,* see this economic condition as the key to the decline of Nkrumaism.

36 Bretton, *op. cit.,* p. 79, and Fitch and Oppenheimer, *op. cit.,* p. 107.

37 Morris Janowitz, *The Military in the Political Development of New Nations* (Chicago: University of Chicago Press, 1964), p. 39; and "Nkrumah's Subversion of Africa: Documentary Evidence of Nkrumah's Interference in the Affairs of other African States," (Accra: Ministry of Information, 1966), *passim.*

38 David Apter, *Ghana in Transition* (New York: Atheneum, 1966), p. 304.

39 Omari, *op. cit.,* p. 2, mentions some of the main titles of Nkrumah: Osagyefo, kantamanto (one never guilty), oyeeadeeyie (one who puts things right), show boy, iron boy, the Messiah, deliverer of Ghana, man of destiny, star of Africa.

40 Some of the most interesting documents on this subject can be found in "Nkrumah's Subversion of Africa," *op. cit.*

41 See Mazrui's conclusions, *op. cit.*

42 Roberta E. Koplin, "Education and National Integration in Ghana and

Kenya," Ph.D. Dissertation, Department of Political Science, University of Oregon, December, 1968, p. 296.

43 Sam K. Akesson, "The Roots of our Democracy," *Africa Today,* IX, 10 (December 1962), p. 13.

44 Omari, *op. cit.,* p. 60.

45 Interviews with students at the University of Ghana conducted in the fall of 1970.

46 Austin, *Politics in Ghana, passim,* and Genoud, *op. cit.* pp. 28, 45.

47 Legum, *op. cit.,* p. 133. Also see N.A. Ollennu's "Introduction" in Omari, *op. cit.*

48 Omari, *op. cit.,* pp. 3—4

ARAB SOCIALISM AND EGYPTIAN-ISLAMIC TRADITION

SHIMON SHAMIR

I

Arab Socialism, as it has evolved in Egypt in the early sixties, has shown an ambivalent attitude toward change. On the one hand, the system was produced by a regime which styled itself "revolutionary." Revolutions are supposed to break away from the past and herald the coming of a new dawn and, indeed, this posture is not missing in Arab Socialism. President Nasser's *National Charter* — the basic manifesto of Arab Socialism — asserted in its first chapter "the determination to set up a new society with new social relations and new moral values." The "total revolution," it said, could be realized only through the "unlimited will of revolutionary change."[1]

On the other hand, there is the attachment to tradition. Arab Socialism, it should be noted, does not speak of "revolution" but of *thawra,* and the two are not entirely synonymous. *Thawra,* unlike "revolution," does not necessarily focus on setting in motion the wheels of change — suppressing the past in order to give birth to a new future and effecting a radical departure from the existing order. The root of *thawra* originally conveyed a furious outburst. Today, in the political sense, *thawra* has also the connotation of unleashing the hidden forces of society to overthrow that which is "revolting." *Thawra,* more easily than "revolution," can imply the substitution of the alien and the novel by the indigenous and the traditional.

Indeed, "liberation" (taḥrīr), the central theme of the July 23rd Revolution from its earliest days, did not refer solely to political and economic emancipation. It also meant the release of genuine social interaction and cultural creativity from the bondage of alien influences and the re-establishment of the indigenous patterns. The system produced by the Revolution was depicted as a unique manifestation of the Egyptian-Islamic-Arab heritage. The National Charter, in the

193

chapter entitled "The Roots of Egyptian Struggle," refers to "Pharaonic civilization," "Islamic spiritual thought and awareness," and "Arab cultural heritage."[2] Muḥammad Ḥasanayn Haykal, the articulate spokesman of the Nasser regime, wrote: "Arab Socialism is a faithful disciple of the history of our nation and the national heritage."[3] A decade later, under President Anwar al-Sādāt, the *Guide for Political Action* asserted: "The Arab Socialism which we uphold and our people accepts is that whose roots emanate from the tenets of this people and the endeavors, experiences, and practices that have enriched them through the ages."[4] The Nasser regime has always stressed its pragmatic approach and readiness to learn from the experience of other societies, but at the same time, the claim to an authenticity based on tradition has remained one of the most persistent features of its Arab Socialism.

This dichotomy between tradition and change – which, in different forms, appears in many other revolutions – was also reflected in the debate as to whether Arab Socialism was a self-contained "Arab" system or merely an "Arab" application of universal socialism. Curiously enough, Nasser himself, in various statements, opted for the latter. However, many exponents of Arab Socialism have pointed out that this did not alter the fact that socialism was a pluralistic movement and Arab Socialism, in essence, a separate entity differing from other socialist systems by its emanation from the unique Egyptian heritage and experience.[5]

Despite such occasional theoretical discrepancies, it is not too difficult to discern the principal modes that Arab Socialism chooses to relate itself to tradition. More difficult to assess is its real relationship to tradition, the actual manifestations of conceptual, social, economic, and political traditions as living forces in Arab Socialism. The two types of relationship are far from being identical. Three generations of Egyptian intellectuals, for purposes of apologetics or self-assertion, have manipulated their history and heritage to the extent that by now even a non-tendentious search for roots could easily lose its way. Nasser's own references to what he regards as Egyptian history, such as his reference to the "Mamluk Jungle" in the *Philosophy of the Revolution* or to "Ottoman Imperialism" in the *National Charter,* illustrate this point.

The purpose of this article is to examine and compare the two types of relationship between Arab Socialism and Egyptian tradition. For this purpose, three aspects of Arab Socialism – however arbitrarily articulated — will be scrutinized: its economic organization, the socio-political system, and its *weltanschauung*.

II

The economic organization of Egypt — the most concrete aspect of Arab Socialism — has evolved from a series of measures originally adopted within an entirely different context and under the banner of an official ideology that categorically rejected all socialist systems as alien to Egypt's experience and unsuited to her needs.

The first step was taken in 1956, as part of Nasser's anti-Western campaign, with the seizure and sequestration of British, French, and much of Jewish-owned property. The government thus found itself in charge of large assets and, in January 1957, founded an Economic Establishment *(mu 'assasa)* to administer them. Its decision to accelerate economic development by direct government action, the need to mobilize resources, and its concomitant Egyptianization-Islamization policy, resulted in the rapid expansion of the government sector by means of nationalization and state-owned corporations. By 1958, the regime's spokesmen were providing rationalizations for these measures by propagating a qualified version of socialism included in a program called the "Democratic Cooperative-Socialist Society." This program was also intended to bring the regime's internal organization into harmony with its neutralist and Third World foreign policies. In the years of the union with Syria, two additional factors were particularly crucial: the wish to hold in check the increasingly hostile bourgeoisie and the growing tendency to tighten government control over all sections of society and all aspects of life. After a series of nationalization measures in 1960, the breakthrough was made with the July 1961 legislation which took over practically all the large industrial, financial, and commercial concerns in the U.A.R. and which extended the land reform of 1952, thereby liquidating the power of the bourgeoisie and further weakening the position of landowners. The collapse of the union with Syria, in September, only intensified the government's campaign against the "enemy within," namely, the "reactionary" capitalists, monopolists, and feudalists who were to blame for the failure of the union. The regime adopted a dynamic revolutionary style and proclaimed Arab Socialism; its first authoritative credo, the *National Charter* of May 1962, outlined the economic system in terms of "the termination of all exploitation of labor" and "the people's control over all the means of production."[6] Though private ownership was not abolished and the Private Sector was assigned a share in the national development, the expansion of the Public Sector continued, and along with it, the size of the bureaucracy. By the mid-sixties, the Public Sector consisted of some fifty establishments (*mu'assasāt*) comprising nearly four hundred companies (*sharikāt*), which covered a broad range of activities from heavy industry, commerce, banking, and insurance, cooperative farming, transportation, and the Suez Canal to tourism, publishing, theater, and music. Between 1962 and 1965 alone, the size of the bureaucracy more than doubled.[7]

A salient point in this process was the predominance of immediate political considerations which shaped the economic system. Characteristic also was the highly pragmatic approach applied to cope with pressing socio-economic problems; leaders of the regime pointed to this as one of the advantages of their system. They also admitted to their external sources of inspiration and, indeed, the economic system's similarity to universal models is striking — whether it be taken to signify a "conversion to Scientific Socialism" as claimed by the *Charter,* or a "non-capitalist road of development" as described by sympathetic Marxists, or merely a "state capitalism" as defined by non-sympathetic ones.[8]

Yet the economic system, somehow, was not accepted in Egypt as an entirely improvised and eclectic innovation. It is noteworthy that, considering its radical nature and that it constituted the most sweeping change introduced by the Nasser regime, the reactions the system generated appear to be remarkably mild for a society which is still predominantly traditional. The explanation partly lies in the fact that it was applied with relative moderation; that its edge was directed against foreigners, minorities, and an unpopular elite; that it was made an indivisible part of the nationalist campaign; and, finally, that it aroused expectations of material progress. But beyond these explanations there is the fact that this reorganization of the economy could be regarded by the Egyptians as a coherent state policy, without their having to accept, of necessity, the radical premises on which the government itself based its actions and without necessarily viewing it as a manifestation of the "unlimited will of revolutionary change."

The state control of the economy introduced by Arab Socialism contrasted sharply with the *laissez faire* of the *ancien régime* but not with the totality of Egyptian historical experience. Following the Arab conquest in the seventh century, the government took possession of a considerable part of the occupied lands — the main source of wealth. It regulated landholdings and controlled revenues through a variety of methods, such as the granting, leasing, or farming out of lands. Many other sources of income, apart from land, were state-controlled and subject to the same systems of regulation. These systems were reorganized, reallocating lands and other sources of income, several times in Islamic history.

In Egypt, state ownership of land was more consistent than else-where in the Middle East. The local feudal method of granting fiefs in return for military service was short-lived and with the Ottoman conquest most of the land became virtually the Sultan's property *(mīrī).*[9] In time, the state lost much of its control to the tax-farmers but the process was again reversed in the early nineteenth century by Muḥammad 'Ali, who initiated Egypt's process of modernization. Muḥammad 'Ali's energetic action in assuming control of all agri-cultural lands and in administering them as, in fact, one large estate, has no parallel in the early history of modernization in other Middle Eastern countries. As has been demonstrated exhaustively, the Egyptian tradition of central control is accounted for by the fact that geography has made Egypt the most perfect case of a "hydraulic society," dependent for its subsistence on the effective operation of a strong central government to regulate the irrigation system and the use of land.[10]

Thus, the Arab Socialist policy of appropriation and state control was neither drastically innovative nor abusive simply because there was nothing in local tradition which contradicted it. On the contrary, tradition allowed great latitude to the state to dispose of the national resources as it saw fit. However, there was also very little in Egyptian tradition to inspire the specific forms that state control assumed under Arab Socialism. Indeed, the leaders of the regime rarely referred to any native roots for these specific forms. Neither the *Charter* nor other authoritative documents relate the economic system, as such, to traditional sources. This task has been undertaken by the Nasserist intellectuals.

In the abundance of Nasserist programmatic literature disseminated in Egypt, particularly in its more conservative trends, there are frequent attempts to point to the compatibility of this system with the regulations and institutions of the early Islamic commun-ity. It is pointed out that both the Prophet Muḥammad and the Caliph 'Umar had appropriated land for the needs of the poor, in accordance with the principle of *ḥimā'*; that a prophetic tradition had established that "people own three things in common: water, grass, and fire," in order to maintain the communalization of basic resources and prevent their monopolization and exploitation; that the Quranic *zakāt* tax was intended to subordinate property ownership to the collective interests of the community, etc.[11]

It is not difficult to show that these arguments had all been taken from the school of thought called Islamic Socialism, which preceded Arab Socialism. The limited validity and practical function of these ideas will be discussed below in the section devoted to the conceptual basis of Arab Socialism. It should, however, be noted that the search for indigenous elements in the Arab Socialist system is not confined to Islamic-oriented Arab Socialist circles, but has been joined by sympathetic Western observers as well. Describing the *mu'assasa* (the Economic Establishment founded in 1957), Jacques Berque wrote that Egypt "has found in state initiative its own original type of enterprise." He pointed out that:

The state control practised in the Arab world is primarily directed toward resistance and recovery.... It has the advantage of being attuned to popular feelings, which call forth the deep-rooted and hitherto unexpressed will of these countries. Hence this singularity of many of its undertakings, the enthusiasm which these arouse and the individual character which, despite analogies which have been over-stressed, differentiate them from the actions of other nations under other systems.[12]

As perceptive as these observations are, they offer little to explain exactly wherein lies the originality of this economic system, what precisely are the autochthonous roots nourishing its specific institutional structure and operational methods, and how the "will of these countries" is embodied in any tangible forms.

III

The socio-political system of Arab Socialism in Egypt can be briefly described as follows. The social order rests on "the alliance (*taḥāluf*) of the five forces of the working people: the peasants, workers, intelligentsia, soldiers, and national capitalists." Social elements that are designated as "anti-national" or "exploitative" are outside the system. Within the system, all class distinctions are expected to dissolve and all clashes of interest to be peacefully settled. Particular attention is devoted to the advancement of two of these "forces" — the peasants and workers — through social legislation and by the guarantee that 50 per cent of the seats in the representative bodies will be reserved for them. The political embodiment of this alliance is the Arab Socialist Union (ASU), the only legitimate political organization functioning in Egypt. It is a popular organization open to all but has a highly selective inner *apparat* of cadres which operate within its ranks.[13] The ASU has a pyramidal structure, with the "basic units" (branches in villages, town quarters, and places of employment) at the lowest level and the national bodies (National Congress, Central Committee, Supreme Executive Committee) at the top. Delegates are elected at each level for the bodies of the level above. This system is regarded as a true democracy for, unlike the parliamentary system of the *ancien régime,* it combines political representation with social justice.[14]

Vague definition of the constituents of this system and its erratic implementation allowed great latitude for interpretation. Thus, the Egyptian Marxists — who, after the self-dissolution of all Communist organizations in 1965, were admitted into the ASU and other institutions of the regime — tended to depict the system as having a broad common denominator with Marxist-Leninist socialism to which, they claimed, it was gradually converting itself.[15] The leaders of the regime, however, did not allow this interpretation to be carried too far. The differences between Arab Socialism and the Communist socio-political system have been defined in many authoritative statements — one of the more recent and noteworthy being the ASU's *Guide for Political Action*, which was formulated by a special committee in the summer of 1972, after several months of intensive deliberations.[16]

That which is disavowed by Arab Socialism has been clearly laid down. The five "forces" which are organized as the component parts of the social order are not to be identified with social classes. The program of the dissolution of class differences is not an indirect endorsement of the class struggle but its categorical denial. The rights of workers and peasants have been specifically institutionalized not because the regime aims at a dictatorship of the proletariat but because it wants to facilitate their advancement to positions commensurate to their share in society. None of the five "forces" is favored over the other. The ASU does not represent any single "force" but the union of all "forces." The internal *apparat* of the ASU is not an *avant-garde* detailed to transform the regime into a Marxist-Leninist one. "Conversion to Socialism" does not mean the promotion of any imported scheme, but the development of Arab Socialism as an indigenous system emanating from the unique experience and heritage of Egyptian society.

This confrontation with Marxism, although contributing little to the crystallization of the Arab Socialist socio-political system in positive terms, accentuates at least its particularity. However, the claim that particularity in this case is also authenticity, embedded in tradition, is not substantiated by the spokesmen of the regime and indeed it is contested by many observers.

To be sure, a good many of the facets of this system can be described as measures devised by the leadership for reasons of political expediency — in a way similar to the development of some of the regime's economic institutions. Their nature acquires its logic either from patterns followed by many developing nations or "objective" local circumstances, and not necessarily from an autochthonous tradition. For example, the choice of "forces" into which the Arab Socialist society is divided can be explained in the following terms: Peasants and workers would be given prominence today by any "revolutionary" regime in any part of the world; the army is there because it happens to be the leadership's power base; the intellectuals, as in all similar regimes, have a particularly important role in legitimizing power and managing the technocracy; finally, the "national capitalist class" is no more than an improvised category into which the government conveniently lumps together all those property-owners and entrepreneurs (certain categories of contractors, merchants, and land-owners) who, at any given moment, are regarded as more useful outside the Public Sector. To the extent that the institutions produced by the Arab Socialist system have a coherent identity, their origin can usually be traced to external sources, such as the Corporate State of Fascist Italy, the Socialist Alliance of Yugoslavia, or various one-party systems of the Third World.

Still, all such explanations fail to account for some intrinsic qualities and consistent features of the socio-political system of Egypt. They are of little assistance in comprehending the patterns of Arab Socialism's diffusion throughout the society, or the extent of its acceptance or rejection. These gaps delineate the area in which the quest for possible links to previous tradition appears relevant.

A striking feature of the Arab Socialist system is that society is not articulated in terms of stratification. It may never have occurred to the Marxists, but when the regime's spokesmen insisted that the "forces" which constitute society are not social classes they may have meant just that. For the Marxists, the regime's attitude could not be

explained other than as an indulgence in verbalism in order to escape
the exigencies of harsh social realities. Surely, they argued, three of
these "forces" — the peasants, workers, and national capitalists —
constitute classes: the two former, of the proletariat, and the latter,
of the bourgeoisie. Yet it may very well be that the Arab Socialists'
position was coherent within their own terms. In this confrontation
the arguments of the Marxists represented the general Western model
of society — namely, a structure horizontally stratified into classes that
are primarily recognized, if not actually determined, by the degree of
their wealth — while the position of the Arab Socialists rested, consciously or unconsciously, on a model drawn from their own, non-
Western, tradition. This proposition is supported by the fact that if
the class concept is applied to Arab Socialism's "alliance of forces,"
the Egyptian middle class — undoubtedly the backbone of Nasserist
society — would be conspicuously absent. It thus seems plausible that
the scheme of "five forces" is of a basically different nature.

As a reflection of historical experience, society in classical Islam
was described as being composed of sectors, or resting on "pillars"
(arkān). These were defined by function rather than by wealth, and
the division was heavily stamped with raison d'état. The sectors were
defined, to a large extent, by the nature and extent of their usefulness
to the state or the government — the two being indivisible and
expressed by one concept: dawla. This model, which apparently had
been influenced by Persian tradition, usually consisted of four or five
sectors, most commonly comprising the soldiers, administrators, men
of religion, merchants, and the laboring masses.

One of the more recent formulations of this concept appears in a
treatise by the celebrated seventeenth-century Ottoman historian and
biographer, Ḥajji Khalīfa. His work typically reflects both the pragmatic outlook of a man of affairs seeking to advise his Sultan on the
good management of the state and the beliefs of an orthodox Muslim,
well versed in authoritative Islamic sources. Ḥajji Khalīfa is perhaps
the last link in a chain of thinkers on questions of society and politics
extending from the philosophers of the classical era through Ibn
Khaldūn (who influenced Ḥajji Khalīfa's writings) up to the scholars
of the Ottoman Empire before its decline. Ḥajji Khalīfa contends that
government was entrusted to the sultans by God, in accordance with
the holy law. To have effective authority they had to have an army.
To maintain the army, they needed revenue, and there can be no
revenue without taxable subjects. Human association, therefore, con-
sists of four "pillars": the 'ulamā' (scholars, interpreters of the holy

law), the 'askar (army), the tujjār (traders), and the ra'āya (the masses). The four groups are "political beings by nature" and the well-being of the state depends on their harmonious interaction.[17]

Thus, though the direct inspiration of the "five forces" system of Arab Socialism may be external, it is the system's compatibility with the traditional scheme that lends it credibility and force. It may be claimed that the Arab Socialist system, like the traditional, is basically a classification into functional groups and not a stratification into classes. It does not cover the whole spectrum of society because it is not concerned with the levels of a social pyramid, but with the "pillars" of a political order. The stress is on those groups which must be organized and controlled because, occupationally, they are best qualified to perform the most vital functions: production, management, coercion, and legitimization. In this scheme the middle class, as such, need not necessarily be included. When it comes to regimentation for the vital purposes of the regime, the small shopkeeper or low-ranking clerk does not have a high priority, despite the fact that their class represents the main bulk of the politically-minded Egyptian public and, as such, may be quite significant for the regime.

The four or five sectors composing traditional society were, of course, too large to serve as the framework for actual social organization. That which characterized the pattern of social organization in traditional society — as it also had existed in Egypt up to the period of modernization (and partly beyond) — was its fragmentation. Traditional society was organized into a vast number of small social groups, defined by such criteria as occupation (guilds), residence (quarters, villages), descent (clans, tribes, ethnic groups), and religion (millets). Of particular importance to our case was the guild system which in Ottoman Egypt, to quote Gabriel Baer, "comprised the whole gainfully-occupied town population."[18] Organization was quite loose and there was much overlapping between groups defined by different criteria, but each group may be said to have constituted a self-contained unit which regulated the lives of its members. Although no uniformity existed in the relations of these groups to each other and although great differences did exist in their social positions, the pattern basically was not that of horizontal, layer-above-layer stratification. There were hierarchical differentiations within each unit, with a chief (usually called shaykh) at its head serving as the link to the government. In the case of Egypt, the chiefs served usually as a channel for government control rather than for the expression of corporate autonomy. Government in this social structure had a decisive role. Since this structure, which is sometimes described as "convergent," was not integrative, it could only exist as a composite whole by virtue of the government holding each component in its proper place. The essential principle of good administration was to see that each group "performed its due functions and did not encroach on the functions of the others."[19]

A simplistic analogy to Arab Socialist Egypt would certainly miss the mark but some associations, nonetheless, are inescapable. It thus appears that the way the Egyptian leadership sees its own role, its relationship with the various components of society, and the latter's mutual relations, is quite compatible with the traditional model.

As seen above, the regime views the various social "forces" concurrently arrayed. Their most meaningful relationship is with the center. As the statute of the ASU puts it: each of the five "forces" operates "with the understanding that they bind themselves to national action [i.e. as prescribed by the government] in close solidarity at all levels."[20]

Here, too, government control is the crucial factor. In addition to the ASU, the government maintains a network of various organizations, each of which is functionally intended; it may be related to one of the social "forces" but has hardly any social role. These include trade unions, cooperative societies, youth and student organizations, professional associations, and chambers of commerce — all tightly controlled by the government. The whole complex of these bodies is somehow expected to be coordinated (although not controlled) by the ASU to form an organism completely in tune with the government's aims and policies.[21]

The regime's cheerful confidence in "the disappearance of all class distinctions" and "the peaceful resolution of class differences" evidently emanates from a conception of society as a corporative system in which the vertical divisions separating the various functional sectors overshadow the horizontal ones which separate the rich from the poor. The government's tendency to arrange — to some degree — the representation of peasants by landowners and state cooperative farming functionaries and the representation of workers by engineers, factory managers, and state trade union functionaries could, apparently, be explained as a matter of political expediency. But the debate that has evolved over this issue has revealed a genuine confusion as to the nature and definition of these groups. The government for its part was inclined to take the corporative view and obscure the differences between management and labor (although on this issue it had to yield some ground under pressure from its leftist wing).[22]

The brief references made above to the structure of traditional society point implicitly to what was, perhaps, the most celebrated trait of Islamic polity in general and Egypt in particular: the deep cleavage that separated the ruler from the ruled, the ḥākim from the maḥkūm. Traditionally, state politics and government were the prerogative of those who, by virtue of their occupational functions, possessed power: the military commanders and the chief administrators, who were also linked to the military establishment. These power-holders in turn clustered around the dynastic or self-appointed sovereign. In a study of the city under the Egyptian Mamluk rulers, the author has pointed out that "The crucial factor in the politics of the Mamluk cities was not the structure of the regime or the bureaucracy as such, but the position in which the powers and facilities which accrued to its individual members placed them in the society at large."[23] Power could lead to the accumulation of wealth but rarely vice versa. Islamic history supplies an abundance of illustrations of the fact that wealth alone could not basically alter the socio-political position of individuals or groups. The mawālī, the non-Arab converts to Islam in its earlier period, were sometimes richer than their Arab rulers but nevertheless were held in contempt. Many a Jewish or Christian dhimmī, members of the protected religious communities, managed to enrich themselves through trade or otherwise, but as a rule they were barred from the governing class and socially were ranked below the humblest Muslim.[24] The monopolization of power was not only imposed by the "men of the sword," but also legitimized by Islamic orthodoxy which demanded complete obedience from all subjects, provided their rulers effectively upheld the institutions of Islam. By this and other means, the 'ulamā' served as a bridge between the two separate layers of society.

It is this distinguishing feature which remains the most constant element in Egyptian political culture. The Arab Socialist regime employs the term "revolution" (thawra) both in common parlance and official usage to express, without distinction, both the new socio-political system and the government that imposes it — just as the traditional term dawla expresses both government and polity.[25] With all its populist features, the Arab socialist system still represents the continuity of the ḥākim-maḥkūm syndrome. Power is in the hands of key technocrats clustered around the ra'īs and is not shared, in any meaningful way, by the regime's popular and representative institutions. Continuity is manifested also in such aspects of the system as the manner in which the leadership employs the bureaucracy and the security machinery; its expectations from the intellectuals; the nature of rivalries among competing factions of the elites; the way socio-economic benefits are bestowed but never legitimately demanded; the broad consent given to the government by the popular classes and the lack of widespread interest in political participation.

To the extent that the introduction of this system signified a departure from that of the *ancien régime,* the import of that departure was, paradoxically, an act of restoration rather than innovation. The July 1952 Revolution succeeded in overthrowing an elite based on landed wealth, which had emerged in the nineteenth century, largely as the result of the anomalies of an unchecked process of Westernization. This elite was intermingled with non-Muslim and foreign elements; it had been ineffective in its disposition of power and had failed to legitimize itself in terms of coherent group solidarity which could command the allegiance of the masses. In contrast, the Revolutionary regime was solidly based on the armed forces, produced effective and stable government, and received its legitimation through the propagation of *qawmiyya* — the Islamic-based Pan-Arab nationalist vision. Thus, Nasser's revolutionary regime was, in fact, more analogous to the traditional system of power and authority than the regime it overthrew.

The commitment to *qawmiyya,* voluntary or imposed, is essential for the cohesion of the Arab Socialist system. Whether in Egypt or elsewhere in the Arab world, this is the feature of Arab Socialism that distinguishes it, more than anything else, from the prototype European socialist movements. According to the ASU's *Guide for Political Action:*

The principle of Alliance (*taḥāluf*) embodies the holy national unity and expresses the consensus of the people, with all its working forces, supporting the movement which endeavors to realize the national hopes and interests.... The principle of Alliance expresses the existence of national interests which are the essence and the foundation and which are not contested — cannot conceivably be contested — among the five working forces of the people. It also expresses the precedence of these interests and the need to uphold them and put them above any private interest or possible self-interest of a social force within the Alliance.[26]

National goals supersede social needs and expectations. A principal function of Arab Socialist institutions is to effect "mass mobilization for national action." The collective is regarded as being in a state of constant emergency, and all resources must be mobilized to encounter the titanic challenges and do battle with the formidable enemies of the nation.*

The stress on *qawmiyya* is intended to accomplish more than the investiture of legitimacy upon the leaders of the "national struggle." It also seeks to give coherence and cohesiveness to the community, to regulate relations between the collective and individuals or groups, to establish a scale of values and set of symbols, to restore identity and status, to endow politics and diplomacy with a sense of purpose, and to create affiliation to a universalistic vision. These are precisely the functions fulfilled by traditional Islam, with its political doctrine, all-embracing belief system, communal gradations, legal and social institutions, spirit of solidarity and total commitment, *jihād*, and universal message.

Just as compatibility with tradition may be proposed as a partial explanation for the successful incorporation of some of the elements of Arab Socialism into the socio-political system, incompatibility may account for the rejection of others. Arab Socialism's most conspicuous failure in Egypt has been its total inability to create a political organization with any substantial existence of its own, rooted into the very structure of society. The ASU – like its two predecessors, the Liberation Rally and the National Union – has not managed to achieve effectively the goals set for it by the regime. Membership is recruited mainly through bureaucratic channels and is characterized by low commitment to the organization's goals and estrangement from its operational methods. The heads of the ASU admitted themselves that, as a result of cumulative failures, the popular attitude toward the ASU is one of ridicule.[27]

It seems plausible that this resulted not only from the ASU's many inherent contradictions – such as that between coercion and participation – but also from its inability to present itself in a way meaningful to the Egyptian public. Although the ASU's objective was to reach the masses and become a genuinely popular organization, the method chosen was the application of an alien model, out of tune with the indigenous political culture and its social tradition. The influence of the Western one-party system is denied by the spokesmen of the

---

* From the outset, mobilization had been an important element in all Arab Socialist programs, and since the Six-Day War it often occupied the central place. See, for example, Nasser's "March 30 Program" of 1968.

regime, but this does not obliterate the fact that it was this very model which has so unsuitably been transplanted to Egypt.

Egypt, like many other Muslim countries, had a long tradition of popular organizations. Thus, as Sir Harold Gibb has pointed out:

It was out of the *ṣūfī* movement that there developed those institutions which gave an organic structure to Muslim society from the twelfth to the nineteenth century. *Ṣūfism* became a mass movement and its leaders founded new forms of organization to meet its new role and responsibilities. This was the creation of brotherhoods or fraternities... [that] ultimately...embraced the whole range of social classes.

The fraternities followed lines of both social and economic functions and gave the individual an appropriate stage on which he could exercise his responsibilities as a full and free Muslim citizen.[28]

The tendency apparent in different Egyptian classes to form a variety of voluntary associations — benevolent, religious, social, or other — is indicative of the search for substitutes to fill the gap created by the decline of the traditional fraternities. The government — whose own organization, the ASU, lacks any real social content — maintains a jealous watch over these associations: in 1966, for example, it abolished hundreds of them which did not conform to the Law of Associations of 1964.

Quantitatively, the extent of social mobilization achieved through the political organizations and other channels — such as the educational system, military conscription, and the communications media — is impressive. As an institution-builder, however, Arab Socialism has staged a poor performance. By and large, its socio-political institutions remain an improvised superimposition, offer no solution to uprootedness and dislocation, and fail to satisfy the genuine need to reestablish a meaningful relationship between the individual and the community.

The Nasserists themselves see it differently. Their claim for the indigenous nature of the Arab Socialist socio-political system and, as such, its effective expression of the community, is molded by their own historical perspective. The crux of their thesis is that the Arab-Islamic community of the Prophet Muḥammad and the early Caliphs — the ideal model of human association — was socialistic and it is on this foundation that contemporary Arab Socialism is built. A characteristic exposition of this argument appears in a series of books published in Cairo during the sixties, with such titles as "The Socialism of Muḥammad," "The Socialism of ‘Umar," and "The Socialism of ‘Uthmān."[29] Maḥmūd Shalabī, the author of these volumes, has painstakingly catalogued the words and deeds which, he felt, establish beyond doubt the socialist outlook of these model Arab leaders. This line of thought, which has many precedents in Arab literature of earlier decades, has apparently won great popularity among the Egyptian public.

A closer examination reveals that the exponents of this view, usually the intellectuals of the regime, do not really attempt to link specific socio-political patterns of contemporary Arab Socialism to their historical heritage. Rather, they try to relate basic premises and broad values to tradition – mostly the concepts of social justice and liberty. The argument, therefore, belongs better to the overall *weltanschauung* of Arab Socialism discussed in the next section.

IV

The conceptual basis of Arab Socialism has never been systematically expounded. Both the leaders of the regime and its intellectuals have repeatedly deliberated on the difficulties involved in such an undertaking, and preferred, instead, to mold their tenets piecemeal, as circumstances warranted. Once again, the challenge of Marxism has served as a catalyst obliging the Nasserists to define the differences between Marxism and Arab Socialism and to articulate their own outlook, positing their ideas against this challenge.

As thus formulated, the tenets of Arab Socialism can be summarized as follows: Arab Socialism adheres to the principles that labor is an honor, both a right and a duty; that the exploitation of man by man must cease; that neither excessive riches nor degrading poverty are tolerable in a just society; that every individual should have an equal opportunity to acquire a fair share of the national wealth; that every individual is entitled to security, self-realization, and dignity.

Arab Socialism propagates a humanistic, quite optimistic outlook on man and society. "Faith in the proper intrinsic value of man," says one of the regime's organs, is "in no way incompatible with the integral application of the socialist principles and objectives."[30] Even in a highly-organized socialist system, the individual has a role to play and is entitled, by right, to liberty and justice. There is no inevitability of the class struggle nor a necessity for harsh measures of coercion, because national solidarity, which supersedes other interests, is capable of bringing about the peaceful resolution of social conflicts and the fusion of all classes.

Arab Socialism rejects historical or social determinism. Although it recognizes the influence of material factors, its concepts are neither materialistic not dialectical. It believes that history and the development of society are shaped by human ideals. Arab Socialism, it is asserted, has faith "in spiritual values and in God,"[31] and maintains that "the eternal spiritual values emanating from the religions are capable of guiding mankind."[32]

Two different strata may be discerned in this conceptual structure. The more recent one comprises socialist ideas and symbols incorporated into the Nasserist program in the late fifties and early sixties. They derive from the broad common denominator of most socialist movements and vaguely reflect certain aspects of Marxist thinking. These are the concepts which, in the main, are asserted by the political leadership and stressed in such official programs as the *National Charter* and the ASU manifestos.

The concepts of the earlier stratum are usually expounded by the intellectuals and appear in the prolific, and somewhat less rigidly regimented, ideological literature disseminated under that regime. This earlier stratum comprises elements from the Liberal-Nationalist ethos that prevailed in Egypt under the monarchy. The contradictions between the two strata and between this idealistic liberalism and the regime's étatistic theory and practice is self-evident but not altogether surprising. It should be remembered that the formative years of the Nasserist spokesmen — mostly but not exclusively intellectuals — were the years when Liberal-Nationalism was equated with progress, modernity, and the vision of national regeneration. The conversion to radical Arab Socialism, which took over these aims, was only gradually effected, thus resulting in an erratic mixture of the two credos.

This dichotomy is salient throughout a large part of Arab Socialist writings. An example in point is an essay by Lewis 'Awaḍ on "Socialism and Literature." Oscillating between materialism and idealism, nationalism and internationalism, individuality and collectivism, civil liberty and state control, 'Awaḍ concludes: "Our Socialism, then, does and must embrace all these meanings. From amid these contradictions, harmony must be established...This is what makes our Socialism a humanist creed that serves the individual and the society, spiritual and material life — past, present and future."[33]

Apart from broad references to history and religion, none of the

components of the conceptual system outlined above establishes a link
to a specific indigenous tradition. The concepts of the first stratum
are admittedly inspired by East European and Afro-Asian ideologies,
while the source of the second is Western by definition. Yet the claim
persists that "Arab Socialism is in keeping with the nation's ancient
spiritual and ethical values,"[34] and various ideologues have ventured
to substantiate it. The most systematic formulations have been proposed by those Nasserists who adhere to the Islamic Socialism school
of thought, which thus may be regarded as forming an optional third
stratum in the conceptual system of Arab Socialism.

Following the path mapped out by the chief exponent of Islamic
Socialism, the Syrian Muṣṭafā al-Sibāʿī, and since trodden by many
Egyptians ranging from devout Azharites to semi-secular intellectuals,
the advocates of this school claim that the social order of Islam and
their socialist system are fundamentally the same. Islam, they say, has
formulated a concept of social solidarity and mutual responsibility —
expressed by the term *takāful* — that is the quintessence of socialism.
Islamic society is conceived as a brotherhood in which the members of
the community and the community at large are responsible for
supporting the deprived. This mutual responsibility applies not only to
material needs but to all aspects of life: moral, social, legal, political,
cultural and so on. *Takāful* is depicted as the conceptual basis of a set
of Arab-Islamic values which, by regulating the life of the community,
do away with all internal conflicts and create a harmonious
organism.[35]

The manner in which some Arab intellectuals elaborate on this
concept of *takāful*, educing from it broad philosophical implications
as well as practical relevance, is quite impressive. Sound, too, are their
efforts to stress *takāful*, whose solid roots in Islamic tradition are
indisputable, at the expense of *ishtirākiyya*, the ill-contrived Arabic
rendering of "socialism" which, for many traditional Egyptians, had
the connotation of heathenism and heresy, and an excessive, not to
say indecent, sharing of private property and life. Some elements of
takāful are also reasonably congruent with certain tenets of Arab
Socialism: for example, the propositions that class conflicts are not
inevitable and can be eliminated by communal solidarity; that private
ownership is legitimate provided it is held in conformity with social
responsibility; and that the desired social order is governed by laws
drawing their sustenance from spiritual values.

The congruence between the two theoretical systems may also be
found in their approach to the question of equality. Although the

equality of man, in the metaphysical sense, has been one of the basic
tenets of Islam, the reality of social inequality has never been put in
question. The values of *takāful* were intended to moderate class differences but not abolish them altogether. Muslim moralists frowned upon
excessive riches and greed for earthly possessions, but at the same time
viewed their existence as part of the natural order. The profound
acceptance of social inequality as inherent in the human condition is
deeply-rooted in Egypt's traditional society and finds expression in its
folklore and folk wisdom. The author recalls that, in interviews with a
considerable number of Egyptians from the popular classes, many of
them responded to questions on socialism by stretching out the palms
of their hands, explaining that just as God created the fingers in different sizes and shapes, so was man created rich and poor.

Concordant with this view, Arab Socialism does not postulate egalitarianism; it propounds such principles as "equal opportunity" and
"sufficiency," but not equality *per se*. Indeed, in view of Egyptian
realities, this would be preposterous. An estimation of the distribution
of income in Egypt in 1958 — the period of the emergence of the first
Nasserist socialist concepts — put the ratio between the per capita
income of the lowest-paid group and that of the "bourgeoisie" at 1:40
in the urban society and at 1:220 in rural society.[36] The socialist laws
of the early sixties fixed a ratio of approximately 1:65 between the
minimum lawful wages for laborers and the maximum wages for
directors, and many observers have noted that both the minimum and
the maximum limits have remained theoretical.[37] Thus, equality is
neither inherent to the social outlook of the political leadership and
the technocratic elite nor propagated by their doctrine.

Nevertheless, congruence between *takāful* and Arab Socialism
remains confined within narrow limits. Traditional *takāful*, after all,
stems from such values as righteousness, piety, and charity[38] — very
different from the premises of modern socialism. It seems quite
obvious that a modern application of *takāful* would lead no further
than the Welfare State. This may well suit those Nasserist intellectuals,
discussed above, who have never detached themselves completely from
their Liberal-Nationalist background. However, for the inaugurators of
Arab Socialism this would be far from adequate.

In order to legitimize those concepts of Arab Socialism which cannot reasonably be co-extensive with *takāful*, the spokesmen of Nasserism often resort to the same methods employed in the previous two or
three generations to legitimize modernism, reform, liberalism, consti-
tutionalism, and nationalism. Fragments of their heritage are taken

from traditional contexts and arbitrarily rearranged so as to fit the latest ideology, without any heed paid to inherent contradictions. Thus, the source for the theory of the nationalization of the means of production is traced to Islamic law (*ḥimā, waqf*), just as the origin of parliamentary representation was formerly traced to the Quran (*shūra*). Such disputation holds its attractions for both traditional Muslims and Arab Socialists: The former hope to render their beliefs more palatable to the prevailing revolutionary movement, whereas the latter expect to make their ideology more acceptable to the traditional and semi-traditional public.

Although in practical terms this method offered a workable formula for change, intellectually it became self-defeating. Like the Islamic-Modernists and Liberal-Nationalists before them, the Arab Socialists have been caught in a cross-fire: for the consistent Islamic thinkers, their traditionalism is counterfeit,[39] and for radical revolutionaries, their socialism is a farce.[40] It may thus be said of Arab Socialist intellectuals, borrowing a phrase from Wilfred C. Smith, that "they try to champion rather than to understand, to buttress rather than to elucidate."[41]

Seen in this light, the hypothesis put forward by such observers as Hanna and Gardner, that the roots of Arab Socialist ideology may be found at society's "core-value level,"[42] does not appear very promising. It seems that the only way to make this proposition plausible is to redefine Arab Socialism, as, in fact, the authors themselves do elsewhere in their book, where they suggest substituting *takāfuliyya 'arabiyya* for *ishtirākiyya 'arabiyya.*[43]

Similar difficulties are encountered in examining the proposition — held by these observers, as well as by Egyptian writers — that Arab Socialism's indigenous nature is proven by the recurrence of socialist ideas in the thinking of local intellectuals throughout the modern period. The writings of such thinkers as the Pan-Islamist leader Jamāl al-Dīn al-Afghānī, the Syrian-Christian Doctor Shiblī Shumayyil, the Islamic reformer Muḥammad 'Abduh and the Coptic Fabian Salāma Mūsā, are often cited to substantiate this argument.[44] However, the very same selections of writings demonstrate the invalidity of the argument. For it seems obvious that the traditional intellectuals, such as Afghānī and 'Abduh, did not go beyond preaching broad human-itarian benevolence, while the intellectuals who seriously embraced socialist concepts, such as Shumayyil and Mūsā, did so as an assertion of their faith in all-encompassing Westernization.

V

The different forms and degrees of interaction between the Egyptian-Islamic tradition and Arab Socialism may be summed up as follows:

a. The persistence of traditional patterns is manifest mainly in the socio-political and economic organization of the Arab Socialist system. Their reflections are found in such aspects of that system as the state control of principal material resources, the highly-centralized administration, the gap between the ruler and the ruled, the subjection of social classification and organization to considerations of political regimentation and control, the superimposition of communal solidarity over other interests, and the preclusion of the legitimacy of class conflict. This persistence of the traditional political culture offers a partial explanation of the remarkable viability and stability of the Nasserist system, in spite of all its shattering losses and setbacks.

b. In its endeavor to build institutions and formulate revolutionary symbols and concepts, Arab Socialism has failed to forge meaningful links to tradition. To the extent that this linking was tried, it took the form of either misinterpretation of tradition or misrepresentation of the principles of Arab Socialism. The ensuing failures are made manifest in such weaknesses of Arab Socialism as the ineffectiveness of the ASU and the vagueness of its doctrine.

A conclusion to be drawn from this synthesis is that the bonds to tradition subsist precisely where they cannot be admitted and fail to materialize where they are solemnly proclaimed. The regime does not only disavow the above-mentioned traditional characteristics of Egyptian political culture (a), but actually seeks to define its own identity in contradistinction to certain regimes of the past to which it attributes those characteristics. At the same time, as has been shown, it often claims indigenous authenticity for Arab Socialist tenets and institutions which can be described as anything but indigenous (b).

Another conclusion is that the fusion of traditional and modern patterns has succeeded better in those general elements of the system which are not necessarily socialistic and less in those which are more specifically associated with universal models of socialist revolution. This raises the crucial question as to what extent Egyptian tradition, and particularly Islam, is receptive at all to socialist revolution in this sense. The question, of course, has been discussed exhaustively by Islamicists and social scientists alike. One of the most outstanding contributions to this discussion was made by Bernard Lewis in his landmark essay on "Communism and Islam." Lewis pointed out that, contrary to popular belief, there are elements in Communism to which Islamic society is prone, namely its authoritarian-totalitarian nature on the political, economic, and intellectual planes, its collectivist spirit, and its quasi-religious organization.[45] There is, however, no difficulty in pointing out elements within Islam which work in precisely the opposite direction: Islam has a transcendental conception of the universe; it draws on revealed truth; it is not anthropocentric; it is past-oriented with no utopian inclinations; founded on community not on class; has no tradition of intellectual dissent and social protest of the type that nurtures a radical socialist movement, and so forth.

The question whether for the spread of socialism Islam is an asset or a liability has not been settled. Nor has the extent to which the incorporation of socialism depends at all on its successful fusion with local tradition definitely been determined. What can be established, however, is that, in the particular case of Nasserist Egypt, whatever the reasons, in more than a decade, socialist revolution has made little headway.

Egyptian society has never produced a viable socialist movement sufficiently detached from the center to develop strong revolutionary ideological motivation and commitment. The officers who made the July 1952 Revolution lacked definite class affiliations. Their disposition has remained reformative rather than revolutionary. The managerial technocratic elite which upholds the regime's structure is embedded in the upper class and its loyalty to socialist revolutionary concepts is often mere lip service. Hence, the depiction of the Nasserist system as "socialism without socialists" is not unfounded. Aware of this contradiction, the regime, at one point, opted for the recruiting of Egyptian Marxists, several hundreds in number, to serve as political cadres in its political institutions, but to no avail.[46] Furthermore, the willingness of the Marxists to be absorbed into the system indicated that they, too, could not be regarded as an alternative force capable of directing the implementation of a Socialist revolution in Egypt within any foreseeable future.

As a socialist system, Nasserism remains vague and superficial. Typical to it is the statement, frequently made by Nasser, to the effect that "whoever contributes to production is a socialist." Indeed, in Nasserist Egypt, socialist ideals have always been secondary to foreign policy goals, considerations of domestic politics, and economic expediency.

Nationalism has been the main driving force behind the Arab Socialist undertaking. In Egypt, Arab Socialism has remained subsidiary to all-embracing nationalism, not its potential alternative. The nationalist struggle against imaginary or real external enemies has overshadowed all internal social conflicts and has hindered the emergence of effective class symbols. The terms of reference of Arab Socialism are the nationalist aspirations for a collective regeneration, the realization of a self-image and attainment of a vision of greatness. It is these concerns, more than any particular aspect of Arab Socialism, that proved capable of unleashing the innate forces of society. Nationalism did manage to mingle traditional Islamic values with modern ones into an effective blend which, even if intellectually faulty, appears vigorous and explosive; socialism did not.

The experience of Arab Socialism's first decade in Egypt has not supported the proposition of some observers that, in a country like Egypt, once a socialist revolution is initiated, it is bound to gain momentum and supersede other systems. Whether due to accidental or essential factors, the trend in Egypt has swung in the opposite direction. After its energetic inauguration in 1961-62, Arab Socialism had lost its impetus by the mid-sixties. Since the defeat of June 1967, it has been assigned an even lower priority and the leftist formulas for recovery have been categorically rejected. The ascendancy of a traditional personality like Sadat in 1970 was in itself a setback for socialism. This was followed, in 1971-72, by a series of practical measures which he took to somewhat liberalize the economic system, curb the influence of the Marxists, and tone down revolutionary socialist themes in the regime's programs.

Although in terms of social transformation, the experience of a decade is probably too short to allow any definite conclusions to be drawn, nonetheless the record is sufficiently indicative to justify the question as to whether a genuine socialist revolution of any kind is at present within the range of possible answers to the problems of Egyptian society. This line of thought, some would argue, leads back to tradition as a possible source of inspiration for better answers. However, there is no escape from the conclusion that if tradition is to be combed to produce more meaningful answers, this would have to be done in a different way than hitherto.

NOTES

1 Jamāl 'Abd al-Nāṣir, *Al-mithāq al-qawmī*, p. 9. Quotations from the *National Charter* are cited from the Arabic edition.

2 *Ibid.*, pp. 17-18.

3 *Al-Ahrām*, August 4, 1961.

4 *Mashrū' dalīl al-'amal al-siyāsī wal-fikrī wal-tanẓīmī, al-Ṭalī'a,* October 1972, p. 101.

5 See, for example, Nasser's statement to a congress convened in Alexandria in August 1966, as given by Muṣṭafā Fahmī, *Al-ishtirākiyya wal-fikr al-ishtirākī al-'arabī* (Alexandria: 1968), pp. 233–236.

6 *Al-mithāq*, pp. 55–61.

7 The Shiloah Center for Middle Eastern and Afrıcan Studies, *Middle East Record* III (1967), p. 549; R.H. Dekmejian, *Egypt under Nasir* (Albany: State University of New York Press, 1971), p. 230. The evolution of the economic system of Arab Socialism is described in Charles Issawi, *Egypt in Revolution* (London: Oxford University Press, 1963), and in Patrick O'Brien, *The Revolution in Egypt's Economic System from Private Enterprise to Socialism* (London: Oxford University Press, 1966).

8 A more sarcastic phrase is used by Hassad Riad: *étatism pharaonique immobiliste.* See his *L'Egypte Nassérienne* (Paris: Editions de Minuit, 1964), p. 231.

9 Gabriel Baer, *Introduction to the History of Agrarian Relations in the Middle East, 1800-1970* (Hebrew)(Hakibbutz Hameuchad, 1971), pp. 9–11.

10 G. Karl Wittfogel, *Oriental Despotism* (New Haven: Yale University Press, 1957), p. 166.

11 See, for example, Sayyid Mursī, *Insāniyyat al-ishtirākiyya al-'arabiyya*, (Cairo: n.d.), p. 133.

12 Jacques Berque, *The Arabs, Their History and Future* (Eng. tr.) (London: Faber and Faber, 1964), p. 134.

13 The inner *apparat (al-jihāz al-sirrī* or *al-ṭalī'ī)* was a secret organization, but since its disbandment in May 1971, much material has been made available. In 1972-73, there was talk of re-establishing it, this time openly. See Shimon Shamir, "The Marxists in Egypt: The 'Licenced Infiltration' Doctrine in Practice," in M. Confino and S. Shamir (eds.), *The U.S.S.R. and the Middle East* (New York: John Wiley and Sons, 1973), pp. 310f.

14 The socio-political system is outlined in the following Egyptian documents: the 1962 *National Charter*, the 1962 Statute of the ASU, the Constitutions of 1964 and 1971, the 1968 "March 30 Program" and the *Guide for Political Action* drafted in 1972.

15 For the Nasserist-Marxist debate see Shamir, *op. cit.*, pp. 293–303.

16 *Al-Ṭalī'a*, October 1972, pp. 90–105.

17 These references to the work of Ḥajji Khalīfa have drawn largely on F.

Rosenthal, *Political Thought in Medieval Islam* (London: Cambridge University Press, 1962), pp. 224–233.

18 Gabriel Baer, *Egyptian Guilds in Modern Times* (Jerusalem: Israel Oriental Society, 1964), p. 5.

19 H.A.R. Gibb, "The Heritage of Islam in the Modern World (II),"*International Journal of Middle East Studies*, Vol. I (1970), p. 222. It should, however, be noted that Gibb employs the term "class" for the groups into which Islamic society is classified. For the structure of traditional society, see H.A.R. Gibb and H. Bowen, *Islamic Society and the West*, Vol. I, Pt. I (London: Oxford University Press, 1950), pp. 208–216. Cf. C.A.O. Nieuwenjuije, *Social Stratification and the Middle East* (Leiden: E. D. Brill, 1965).

20 The English translation is in S.A. Hanna and G.H. Gardner, *Arab Socialism* (Leiden: E.D. Brill, 1969), pp. 373–385.

21 See the "Working Paper" of ASU First Secretary Sayyīd Mar'ī in *al-Ṭalī'a*, May 1972, pp. 18–20.

22 *Middle East Record* III (1967), p. 533.

23 I. Lapidus, *Muslim Cities in the Later Middle Ages* (Cambridge, Mass.: Harvard University Press, 1967), p. 48.

24 G.E. von Grunebaum, *Medieval Islam* (Chicago: University of Chicago Press, Phoenix ed., 1961), pp. 181–182, 200–201; James A. Bill, "Class-Analysis and the Dialectics of Modernization in the Middle East," *International Journal of Middle East Studies*, Vol. III (1972), p. 424.

25 For another kind of relationship between *dawla* and *thawra* see Bernard Lewis, "Islamic Concepts of Revolution" in P.J. Vatikiotis (ed.), *op. cit.*, pp. 30–40.

26 *Al-Ṭalī'a*, October 1972, pp. 99–100.

27 Mar'ī's "Working Paper," *op. cit.*, lists eleven failures of the ASU, pointing out that ordinarily any five of them would have been sufficient to wreck any political organization.

28 Gibb, *Heritage*, pp. 225–227.

29 Published by *Maktabat al-qāhira al-ḥadītha.*

30 "Arab Socialism and Communism," *Scribe* (Cairo), July 23, 1962, quoted from Hanna and Gardner, p. 338.

31 *Ibid.*, p. 339. Cf. Fahmī, p. 288.

32 *Al-mithāq*, p. 75. For "the theoretical structure of Arab Socialism" see Fayez Sayegh's article in *St. Antony's Papers* XVII (1965), pp. 9–55.

33 See the articles of Lewis 'Awaḍ, *Al-ishtirākiyya wal-adab wa-maqālāt ukhrā* (Beirut: 1963); quoted from K.H. Karpart (ed.), *Political and Social Thought in the Contemporary Middle East* (New York: Praeger, 1968), p. 178.

34 'Abd al-Raḥmān Shākir in *al-Katib.*

35 See the views of Sība'ī and Maẓhar in Hanna and Gardner, pp. 149–204; Hamid Enayat, "Islam and Socialism in Egypt," *Middle Eastern Studies*, Vol. IV (1968), pp. 153–166.

36 Issawi, *op. cit.*, p. 120.

37   The minimum daily wage was raised in February 1962 from PT 16-22 to PT 25, which would amount to an annual income of approximately £E75; the maximum salary of directors was fixed by the July 1961 laws at £E5,000.

38   Sibā'ī in Hanna and Gardner, pp. 150–152.

39   See, for example, the criticism of Ṣalāḥ al-Dīn al-Munajjid in his *Al-taḍlīl al-ishtirākī* (Beirut: 1965).

40   See, for example, the criticism of Jalāl Ṣādiq al-'Aẓm in his *Al-naqd al-dhātī ba'd al-hazīma* (Beirut: 1968).

41   Wilfred C. Smith, *Islam in Modern History* (New York: Mentor ed., 1959), p. 15.

42   Hanna and Gardner, *op. cit.*, p. 15.

43   *Ibid.*, p. 147.

44   In addition to Hanna and Gardner, see, for example, Rif'at al-Sa'īd, *Ta'rīkh al-fikr al-ishtirākī fī misr* (n.p., 1969).

45   Bernard Lewis, "Communism and Islam," *International Affairs*, Vol. XXX (1954), pp. 311–324. The author's conclusion, however, is that "Communism thus has many features in common with religion, but those that are lacking are perhaps the most important" (p. 323).

46   See Shamir, *op. cit.*, pp. 294–307.

SOME ASPECTS OF THE ANALYSIS OF THE SPREAD OF SOCIALISM

S.N. EISENSTADT AND YAEL AZMON

INTRODUCTION

The materials presented in the preceding chapters provide some interesting indications about the patterns of diffusion of different aspects of socialism and communism and of their incorporation into the social, political, and cultural frameworks of their respective societies, as well as about the conditions under which such differential diffusion and selective incorporation take place. As mentioned above, the major problems of such incorporation with which we shall concern ourselves are: first, which societies, social groups, or elites are prone to incorporate some of the symbolism of socialism into the central symbols of their collective (cultural and political) identity; second, the degree to which it is the whole "package deal" of the socialism symbolism — its model of society, political program, and Weltanshauung — or only some of its aspects that are so incorporated; third, the degree to which it is the symbolic and/or institutional and/or organizational aspects of the socialist tradition or programs that are so incorporated; fourth, the degree to which it is the reformist, revolutionary and conflicting aspects or the harmonious and solidary as well as the class aspects of socialist symbolism that are so incorporated.

Such incorporation need not, of course, be the same among all the groups or elites within the same society. Indeed it has been very characteristic of the spread of socialism and communism that different groups and elites within the same society have picked up different aspects or packages of such aspects from within the socialist tradition — thus presumably having different perceptions of such discrepancy.

But yet these different modes of incorporation have not been entirely random. They were influenced by several basic aspects of the situation of historical change in which these societies and groups were caught, by a combination of their "objective" situation within their own society and of their society's situation on the international scene, and of their evaluation of such situations. While it would be out of place to attempt a full analysis of all forces which may influence such perception, we may yet attempt here some tentative indication of the most important among them.

Among such forces of special importance are first, the structure and "contents" of the political and cultural centers of these respective societies, the degree of their internal cohesion and continuity in the new situation, and the degree to which they were impinged upon and weakened by the various processes of modernization.

Second, and closely connected with the former, is the continuity of collective identity of these societies and the degree of impingement of the forces of modernity on them; the degree to which these processes in their respective traditions (and accordingly also the degree to which they could seize upon such theories in the socialist tradition) undermined some of the components of such identities, and the degree to which they could be drawn to some components, symbols, or orientations in the new settings.

The third force is the extent to which there existed among the various groups and elites of a society a strong orientation and tradition toward participation in some Great Traditions in general and some universalistic setting in particular; and the degree to which they aspired, when drawn into the orbit of the new "European" international type of tradition to attain some place within it according to universalistic premises of their own and/or of the new civilization.

Fourth is the degree of importance of utopian and millenarian orientations in their tradition.

Fifth is the evaluation by the different groups of the society's prospects of attaining some of the "ideals" or premises of modernity within the given setting. This in its turn is greatly influenced by the internal cohesion of the groups, by their vision of modernity, by the degree of a society's social and cultural openness in general and by its attitude to change in particular, as well as by its relative emphasis on power or prestige as its basic social orientation. This evaluation was also influenced by the degree of dislocation of the given groups from within their own society as caused by the impingement of internal and external social, political, and economic forces, and by the relative place of the groups in the emerging power structure.

Part One

THE PATTERNS OF INCORPORATION OF DIFFERENT
DIMENSIONS OF SOCIALIST TRADITION

S.N. EISENSTADT

With regard to all the aspects specified above, certain patterns of diffusion can be discerned in different societies — whether those analyzed here in the different case studies or others. We shall first present very brief outlines of some of these major patterns.

In Western Europe, and to some degree Central Europe, many elites and groups have incorporated into the symbols of collectivity which they forged out in the nineteenth and twentieth centuries several socialist orientations and symbols (such as social security and justice). Among these groups only a few secondary or marginal extremist elites have accepted the entire package of socialist tradition.

Socialism's "package deal" was accepted in these countries primarily in the initial phases of its development by marginal groups, while with the growing institutionalization of socialism in Europe it was mostly the general social and cultural symbols of socialism, as well as concrete political and social programs, that were incorporated into the new emerging political and collective symbolism.

At the same time there tended to develop here a certain mode of continuity between the symbols of socialism and those preceding European traditions, whether modern or premodern. This mode was characterized by the willingness to use the existing tradition to find answers to new problems within the realm of the social and cultural order. Hence these groups tended to differentiate between different layers of traditional commitments and motivations and to use them and the available organizations for the implementation of new concrete goals, tasks, and activities.

This illustration also indicates the two major foci of continuity of tradition that developed in Europe. The first is the persistence — even if a flexible one — of some basic poles or modes of perception of cosmic, cultural, and social order. The second focus of such continuity lies in the persistence of autonomous symbols of

collective identities of the major sub-groups and collectivities —
however great may be the concrete changes in their specific
contents.

Such continuity seems to have been maintained here even when the
elites tend to change or redefine the major problems of social and
cultural order and to broaden greatly the scope of the available and
permissible answers to them. Hence they tend to maintain continuity
of tradition mostly on the levels of commitment to central symbols of
the social and cultural orders and some very general orientations to
these orders, but not to the overall content of these orders which, in
such situations, continuously change.

In Russia and China, the elites which established the revolutionary
regimes have incorporated the whole package deal of socialist symbolism into the central symbols of political and cultural identity of their
respective societies and made it a central component of their symbolism. In these regimes there also developed some different patterns of
continuity between the new socialist symbols and orientation and
various patterns of tradition.

On the one hand such revolutionary elites tended, by definition, to
destroy most of the concrete symbols and structures of existing traditions, strata, and organizations and to emphasize new contents and
new types of social organization. Yet at the same time such an elite
may evince a great continuity with regard to what may be called some
basic modes of symbolic and institutional orientations.

They tend to pose some of the basic problems of social and cultural
order and of their interrelations in broad terms (e.g., emphasis on
power, etc.) not very different from those utilized by their predecessors — although both the concrete working out of these problems
(e.g., how to establish a "strong" autocratic absolutist society as
against a "strong" industrial one) and the concrete answers would
differ greatly from those of the preceding order.

They attempt to utilize many of the traditional orientations — but
shorn of much of their concrete contents and of their identification
with and connection to the older order or parts thereof. In other
words, the basic attempt here is to unleash — and to control in a new
way — the basic motivational orientations inherent in the older systems while changing their contents and basic identity.

A similar process takes place here with regard to the incorporation
of symbols of partial groups or even some of the older central symbols
(especially "patriotic" ones). On the one hand we find here an almost
total negation of these symbols; but on the other hand, because of the

similarity of problems posed revealing to us the nature of the social order, there tends also to develop parallel attempts to use or uphold such symbols — or general symbolic orientations — shorn of their former context, and denied almost any partial autonomy of their own.

Within several other Asian countries, like Ceylon and Burma, as well as some of the Muslim (Arab) countries, there have also arisen groups which have attempted to incorporate into the symbolism of their society some socialist symbols. They tended to select out of these socialist symbols some broader cultural orientations of general political and social symbols, or sometimes even political programs. But only rarely — even among the politically revolutionary groups, as in the case of the more extreme Ba'th elites in the Middle East — have they attempted to accept the whole "package deal" of socialism, or to make it the predominant element in the symbols of their collective identity.

Moreover, unlike in either the Eastern European or the Russian and Chinese cases, in most of these countries the socialist orientation did not entail, except among marginal extremist elites, a high degree of commitment to its premises or a very high degree of institution-building. In these societies the relation with existing traditions was characterized by emphasis on continuity, with many of the existing symbols of collective identity, as well as a de facto continuity in many modes of perception of social and political problems and with but little feasibility in adaptation to new problems and settings.

The picture of African socialism is even more complicated. On the one hand we find among some of the most central elites a very strong predilection to incorporate the symbols of socialism into their central symbols of identity. But this is done mostly on the symbolic level, especially with regard to general political symbols or orientations but with a predilection to accept the ideological scientific "package deal" or even the political programs of societies. At the same time there tended to develop in many of these African countries — and in many cases also countries with Islamic traditions — a strong conscious emphasis on the continuity between some of the symbols of socialism, especially those of solidarity and of harmony with the presumed symbols of these respective societies.

As against all these cases we find several other societies, of which Japan is the best example, in which only extreme groups which never fully succeeded in getting even near the center have accepted the incorporation of the symbolism of socialism as a basic component of their collective orientations.

Latin American countries present a much more complicated picture. Originally only marginal groups in Latin America developed some commitment to socialist symbols, but lately — especially since the Cuban revolution and the recent developments in Chile — such symbols moved, as it were, into much more central spheres of society and culture.

In India there developed a situation which was rather the obverse from that in many of the Middle Eastern or African countries. The symbols of socialism were not central in the new symbols of collective identity that developed throughout the movement toward independence and after the attainment of independence, even though that symbolism played an important role in the world-view of a leader such as Jawaharlal Nehru. At the same time many socialist programs were adopted in terms of social ideology and institution-building.

How can we then explain these patterns of incorporation of different aspects of the socialist tradition in various societies and civilizations? What constellations of the factors enumerated above influenced the degrees to which different aspects of socialist tradition and symbolism were incorporated into different societies?

The materials presented above enable us to offer some tentative hypotheses. It seems that the receptivity to socialist symbols as components of central symbols of collective identity is dependent, first, on the degree to which the traditions of the respective societies (or of their respective elites) contain within themselves strong universalistic elements which transcend the given tribal, ethnic, or national community, as well as strong utopian elements and orientations. Thus, it was in Western Europe, Russia, and China, and to some degree in the Middle Eastern countries, in which such universalistic and utopian elements were predominant (but not in Japan or India, where they were missing) that there developed a strong predisposition to the incorporation of socialist symbols.

Second, such receptivity to the central symbols of socialism is dependent on the degree to which these universalistic orientations and elements existed in their own Great Tradition, as well as their own security and cohesion as such Great Tradition became undermined by the process of being drawn into the new international system; or it is dependent on the degree to which in this process there develops a discrepancy between their aspirations to participate in the universalistic Great Tradition and their own ability to forge out, continue, or maintain such a Great Tradition with strong universalistic elements.

Thus, in Europe, such symbols were forged out, as we have seen, as part of European tradition and of the processes of its reshaping in the nineteenth and twentieth centuries. In other countries it was the ways of incorporation into the new European-dominated international settings that influenced the strength of such predispositions to incorporate the socialist symbols into their symbols. Thus, here again we see that it was Russia and China — where their own strong tradition as centers of a Great, potentially universalistic, Tradition were very sharply undermined — that were highly predisposed to the incorporation of such symbols.

On the other hand the cases of Japan, Latin America, and to some degree Africa indicate that as long as their cultural identity was maintained in some positive way in relations with the West and its international system — whether through attainment of strong standing without any major changes in their own self-conception, as was the case in Japan, or through the acceptance of their own part in it, as was the case for a very long time in Latin America — the predisposition toward the incorporation of socialist symbols into their central symbols was very small and limited to some extremely marginal elites which were not successful in influencing the center and/or broader groups.

The picture in African and Middle Eastern societies indicates some different constellations of the factors for predilection to incorporate different aspects of socialism. In most African societies, the process of colonialism has drawn relatively simple political and cultural units with very weak — if any — Great Traditions into the new international orbit and has implanted, at least among the more educated and urbanized elites, a very strong predisposition to participation in the new broader setting of such New Great Traditions. It was in this context that the ideology of African socialism tended to develop among some of these groups.

In the central Islamic countries the predilection of some elites to incorporate into the central symbols of their societies those of socialism was also very strongly connected with the weakening of many elements of their own Great Traditions — and especially the uncertainty about the relations between the new emerging political centers and the universalistic class of Islam. At the same time, given the persistence of this ambivalence as well as that of Islam as a universalistic tradition, this resulted here also in the selection of some general socialist symbols as well as of broad nationalistic political programs — though not in the development of the institutional and organizational aspect of societies.

Here it is indeed very significant that the predisposition to the incorporation of socialist symbols has been weakest in those African groups or societies within which there persisted or developed a strong Islamic identity which assured them of the possibility to participate in an already existing Great Tradition. At the same time the fact that these groups stood on the relative periphery of the centers of Islam saved them from the turbulence and problems of the more central Islamic countries. In many such countries symbols of socialism were simply incorporated into the general Islamic symbols of the collectivity, while at the same time such groups, with their relative security of participation in a Great Tradition, did not share the turbulence of the center.

A number of conditions influenced whether the whole "package deal" of socialist Weltanshauung or only the political, social, or cultural symbolism and/or program were incorporated into the central political symbols of their respective societies: the degree of motivational commitment which such symbols evoked; and the extent to which symbolism and/or concrete center-formation and institution-building or of rebellion were emphasized in the incorporation of socialist traditions.

Among the most important of these conditions — in addition to the universalistic and utopian elements in the respective traditions of these societies or of their elites — have been the strength or weakness of their centers, i.e., the degree to which these centers have commanded a high degree of commitment; the degree of the nature of the major orientations of these centers and especially the differential emphasis within them on prestige and power; and the degree of internal solidarity of their respective elites and the degree of internal pluralism within them.

The propensity to accept all of socialism as a package deal into their central symbols was greater in those societies insofar as universalistic orientation and the utopian elements in their respective traditions were stronger, and insofar as the actual process of undermining impinged on strong cultural and political centers which commanded a high degree of commitment and whose undermining gave rise to strong "totalistic" movements.

While such tendencies could develop among almost any elite or group, yet on the whole, the influence and pervasion of such elites could be greater insofar as they developed in societies with strong but relatively closed centers, i.e., societies which placed a strong emphasis on power and prestige orientations — of which Russia and China provide the clearest illustrations.

In Burma and Ceylon the tradition of "weaker" centers with greater emphasis on passive and adoptive attitudes to the center — as well as in Latin America with its Spanish patrimonial heritage — the predilection to accept the package deal of socialism was weaker. Except among very marginal groups which attempted to forge out new far-reaching symbols of collective identity, it was mostly a broad cultural orientation that was selected here.

Similarly, given the relatively low degree of intra-elite solidarity and the strong emphasis on power and closed prestige there developed here only relatively weak tendencies to institution-building or concrete center-formation, while at the same time there developed a strong tendency to emphasize the symbols of collectivity and center-formation.

In contrast, in Europe the more pluralistic tradition of the center — combined as it was with relatively strong commitments to it — worked on the whole against the tendency to acceptance of the package deal of socialism and contributed to the differential selection of different aspects of socialism. Given the strong universalistic tradition, the selection that took place here was, first, toward incorporation, especially of social and social-political programs, into the existing political symbols. Secondly, given also the relatively strong cohesion and solidarity of these groups, there developed here also a relatively strong emphasis on the institutional and organizational as well as the motivational aspects of socialism.

The relative emphasis on protest as against center-formation and institution-building was mostly influenced by the position of respective groups in their internal social or international power situation and by their perception of their place in their own society or in the international setting.

Thus, very often — as in Russia or Africa — elites changed their respective emphasis from protest to center-formation when they became ruling elites and new "oppositionary" groups within the society tended to develop a strong protest orientation couched in the terms of socialism to use against the ruling elites and their interpretation of socialism.

Part Two

TRADITIONAL ELEMENTS IN SOCIALIST SYSTEMS: COMPARATIVE REMARKS

YAEL AZMON

During the first emergent phases of socialism in Western Europe, the main development was that of a revolutionary orientation with a strong emphasis on class conflict. Later, the symbolism of "class," especially among the more "established" socialist groups, began to dissociate itself from the revolutionary orientations. Reformatory tendencies became predominant, with varying degrees of emphasis on class conflict. Class symbolism became institutionalized as part of the Western European political tradition.

In the process of diffusion of socialist ideas, non-European countries responded differently to these two basic orientations in socialism. The process of selective diffusion which the expanding socialist ideology has undergone expressed itself in two ways: in acceptance or rejection of specific socialist content, and also in different ways of relating socialist ideas to other ideas. We shall concern ourselves with these two modes of selection, the aim being twofold:

A. Examination of typical combinations of selective tendencies, especially those concerning class conflict as against social harmony, revolution as against continuity; and,

B. Identification of some characteristics of the pre-socialist system which are likely to be related to the existence of such typical combinations.

A central idea in the socialist world-outlook — despite its various transfigurations — is the definition of the relationship between socialism and capitalism as a situation of conflict. This assumption is basic to African socialism, just as it is to the socialism of Russia, China, or Burma. But alongside this similarity, there are obvious differences among various socialist systems in the selection of the concrete social object designated as the subject of conflict. In other words, socialist systems differ in the identification of the capitalist enemy. From this point of view, the major distinction is between objects outside the

228

system, such as "international capitalism" and "neo-colonialism," versus groups within the system itself, variously designated as "cosmopolites," "parasites," and so on. The identification of the social object defines the actual meaning of the general concept of conflict — which makes it essential to the characterization of the different socialist systems.

We shall present three complexes of selection of socialist ideas, the differences among which can be partly related to some elements in the pre-Communist situation. Some of these elements which possess a special interest, though the list is by no means complete, are the following:

A. The continuous existence of some cultural precepts; of certain basic unifying principles underlying motivations and commitments. Even if revolution were to lead to a rejection of traditional contents on different institutional and symbolic levels, a continuity of tradition in this sense can still exist and influence, to a great extent, the processes of selection — mainly by assuming a minimal level of commitments toward various collectives. The political national collective is of special importance in this context.

B. The degree of universal orientation to the "outer world" which exists in the pre-modern societies. Traditional universalism was found in ethnocentrism, like that of Imperial China, and in rivalry relations composed of inferiority-superiority attitudes toward Europe, such as those of Czarist Russia. Common to both is the preoccupation with the evaluation of the outer world and of the place of Chinese or Russian culture within it.

The argument stated here is, first, that continuity of traditional elements in this sense — of continuity of some basic unifying principles — is paradoxically related to revolutionary anti-traditional orientations. And second, that the existence of an out-worldly universalistic orientation in pre-modern times is related to the militant character of Messianic Communist systems — such as those of Russia and China.

The existence of a universalistic orientation in earlier periods functions as a pattern of thought orienting elites toward those social ideas which might have a universal meaning and serve as a model for other nations. The militant Messianism of Russia and China is, according to this view, not just an expression of power politics but a part of a basic orientation inherited from past generations.

The continuity in unifying principles functions as a pre-condition enabling elites to select revolutionary orientations without taking too great a risk from the point of view of maintaining some minimal level of solidarity. Revolutionary orientations are expressed both in anti-traditionalism and in conflict-oriented attitudes toward inner social groups — the first being a negation on a time dimension, the second a negation on a social-spatial dimension.

THE FIRST COMPLEX: SOME OF THE SOCIALIST COUNTRIES OF AFRICA

The first complex of socialist systems to be discussed is that of some — though not all — socialist nations in Africa, specifically Ghana, Tanzania, and Guinea. In African countries a major objective in the selection of socialist ideas and the manner of their implementation is the creation of national integration: the development of a political commitment and the enrichment of the new political framework with cultural content.

In creating a new collective identity, these socialist African states emphasize the connection of socialist ideology with local particularistic content. Socialism's universal orientations have little influence on African Socialism. It is the application of socialist ideology to the unique characteristics of Africa that plays a dominant role.

An outstanding example of this is the concept of the "African personality," which expresses a search for early egalitarian and communalistic traditions in the attempt to build a new political identity on the basis of a synthesis between modern socialist ideas and local primitive traditions.

Although African socialist states have adopted diverse socialist patterns, still a similarity can be found in the selection of socialist ideas and in their role in the creation of political integration in the three countries to be discussed.

In Tanzania especially, local conditions promoted the selection of those socialist ideas which emphasize integration rather than conflict. The introduction of socialism in Tanzania after independence was connected with the drive to achieve greater national integration. Moreover, Tanzanian protests against the colonial government during the struggle for independence had little bearing on the manifestations of its socialism. This resulted in relatively little stress on anti-colonialism which, in other cases, is a main focus of defining relations among social groups in terms of conflict. Furthermore, Tanzania, one of the least developed countries in Africa, does not have any right-wing opposition to the socialist government of President Julius Nyerere — a factor bearing a potential for encouraging the emergence of a positive orientation toward conflict.

Nyerere's motto — "Ujamaa" — best characterizes this trend of emphasizing integration rather than conflict. Ujamaa expresses belief in equality and communality, traditional African values which are also socialist values. Thus in Tanzania those socialist ideas were selected which promote interaction rather than conflict in inter-group relations and which can at the same time be presented as traditional values.*

In contrast to the situation in Tanzania, certain conditions in Ghana were likely to encourage an orientation of conflict in the process of selection of socialist ideas. The socialist movement in Ghana developed as part of the anti-colonialist protest during the pre-independence period, and some emphasis on conflict persists to this day. But, particularly since independence was gained in 1957, conflict in Ghana has been redefined in terms of a contrast between socialist states and colonial ones, that is, the use of conflict in the contents of Ghana's ideology is more relevant to the international level than to the level of inner politics. This trend of selection is part of the striving for autonomy — a popular theme in Ghana's thought. The use of the term "autonomy" as a societal goal carries with it not only political and economic connotations, but symbolic ones as well. It means creating a new political culture uniquely African, instead of imitating the colonial nations.

The emphasis on anti-colonialism in Nkrumian ideology is, therefore, not only an expression of the actual fear of the presence of non-African political power: it is also an attempt at self-expression by negating Western culture and accepting the alternative offered by socialism. The idea of conflict between socialism and capitalism is thus transferred to the international level. But the negation of Western culture does not go as far as attacking the value of Western democratic political institutions in the European context: "African Socialism" is not addressed to other continents but to Africa alone.

Moreover, the presence of right-wing opposition (in the preliminary stages of attaining independence in Ghana) was an additional factor capable of promoting an orientation toward conflict. In spite of these conditions, however, conflict was not stressed. Nkrumah's party did not "take sides" with any one specific group, in contrast to the socialist identification with the proletarian class — as opposed to the bourgeoisie — in European socialist thought. This attitude finds

* This was especially true for the initial period after Tanganyika achieved independence. The Union of Tanganyika with Zanzibar in 1964 partly changed this trend.

expression in the concept of "tribalism" — one of the major focal points of anti-colonialism in Nkrumian ideology. Tribalism is a general term used to cover tribal decentralization, conflict between different economic groups, parochiality, political apathy, lack of commitment to the central power — in short, anything which disturbs political integration.

Yet traditionalism was not totally rejected, and tribal customs which could be accommodated to the Ghanaian socialistic ideology were supported by Nkrumah. Nkrumah used local pagan and Christian symbols, ceremonies, and rituals in creating his own self-image as a leader and in strengthening commitment to the new state.

Conditions in Guinea, even more than those in Ghana, carried a potential of advancing an orientation of conflict. During the colonial period, the French Communist Party was very influential in Guinea, as a result of its intensive efforts to create a leftist political movement and to educate a revolutionary elite. Moreover, the fact that the Guinean Socialist Movement never participated in the governing bodies of the colonial structure as did traditional-conservative elements and the conflict with France in the post-independence period were factors potentially promoting conflict with regard to both the colonial structure and local, traditional elements. But still the conception of socialism as a historical conflict between the proletariat and the bourgeoisie was externalized to the international level.

The ideology which developed in Guinea in the pre-independence period — and even more so in the initial period after attaining independence — is vastly different from the European communist ideology. Guinea encouraged a populist ideology where the unity of the nation was a major factor. The party was thought of as a tool — a means for making the nation politically aware — and also as a framework for participation which could encompass all social groups. Although in the past decade the beginnings of radicalism can be observed in phraseology as well as in the economic policies of nationalization, this radicalism has been expressed in a manner similar to that of Ghana — as a conflict between colonialism and socialism on the international level, and not as an outgrowth of inter-group differences. Nationalization also served an additional purpose as a means of attacking foreign ethnic groups.

In conclusion, Tanzania, Ghana, and Guinea differ in historical development; in the existence or non-existence of strong, traditional groups and/or newly-founded economic groups capable of posing right-wing opposition; in the intensity and length of time of the conflict between the colonial power and the country under rule; in the amount of influence shown by the European communist movements; and other factors. These different conditions have resulted in the creation of a diversity of socialist patterns. Nevertheless, one general principle is common to all three systems: the selection of socialist contents which are characteristically integrative and are easily assimilated together with traditional traits. This particular choice is motivated by the common need for successfully integrating the political framework and creating a viable new political identity. In this connection, one important traditional aspect has negative connotations — the absence of strong continuity of unifying principles organizing motivations and commitments on traditional bases. Paradoxically, the weakness of tradition, in this sense, is a pre-condition for the appearance of newly-adopted "traditional" ideas, manners, and organizational patterns.

THE SECOND COMPLEX: BURMA

In the collective identity of Burma, Buddhism not only plays a central role as the state religion: it is also a basis of social and political thought. The ethical conception of the "good" society, which is used in defining social goals, stems from the traditional Buddhist view that the citizen's well-being is the principal stated objective of the government, though the government may — and Burmese governments often did — fall far short of achieving that aim. The declared mission of the government was to provide the economic conditions necessary for the attainment of basic needs, so that each citizen will have ample time and opportunity for the fulfillment of his spiritual needs.

U Nu's socialism, and that of his successors, was presented to a great extent as a modern version of traditional thinking, not as a modern alternative to old ideas. The relationship between Buddhism and socialism is comparable to the one between "means" and "ends." The "ends" can be seen as the achievement of Buddhist ideas, and the suitable "means" of achieving them in the modern world is socialism. Socialism is a political and economic tool utilized in reaching the aim attached to the traditional image of the "good" society. Thus, socialist ideology has a distributive nature rather than a productive one: emphasis is put on governmental functions of allocation. The ultimate stated motive is achieving individual goals and not those of the collective as an entity.

There is a basic similarity between the views of U Nu and Ne Win in this respect, but emphasis on the "means" and "ends" relationship is put differently. In his writings and speeches U Nu dealt, mainly, with the "ends" — the vision of the ideal Buddhist state, which he discussed in terms of the "human golden age" of the past and which will return in the form of socialism. Ne Win, on the other hand, preaches much less the millenaristic orientation; he dwells on administrative and economic efficiency rather than on religion and ritual. His activity is focused on building the political center on the institutional level and on strengthening the bureaucracy and the army. Nevertheless, the basic affinity between Buddhism and socialism allows for self-identity on the basis of tradition, while also being part of the modern world.

This affinity between Buddhism and socialism is related to another main feature of Burmese socialism — its particularism and lack of Messianism. The Burmese way to socialism is not intended to be the solution to world problems, but a particular way of life for Burma.

What are the sources of this particularistic conception of socialism, which combined traditional with modern terms in forming the basis of collective self-identity? Traditional Burma was a distinctive political unit that had a centralized government, where the king ruled "with the grace of Buddha." Modern Burma is in many ways a continuation of the same traditional political structure. Hence the definition of the political collective is, to a great extent, given. In keeping with the past, even after gaining independence, the political structure is still largely defined in religious terms. This religious tradition, focused within a continuous socio-political system, is the basis of continuity in the unifying principles organizing commitments to the modern polity.

Viewing Burmese socialism as particularistic is connected with the nature of the traditional Burmese structure. In contrast to China, Burma was not a large empire with expansionist goals, but rather a closed structure which concentrated on its religious-cultural individuality. Development of this Burman uniqueness was aided by Theravada Buddhism, which holds a special place in Buddhism and was the basic cause of Burma's becoming an independent religious center. True, dreams of a universal kingdom had existed in which one of Burma's royalty, prophesied to be the future Buddha, will be king of the entire world. This, though, is a millenaristic belief understood in terms of the Golden Age which will begin at the end of the present cycle and which had no practical application. The absence of any real universal orientation in this sense during the traditional period might be related to the separatist trend in Burmese socialism today, as well as to the lack of Messianic pulse prevalent in some of the other socialist ideologies in this part of the world.

* * * * * * * *

Socialism in Burma differs from that in Africa in being the component introducing modernity into an existing cultural and political tradition, while in Africa socialism is more a basis of initially establishing a political-social framework. Yet the orientation of socialism in these African countries, as in Burma, is particularistic: It is not offered as a universal alternative. In other words, there is no claim for universal appeal. Burmese socialism — like "African" socialism — stresses its individuality and its uniqueness to a specific culture. Burmese socialism — again like "African" socialism — rejects inter-class conflict. The kind of socialism which tended to develop in both areas was predominantly of a harmonious solidary nature. The symbolism of conflict when used by institutionalized elites is mostly directed toward outside enemies: "colonialism" and "imperialism" as universal powers.

Still, the difference between these two complexes is mainly a difference of emphasis. Both conceptualize socialism as a major social change which is at the same time based on cultural continuity. But "African" socialism is mainly concerned with establishing a sense of continuity, while Burmese socialism is more concerned with proving the country's modernity by presenting socialism as the point of departure from the traditional past.*

Both similarities and differences are linked to the two main conditions presented above: the strength of the traditional unifying factors and the degree of existence of a universalistic orientation in the traditional period. The weakness of traditional unifying principles of "African" socialism leads to the search for traditional contents in socialism, while the prominence of such continuity of unifying factors of a special content in Burma is associated with the preoccupation with defining socialism as a proof of modernity. The absence of a universalistic orientation in the past in both complexes is connected with the inner-oriented particularistic character of socialism in Africa and in Burma.

* Since there is only a difference in emphasis, the boundaries between the two complexes are not very clearly marked. There are different shades of socialism in this respect, such as the types adopted in Mali and Senegal.

THE THIRD COMPLEX: RUSSIA AND CHINA

Two distinct characteristics typical of Russian socialism pertinent to our subject matter are, first, the central role held by ideas of conflict, as expressed in the priority given to concepts of class struggle in different periods. Enemies of the proletariat in Russia have been variously called Kulaks, parasites, intellectuals, cosmopolites – but they are all inner groups. The second characteristic is Messianism: viewing socialism – meaning the Russian brand of socialism – as the universal model of the good society, to be introduced into other countries.

What connection is there between the above-mentioned characteristics representative of Russian socialist ideology and the Russian heritage of the past? The continuity of the state framework has been a major influence here, in spite of changes in regime, borders, values, and social structure. But this is not the only important element of continuity. A wide range of commitments and motivations are inherited from the past as well. To take just one example, the relationship between nationalism and socialism in Russia, in a way, is contrary to that typifying socialistic Africa. In Russia, nationalism sustains socialism rather than the other way around. The socialistic regime's demands on individual liberties and economic interests are based, to a large degree, on loyalty to the Russian motherland. In short, Russian socialistic commitment greatly depends upon the fact that it is Russian.

Since commitments to the modern frames are to a great extent already given, Russian socialism – relative to the African type – need not assume integrative functions to such a great degree. In Russia, socialism can endure, to an extent, the elaboration of class-conflict ideas.

The second prominent feature typical of Russian socialism is Messianism, a concept also rooted in Russian tradition. The idea of being an active part of universal society is a renewal of the old Czarist Russian social concept of the place of Russia in the international European framework. A political-military struggle, combined with strong Western cultural influences (particularly German and French), led the Russian intelligentsia to develop an inferiority-superiority complex toward the West. The inferiority focused, mainly, on the technological level. Russian moral values were felt by many at the time to be equal, if not superior, to those of the West. This phenomenon is connected with the Messianic drive, the feeling of mission, that socialist Russia wishes to project: to build and then bestow to the world a

Russian model of a society more just than that of the West yet at the same time as modern as Western society.

These two characteristics also are important in Chinese socialism. The role of conflict is not only central in Maoist ideology but is even more distinct than in Russian socialism. According to Mao's definition, conflict exists not only in capitalist society but also in socialist society — and necessarily so. This view is opposite to the official Russian version of the problem. Conflict is the driving power which promotes progress and prevents reaction: hence, it gives vitality to socialist society.

The second characteristic — a strong Messianic drive — is also typical of Maoism, just as it is of Russian socialism. Maoist ideology defines itself as holding the solution to all social injustice. The Chinese regime has shown marked militancy, expressed in attempts to set forth the Chinese concept of socialism with every possible means at its disposal, ideological, military, or both. One of the outstanding expressions of the ideological militancy is the redefinition of conflict in terms of a universal war between the underdeveloped nations and the developed nations — non-Caucasians versus the white "race."

Here one must differentiate between missionary consciousness and power politics. Beyond the obvious political goals which the dissemination of Chinese or Russian influence helps to achieve, an independent sense of an ideological mission exists in both cases with regard to fulfilling an historical role in the development of mankind. The major traditional factor which makes the emphasis on conflict possible is the continuity in tradition in the sense presented above. The revolution in China, as in Russia, led to a re-evaluation of social values and goals, social institutions, and the comparative positions of different groups. But still there was a great continuity on all these levels, especially relevant to this problem — the continuity in commitments to the state. These have set the conditions allowing for the furthering of the element of conflict in social life. However, this element is only a necessary condition, as are other factors, such as those associated with the polarization of strata in traditional Chinese and Russian society, which also directly influence conflict formation.

The factor in traditional Chinese culture directly involved with the missionary orientation representative of socialist China is the traditional orientation of universality, the traditional concept of mankind in terms of its affinity to Chinese culture. In the Chinese view — in which China is "the center of the universe" — Chinese culture is the "only" culture. Other societies are judged according to their proximity to Chinese culture. This concept was transmitted to the revolutionary period and is related to the formation of militant socialism.

CONCLUSION

We have raised two questions: Are there meaningful combinations of different trends in the selection of socialist ideas and in relating them to other idea systems? And, which aspects of pre-modern societies influence these trends in selection?

If the three typical complexes of patterns of selection are distinguished, the second problem can be defined more concretely: Is it possible to discern pre-modern qualities which contribute to the creation of a self-contained socialist self-definition — either by establishing a new political framework or by constructing the modernity of an existing political framework — and other traditional qualities which contribute to the creation of socialist identity of a Messianic-militant nature which breaks out of its own boundaries? Or, to put it differently, what factors are associated with the manner in which each type of socialism addresses itself — particularistically, to a national or racial group, or universally, to the whole world? Another question which partly (but not fully, as will be seen later) merges with the previous one is: What factors are associated with class-conflict consciousness, as against an emphasis on integrational solidarity orientations?

Two characteristics function as a kind of pre-condition with relation to these different tendencies of selection:

1. The degree of continuity in the unifying principles which organize motivations and commitments on the individual and collective levels. Continuity in this sense does not exclude concrete value change, or even the emergence of a general anti-traditional orientation. On the contrary, the argument here is that, paradoxically, a certain amount of continuity in these traditional unifying principles is a kind of pre-condition for the development of an anti-traditional orientation in the selection processes.

2. The existence or non-existence of universalistic orientations in the pre-modern society. Universalistic orientations may be expressed in an ethnocentric outlook such as that of Imperial China or in relations of conflict and competition such as those of Czarist Russia. But both attitudes express self-conception in a wider universal context. The existence or non-existence of this outward orientation is related to the degree of militance in the specific socialist outlook.

Three complexes of selection have been described:

A. The first complex is typical of some African states, such as Ghana, Guinea, and Tanzania. In this "African"* complex, integrative rather than conflict orientations are dominant. The concept of the "capitalist enemy" is projected to the international level — rather than to inner-group conflict; there is an active search for traditional patterns which can be introduced as the common source of the modern socialist state. But the whole set of ideas characterizing "African" socialism is addressed to the African continent only. It is of a particularistic nature.

B. The second complex — typical especially of Burma but also of Ceylon — is similar to the first, except for a difference of emphasis given to different aspects of the connection between socialism and tradition. While in the African type the main effort is directed toward the search for continuity, in the Burmese system, from the same standpoint of assumed continuity with the past, the main emphasis is on the idea of socialism as the turning point for traditional Burma on its way toward modernization. But analogously with "African" socialism, the Burmese pattern is typically integrative in nature and inner-directed.

C. The third complex is that of the militant Communist great powers, Russia and China. Apart from power politics on the international level, they both possess a Messianic outlook toward the outer world, so that both the Russian and the Chinese ways to socialism are universally oriented. In both cases conflict orientation is very prominent, while the integrative aspects of socialism are weaker than in the previous instances. The main trend is revolutionary in yet another respect — the total rejection, on the ideological plane, of tradition.

Various factors — such as different aspects of modernization processes — occurring differently in various elites and classes are associated with these different trends in socialism. But it seems that the combination of these two factors — continuity in traditional unifying principles and universalistic orientation toward the outer world in the traditional society — have a special weight in relation to selection processes in socialism. In countries which have gone through the first phases of modernization — where erosion processes in the traditional society are intense but the old unifying principles are strong enough to check the threatening erosion and the universalistic outward orientation still exists — there is a good chance that militant, conflict-

---

* As stated above, adherents do not include all African socialist countries.

oriented socialism will occur. This kind of ideology is at the same time a phase of modernization and an act of protest against the threatening leading modern nations — the industrial democratic West.

In the first two complexes the characteristic emphasis is on integration through socialism and not on conflict. But the missionary orientation characteristic of the third type is not necessarily related to a complementary selection of conflict-type contents. The typical cases, Russia and China, are examples of socialism having tendencies toward both conflict and Messianism.

Czechoslovakia, however, is different and is characterized by the combination of an integrating tendency in the selection of socialist ideas with a Messianic tendency — expressed in the conception of the "Czechoslovak way" to socialism. Czechoslovak traditional culture contains the factor which is associated with the socialist-missionary orientation: a universalistic orientation. Indeed the Czech way to socialism views itself as a potential universal solution. Nevertheless, compared with Russia and China there is less focus on conflict. Other factors, not discussed here, also condition this characteristic combination.

Thus, the first two complexes are typically oriented toward a selection of integration content and are of a particularistic nature. But the third complex includes socialist systems having a universal missionary tendency in which the central place may be taken either by conflict-content or integration-content tendencies of selection. In this third complex, the most important examples of missionary orientation are Russia and China, both oriented to conflict. But the case of Czechoslovakia proves that there is nothing inevitable in the combination of conflict orientation with Messianism.

A SELECTED BIBLIOGRAPHY ON SOCIALISM

A. Comparative Socialism

de George, Richard. *The New Marxism,* New York, Pegasus, 1968.

Drachkovitch, Milorad (ed.). *Marxist Ideology in the Contemporary World,* New York, Praeger, 1966.

Drachkovitch, Milorad (ed.). *Marxism in the Modern World,* Stanford, Stanford University Press, 1965.

Fleron, Frederick (ed.). *Communist Studies in the Social Sciences,* New York, Rand McNally, 1969.

Friedrich, C. & Brzezinski, Z. *Totalitarian Dictatorship and Autocracy,* New York, Praeger, 1966.

Griffith, W.E. (ed.). *Communism in Europe,* Cambridge, Mass., M.I.T. Press, 1964.

Jacobs, Dan (ed.). *The New Communisms,* New York, Harper & Row, 1969.

Johnson, Chalmers (ed.). *Change in Communist Systems,* Stanford, Stanford University Press, 1970.

Kautsky, J. *Communism and the Politics of Development,* New York, John Wiley & Sons, 1968.

Kautsky, J. (ed.). *Political Change in Underdeveloped Countries: Nationalism and Communism,* New York, John Wiley & Sons, 1962.

Meyer, Alfred. *Communism,* New York, Random House, 1967.

Rubenstein, Alvin. *Communist Political Systems,* Englewood Cliffs, N.J., Prentice-Hall, 1966.

Scalapino, Robert. *The Communist Revolution in Asia,* Englewood Cliffs, N.J., Prentice-Hall, 1969.

Skilling, H.G. *The Governments of Communist East Europe,* New York, Thomas Y. Crowell, 1966.

Skilling, H.G. & Griffiths, F. *Interest Groups and Communist Politics,* Princeton, N.J., Princeton University Press, 1970.

Staar, Richard (ed.). *Aspects of Modern Communism,* Columbia, S.C., University of South Carolina Press, 1968.

B. Socialism in Russia and Eastern Europe

Russia

BOOKS

Armstrong, J.A. *The Soviet Bureaucratic Elite,* New York, Praeger, 1959.

Barghoorn, F.C. *Soviet Russian Nationalism,* London, Oxford University Press, 1956.

Benz, E. *The Eastern Orthodox Church,* New York, Doubleday, 1963.

Berdyaev, Nicolas. *The Origins of Russian Communism,* Ann Arbor, University of Michigan Press, 1955.

Berman, Harold. *Justice in the USSR,* New York, Vintage, 1963.

Black, Cyril (ed.). *The Transformation of Russian Society,* Cambridge, Mass., Harvard University Press, 1960.

Blum, Jerome. *Lord and Peasant in Russia,* Princeton, Princeton University Press, 1961.

Friedrich, C. and Brzezinski, Z. *Totalitarian Dictatorship and Autonomy,* New York, Praeger, 1965.

Carr, E.H. *The Bolshevik Revolution,* Vol. III, London, Macmillan, 1953.

Curtiss, John. *The Russian Church and the Soviet State,* Boston, Little, Brown, 1953.

Dinerstein, H.S. *Communism and the Russian Peasant,* New York, The Free Press, 1965.

Erikson, John. *The Soviet High Command,* New York, Macmillan, 1962.

Fainsod, Merle. *How Russia is Ruled,* Cambridge, Mass., Harvard University Press, 1967.

Florinsky, Michael. *Russia,* Vols. I-II, New York, Macmillan, 1969.

Haimson, Leopold. *Russian Marxists and the Origins of Bolshevism,* Cambridge, Mass., Harvard University Press, 1955.

Hazard, John. *The Soviet System of Government,* Chicago, University of Chicago Press, 1957.

Inkeles, A. and Bauer, R.A. *The Soviet Citizen,* Cambridge, Mass., Harvard University Press, 1959.

Karpovich, Michael. *Imperial Russia 1801-1917,* New York, H. Holt, 1932.

Kassof, Allen. *The Soviet Youth Program,* Cambridge, Mass., Harvard University Press, 1965.

Kolkowicz, Roman. *The Soviet Military and the Communist Party,* Princeton, Princeton University Press, 1967.

Lapenna, Ivo. *State and Law: Soviet and Yugoslav Theory,* New Haven, Yale University Press, 1964.

Lenin, V.I. *State and Revolution.*

Lenin, V.I. *What is to be Done.*

Marx, Karl. *Capital,* Vol. III.

Marx, Karl. *Critique of the Gotha Programme.*

Meyer, Alfred. *Leninism,* New York, Praeger, 1963.

Meynard, Sir John. *The Russian Peasant,* New York, Collier Books, 1942.

Pipes, Richard. *The Formation of the Soviet Union,* New York, Atheneum, 1968.

Pipes, Richard. *The Russian Intelligentsia,* New York, Columbia University Press, 1961.

Pushkarev, Sergei. *The Emergence of Modern Russia 1801-1917,* New York, H. Holt, 1963.

Schachtman, M. *The Bureaucratic Revolution: The Rise of the Stalinist State,* New York, 1962.

Schapiro, Leonard. *The Communist Party of the Soviet Union,* London, University Paperbacks, 1970.

Schapiro, Leonard. *The Government and Politics of the Soviet Union,* New York, Vintage, 1967.

Schapiro, Leonard. *The Origin of the Communist Autocracy,* New York, Praeger, 1965.

Schlesinger, R. *The Nationalities Problem and Soviet Administration,* London, Routledge and Kegan Paul, 1956.

Scott, Derek. *Russian Political Institutions,* New York, Praeger, 1961.

Spinka, Matthew. *The Church in Soviet Russia,* New York, Oxford University Press, 1956.

Stalin, I.V. *Economic Problems in the USSR,* New York, International Publishers, 1952.

Stalin, I.V. *Foundations of Leninism,* New York, International Publishers, 1939.

Stalin, I.V. *Problems of Leninism,* Moscow, Foreign Language Publishing House, 1953.

Treadgold, Donald (ed.). *Soviet and Chinese Communism,* Seattle, University of Washington Press, 1967.

Treadgold, Donald (ed.). *Twentieth Century Russia,* Chicago, Rand McNally, 1964.

Ulam, Adam. *The New Face of Soviet Totalitarianism,* New York, Praeger, 1963.

Ulam, Adam. *The Unfinished Revolution,* New York, Random House, 1960.

Venturi, Franco. *Roots of Revolution,* New York, Grosset and Dunlop, 1966.

Vernadsky, George. *A History of Russia,* New Haven, Yale University Press, 1948.

Yarmolinsky, Adam. *Literature Under Communism,* Bloomington, Ind., Indiana University Press, 1960.

Czechoslovakia and Yugoslavia

BOOKS

Avakumovic, Ivan. *History of the Communist Party of Yugoslavia,* Aberdeen, Aberdeen University Press, 1964.

Bauer, Otto. *Die Nazionalitatenfrage und die Sozialdemokratie,* Vienna, Wiener Volksbuchhandburg, 1924.

Benes, E. *Democracy, Today and Tomorrow,* London, Macmillan, 1939.

Benes, E. *My Memoirs, From Munich to New War and New Victory,* London, Allen, 1959.

Borkenau, Franz. *World Communism,* Ann Arbor, University of Michigan Press, 1962.

Brock, Peter. *The Political and Social Doctrines of the Unity of Czech Brethren,* The Hague, Mouton, 1967.

Brzezinski, Z.K. *The Soviet Bloc,* Cambridge, Mass., Harvard University Press, 1967.

Chmelap, Josef. *Political Parties in Czechoslovakia,* Prague, 1926.

Clisshold, Stephen (ed.). *A Short History of Yugoslavia,* New York, Cambridge University Press, 1966.

Dedijer, Vladimir. *Tito Speaks,* New York, 1953.

Denis, Ernst. *La Boheme Depuis La Montagne Blanche,* Vol. II, Paris, 1930.

Drachkovitch, M. (ed.). *Marxism in the Modern World,* Stanford, Stanford University Press, 1965.

Erlich, Vera. *Family in Transition,* Princeton, Princeton University Press, 1966.

Feierabend, Ladislav. *Agricultural Cooperatives in Czechoslovakia,* New York, Mid-European Studies Center, 1952.

Fisher, Jack. *Yugoslavia: A Multinational State,* San Francisco, Chandler, 1966.

Footman, David (ed.). *International Communism,* London, 1960.

Golan, Galia. *The Czechoslovak Reform Movement,* Cambridge, Cambridge University Press, 1971.

Golan, Galia. *Reform Rule in Czechoslovakia,* Cambridge, Cambridge University Press, 1973.

Griffith, William. *Communism in Europe,* Vol. I, Cambridge, Mass., M.I.T. Press, 1964.

Heymann, F.G. *John Zizka and the Hussite Revolution,* Princeton, Princeton University Press, 1955.

Hoffman, G. and Neal, F.W. *Yugoslavia and the New Communism,* New York, Twentieth Century Fund, 1962.

Jackson, George. *Comintern and Peasant in East Europe 1919-1930,* New York, Columbia University Press, 1966.

Jelavich, Chas. and Barbara (eds.). *The Balkans in Transition,* Berkeley, University of California Press, 1963.

Kann, Robert. *Multi-National Empire: Nationalism and National Reform in the Habsburg Monarchy,* Vol. I, New York, Columbia University Press, 1950.

Kerner, R. (ed.). *Czechoslovakia: Twenty Years of Independence,* Berkeley, University of California Press, 1940.

Kohn, Hans. *Nationalism: A Study in its Origins and Background,* New York, Collier, 1944.

Korbel, Josef. *The Communist Subversion of Czechoslovakia 1938-1948,* Princeton, Princeton University Press, 1959.

Kozak, Jan. *How Parliament Can Play a Revolutionary Part in the Transition to*

Socialism and the Role of the Popular Masses, London, Independent Information Center, 1961.

Krofta, Kamil. *The Nationalities Development of the Czechoslovak Land,* Prague, 1934.

Kusin, V.V. *The Intellectual Origins of the Prague Spring,* Cambridge, Cambridge University Press, 1971.

Lendvai, Paul. *Eagles in Cobwebs,* London, MacDonald, 1965.

Lenin, V.I. *A Contribution to the Question of a National Policy.*

Lettrich, Josef. *History of Modern Slovakia,* New York, Praeger, 1965.

London, Kurt (ed.). *Eastern Europe in Transition,* Baltimore, Johns Hopkins Press, 1966.

Macartney, C.A. *Hungary and Her Successors,* New York, 1937.

Macartney, C.A., and Palmer, A.W. *Independent Eastern Europe,* London, Macmillan, 1962.

Macek, J. *The Hussite Movement in Bohemia,* Prague, 1958.

McClellan, W.D. *Svetozar Markovic and The Origins of Balkan Socialism,* Princeton, Princeton University Press, 1964.

McKenzie, Kermit, *Comintern and World Revolution 1928-1943,* New York, Columbia University Press, 1964.

Marx, Karl, and Engels, Friedrich. *Revolution and Counter-Revolution.*

Masaryk, T.G. *The Making of a State,* New York, H. Fertig, 1969.

Masaryk, T.G. *Les Problemes de la Democratie,* Paris, Riviere, 1924.

Masaryk, T.G. *The Spirit of Russia,* New York, H. Fertig, 1967.

Materijali za Ideoloski Odgoj Clanova Narodnog Fronta, Zagreb, 1969.

Odlozilik, O. *Jan Amos Komensky,* Chicago, Czechoslovak National Council of America, 1942.

Pelikan, J. (ed.). *The Political Trials in Czechoslovakia.* London, 1971.

Peroutka, Ferdinand. *Jaci Jsme,* Prague, 1924.

Popovic, Nenad. *Yugoslavia, The New Class in Crisis,* Syracuse, N.Y., Syracuse University Press, 1968.

Programme of the Communist Party of the Soviet Union. Moscow, Foreign Language Publishing House, 1961.

The Programme of the League of Yugoslav Communists, April 1958, Belgrade, 1958.

Remington, Robin A. (ed.). *Winter in Prague,* Cambridge, Mass., M.I.T. Press, 1969.

Seton-Watson, Hugh. *Eastern Europe Between the Wars 1918-1941,* New York, Harper and Row, 1967.

Seton-Watson, Hugh. *The Eastern European Revolution,* London, 1952.

Seton-Watson, R.W. *History of the Czechs and Slovaks,* Hamden, Conn., Archon Books, Shoe String Press, 1965.

Seton-Watson, R.W. *Slovakia Then and Now,* London, Allen, 1931.

Seton-Watson, R.W. *The Southern Slav Question and the Habsburg Monarchy,* New York, H. Fertig, 1969.

Shoup, Paul. *Communism and the National Question,* New York, Columbia University Press, 1968.

IV Sjezd Svazu Czechoslovenskych Spisovatelu, Prague, 1968.

Spinka, Matthew. *John Amos Comenius,* Chicago, University of Chicago Press, 1943.

Spinka, Matthew. *John Hus and the Czech Reform,* Chicago, University of Chicago Press, 1941.

Stalin, V.I. *Marxism and the National and Colonial Question,* Moscow, Foreign Language Publishing House, 1935.

Taborsky, Eduard. *Communism in Czechoslovakia,* Princeton, Princeton University Press, 1961.

Taborsky, Eduard. *Czechoslovak Democracy at Work,* London, 1945.

Thomson, S.H. *Czechoslovakia's European History,* Princeton, Princeton University Press, 1963.

Tito, J.B. *Selected Speeches and Articles,* Zagreb, 1963.

Tomasevich, J. *Peasant Politics and Economic Change in Yugoslavia,* Stanford, Stanford University Press, 1955.

Trouton, Ruth. *The Peasant Renaissance in Yugoslavia,* London, Routledge and Kegan Paul, 1952.

Ulam, Adam. *Titoism and the Cominform,* Cambridge, Mass., Harvard University Press, 1952.

Vucinich, Wayne (ed.). *Contemporary Yugoslavia,* Berkeley, University of California Press, 1969.

Wiskemann, Elizabeth. *Czechs and Germans,* London, Oxford University Press, 1938.

Wolff, Robert. *The Balkans in Our Time,* Cambridge, Mass., Harvard University Press, 1956.

Zaninovich, George. *The Development of Socialist Yugoslavia,* Baltimore, 1968.

Zeman, Z.A.B. *Prague Spring,* London, 1968.

Zinner, Paul. *Communist Strategy and Tactics in Czechoslovakia, 1918-1948,* London, Pall Mall, 1963.

ARTICLES

Aczel, Tamas. "Spokesman of Revolution," *Problems of Communism,* Vol. XVIII, No. 4-5, 1969.

Burkes, R.V. "The Removal of Rankovic: An Early Interpretation of the July Yugoslav Party Plenum," Rand Corporation Memorandum, Santa Monica, 1966.

Bushkoff, Leonard. "Marxism, Communism and the Revolutionary Tradition in the Balkans," *East European Quarterly,* Vol. I, No. 4.

Golan, Galia. "The Road to Reform," *Problems of Communism,* Vol. XX, No. 3.

Golan, Galia. "The Short-Lived Liberal Experiment in Czechoslovak Socialism," *Orbis,* Vol. XIII, No. 4.

Hykisch, Anton. "The Everyday Routine of the Younger Brother," *Plamen,* 1, 1968.

Isaacs, H. "Group Identity and Political Change," *Survey,* No. 69, October, 1968.

Kaplan, Karel. "Deliberations on the Political Trials," *Nova Mysl* 6-8, 1968.

Rubenstein, Alvin. "Yugoslavia's Opening Society," *Current History,* Vol. XLVIII, No. 283.

Taborsky, Edward. "Local Government in Czechoslovakia 1919-1948," *The American Slavic and East European Review,* Vol. 10, No. 3.

Tomasic, D.A. "Nationality Problems and Partisan Yugoslavia," *Journal of Central European Affairs,* Vol. 6, No. 2.

"2000 Words," *Literarni Listy,* 27 June 1968.

C. Socialism in China

Barnett, A. Doak. *China After Mao,* Princeton, Princeton University Press, 1967.

Barnett, A. Doak. *Communist China in Perspective,* New York, Praeger, 1962, especially Ch. II, "Continuity and Change," pp. 27–50.

De-Bary, William T., et al. (comps.). *Sources of Chinese Tradition,* 2 vols., New York, Columbia University Press, 1967.

Bernal, Martin. "Chinese Socialism before 1913," in Jack Gray (ed.), *Modern China's Search for Political Form,* Oxford, 1969, pp. 66–96.

Bowie, R.R. and Fairbank, J.K. (eds.). *Communist China 1955-1959, Policy Documents with Analysis,* Cambridge, Mass., Harvard University Press, 1962.

Ch'en, Jerome (ed.). *Mao,* Englewood Cliffs, N.J., Prentice-Hall, 1969.

Cohen, Arthur A. *The Communism of Mao Tse-Tung,* Chicago, University of Chicago Press, 1964.

Compton, Boyd. *Mao's China: Party Reform Documents, 1942-1944,* Seattle, University of Washington Press, 1967.

Crozier, Ralph G. (ed.). *China's Cultural Legacy and Communism,* New York, Praeger, 1970.

Eisenstadt, S.N. "Tradition, Change, and Modernity: Reflections on the Chinese Experience," in Ping-ti Ho and Tang Tsou (eds.), *China in Crisis,* Vol. 1, Chicago, University of Chicago Press, 1968, pp. 753–74.

Fairbank, John K. "The People's Middle Kingdom," *Foreign Affairs,* July 1966, pp. 574–86.

Fairbank, John K. *The United States and China,* Cambridge, Mass., Harvard University Press, 1971.

Feuerwerker, Albert. "China's History in Marxian Dress," *American Historical Review,* LXVI:2, January 1961, pp. 323–53.

Feuerwerker, Albert. "From 'Federalism' to 'Capitalism' in Recent Historical Writing from Mainland China," *Journal of Asian Studies,* XVIII, November 1958, pp. 107–16.

Fitzgerald, C.P. *The Birth of Communist China,* Harmondsworth, Penguin, 1964.

Ho, Ping-ti. "Salient Aspects of China's Heritage," in Ping-ti Ho and Tang Tsou, *China in Crisis,* Vol. 1, pp. 1–92.

Johnson, Chalmers. *Peasant Nationalism and Communist Power,* Stanford, Stanford University Press, 1962.

Levenson, Joseph R. "Communist China in Time and Space: Roots and Rootlessness," *China Quarterly,* 39 (July-September 1969), pp. 1—11.

Levenson, Joseph R. *Confucian China and Its Modern Fate: A Trilogy,* Berkeley, University of California Press, 1968, especially Pt. I, pp. 134—45, 156—63; Pt. III, pp. 47—82, 110—25.

Levenson, Joseph K. "Marxism and the Middle Kingdom," *Diplomat,* September 1966, pp. 48—51.

Lifton, Robert J. *Revolutionary Immortality: Mao Tse-tung and the Chinese Cultural Revolution,* New York, Random House, 1968.

Lifton, Robert J. *Thought Reform and the Psychology of Totalism,* Harmondsworth, Penguin, 1961.

Lowe, Donald M. *The Function of 'China' in Marx, Lenin and Mao,* Berkeley, University of California Press, 1966.

MacFarquhar, R. *The Hundred Flowers Campaign,* New York, Praeger, 1960.

Mao Tse-tung. *Selected Works,* 4 vols., Peking, Foreign Languages Press, 1965.

Meisner, Maurice. *Li Ta-chao and the Origins of Chinese Marxism,* Cambridge, Mass., Harvard University Press, 1967.

Munro, Donald J. *The Concept of Man in Early China,* Stanford, Stanford University Press, 1969.

Needham, Joseph. "The Past in China's Present," *The Centennial Review,* Vol. 4, 1960, pp. 145—78, 281—308.

Nivison, David S. "Communist Ethics and Chinese Tradition," *Journal of Asian Studies,* 16, November 1956, pp. 51—74.

Pandit, Tooshar. "Totalitarianism vs. Traditionalism," *Problems of Communism,* XII:6, November-December 1963, pp. 10—14.

Pye, Lucian W. *The Spirit of Chinese Politics,* Cambridge, Mass., M.I.T. Press, 1968.

Scalapino, Robert A. "Prelude to Marxism — The Chinese Student Movement in Japan, 1900-1910," in A. Feuerwerker et al. (eds.), *Approaches to Modern Chinese History,* Berkeley, University of California Press, 1967, pp. 190—215.

Scalapino, R.A., and Schiffrin, Harold. "Early Socialist Currents in the Chinese Revolutionary Movement," *Journal of Asian Studies,* XVIII: 3, May 1959, pp. 321—42.

Schiffrin, Harold Z. "The 'Great Leap' Image in Early Chinese Nationalism," *Asian and African Studies,* Vol. 3, 1967, pp. 101-19.

Schram, Stuart R. "Chinese and Leninist Components in the Personality of Mac Tse-tung," *Asian Survey,* III: 6, June 1963, pp. 259—73.

Schram, Stuart R. *Mao Tse-tung,* Harmondsworth, Penguin, 1966.

Schram, Stuart R. *The Political Thought of Mao Tse-tung,* Harmondsworth, Penguin, 1969.

Schram, Stuart R. et al. "What Is Maoism: A Symposium," *Problems of*

Communism, XV:5, September-October 1966, pp. 1–30. See also Vol. XVI:2, April-March 1967, pp. 91–99.

Schram, Stuart R. and d'Encausse, Helene Carrere (eds.). *Marxism and Asia*, London, Allen Lane, 1969.

Schurmann, Franz. *Ideology and Organization in Communist China*, Berkeley, University of California Press, 1968, esp. pp. xxxiv-lii, pp. 1–104, 506–31.

Schurmann, Franz. "On Revolutionary Conflict," *Journal of International Affairs*, XXIII:1, Winter 1969, pp. 36–53.

Schwartz, Benjamin I. "China and the West in the 'Thought of Mao Tse-tung,' " in Ping-ti Ho and Tang Tsou (eds.), *China in Crisis*, Vol. 1, pp. 365–96.

Schwartz, Benjamin I. *Chinese Communism and the Rise of Mao*, New York, Harper, 1967.

Schwartz, Benjamin I. *Communism and China: Ideology in Flux*, Cambridge, Mass., Harvard University Press, 1968.

Schwartz, Benjamin I. "Modernization and the Maoist Vision – Some Reflections on Chinese Communist Goals," *China Quarterly*, 21, January-March 1965, pp. 3–19.

Snow, Edgar. *Red Star Over China*, New York, Random House, 1938.

Taylor, George E. "Communism and Chinese History," in Donald W. Treadgold (ed.), *Soviet and Chinese Communism*, Seattle, University of Washington Press, 1967, pp. 24–36.

Torr, Dona. *Marx on China 1853-1860*, London, Lawrence and Wishart, 1967.

Tsou, Tang. "Revolution, Reintegration and Crisis in Communist China: A Framework for Analysis," in Ping-ti Ho and Tang Tsou (eds.), *China in Crisis*, Vol. 1, pp. 277–364.

Van Slyke, Lyman P. *Enemies and Friends, the United Front in Chinese Communist History*, Stanford, Stanford University Press, 1967.

Wright, Arthur F. "Struggle vs. Harmony – Symbols of Competing Values in Modern China," *World Politics*, VI: 1, October 1953, pp. 31–44.

Zagoria, Donald S. *The Sino-Soviet Conflict 1956-61*, New York, Atheneum, 1966.

D. Socialism in Burma

Ady, Peter. "Economic Basis of Unrest in Burma," *Foreign Affairs*, 1951.

Andrus, Russell J. *Burmese Economic Life*, Stanford, Stanford University Press, 1947.

Badgley, John H. "Two Styles of Military Rule: Thailand and Burma," *Government and Opposition*, 1969.

Badgley, John H. "Burma: The Nexus of Socialism and Two Political Traditions," *Asian Survey*, 1965.

Badgley, John H. "Burma's Zealot Wungyi's: Maoists or St. Simonists," *Asian Survey*, 1965.

Bechert, Heinz. "Theravada Buddhist Sangha: Some General Observations on Historical and Political Factors in its Development," *Journal of Asian Studies,* 1970.

Benda, Harry J. "The Structure of Southeast Asian History," in R.O. Tilman (ed.), *Man, State and Society in Contemporary Southeast Asia,* London, Pall Mall, 1969.

Butwell, Richard. *U Nu of Burma,* Stanford, Stanford University Press, 1960.

Butwell, Richard. "Civilians and Soldiers in Burma," *Studies on Asia,* 1961.

Butwell, Richard. "The Four Failures of U Nu's Second Premiership," *Asian Survey,* 1962.

Butwell, Richard, & von der Mehden, F.R. "The 1960 Election in Burma," *Pacific Affairs,* 1960.

Cady, John F. *A History of Modern Burma,* Ithaca, N.Y., Cornell University Press, 1958.

Cady, John F. *Southeast Asia: Its Historical Development,* New York, McGraw-Hill, 1964.

Cady, John F. *Thailand, Burma, Laos and Cambodia,* Englewood Cliffs, N.J., Prentice-Hall, 1963.

Emerson, Rupert. *From Empire to Nation,* Cambridge, Mass., Harvard University Press, 1960.

Emerson, Rupert. "Paradoxes of Asian Nationalism," in R.O. Tilman (ed.), *Man, State and Society in Contemporary Southeast Asia,* London, Pall Mall, 1969.

Furnivall, John S. *Colonial Policy and Practice: A Comparative Study of Burma and Netherlands India,* New York, New York University Press, 1948.

Furnivall, John S. *An Introduction to the Political Economy of Burma,* Rangoon, Peoples Literature Committee and House, 1957.

Guyot, D. "The Burma Independence Army: A Political Movement in Military Garb," in J. Silverstein (ed.), *Southeast Asia in World War Two,* New Haven, Conn., 1966.

Guyot, James F. "Bureaucratic Transformation in Burma," in Ralph Braibanti et al., *Asian Bureaucratic Systems Emergent From the British Imperial Traditions,* Durham, N.C., Duke University Press, 1966.

Guyot, James F. "Political Involvement in Burma," *Journal of Contemporary Administration,* 1970.

Hagen, Everett E. *The Economic Development of Burma,* Washington, National Planning Association, 1956.

Harvey, G.E. *History of Burma,* London, Longmans Green, 1925.

Harvey, G.E. *British Rule in Burma 1824-1942,* London, Faber & Faber, 1949.

Hatley, R. "The Overseas Indian in Southeast Asia: Burma, Malaysia and Singapore," in R.O. Tilman (ed.), *Man, State and Society in Contemporary Southeast Asia,* London, Pall Mall, 1969.

von Heine-Geldern, Robert. *Conceptions of State and Kingship in Southeast Asia,* Ithaca, Cornell Data Paper No. 18, 1956.

Hlaing, U Aye. *A Study of Economic Development of Burma 1870-1940,* Rangoon, 1964.

Johnstone, W.C. *Burma's Foreign Policy: A Study in Neutralism,* Cambridge, Mass., Harvard University Press, 1963.

King, Winston L. "Buddhism and Political Power in Burma," *Studies on Asia,* 1961.

Lissak, Moshe. "Social Change, Mobilization and Exchange of Services Between the Military Establishment and the Civil Society: The Burmese Case," *Economic Development and Cultural Change,* 1964.

Lissak, Moshe. "The Military in Burma: Innovations and Frustrations," *Asian and African Studies,* 1968.

Luce, G.H. "Economic Life of the Early Burmese," in *Burma Research Society,* Fiftieth Anniversary Publications, 1960.

Maung, Maung (ed.). *Aung San of Burma,* The Hague, Martinus Nijhoff, 1962.

Maung, Maung. "Cultural Values and Economic Change In Burma," *Asian Survey,* 1964.

Maung, Maung, *Burma and General Ne Win,* New York, Asia Press, 1969.

Maung, Mya. *Burma and Pakistan: A Comparative Study of Development,* New York, Praeger, 1971.

Maw, Ba. *Breakthrough in Burma: Memoires of a Revolution, 1939-1946,* New Haven, Conn., Yale University Press, 1968.

von der Mehden, Fred R. "The Changing Pattern of Religion and Politics in Burma," *Studies on Asia,* 1961.

Mendelsohn, Michael. "A Messianic Buddhist Association in Upper Burma," *Bulletin of the School of Oriental and African Studies,* 1961.

Mootham, O.H. *Burmese Buddhist Law,* London, Oxford University Press, 1939.

U Nu. *Towards a Welfare State,* Rangoon, 1952.

U Nu. *Towards a Socialist State,* Rangoon, 1958.

U Tan Pe. *Sun Over Burma,* Rangoon, 1949.

Nash, Manning. *The Golden Road to Modernity: Village Life in Contemporary Burma,* New York, John Wiley, 1965.

Nash, Manning. "Burmese Buddhism in Everyday Life," in R.O. Tilman (ed.), *Man, State and Society in Contemporary Southeast Asia,* London, Pall Mall, 1969.

Pfanner, M.R. "Burma," in Frank H. Golay, et al. *Underdevelopment and Economic Nationalism in Southeast Asia,* Ithaca, New York, Cornell University Press, 1969.

Pye, L.W. "The Army in Burmese Politics," in J.J. Johnson (ed.), *The Role of the Military in Underdeveloped Countries,* Princeton, Princeton University Press, 1962.

Pye, L.W. *Politics, Personality and Nation-Building: Burma's Search for Identity,* New Haven, Conn., Yale University Press, 1962.

Pye, Maung Maung. *Burma in the Crucible,* Rangoon, 1951.

Redfield, Robert. *Peasant Society and Culture,* Chicago, University of Chicago Press, 1956.

Sarkisyanz, M. "On the Place of U Nu's Buddhist Socialism in Burma's History of Ideas," *Studies on Asia,* 1961.

Sarkisyanz, M. *Buddhist Backgrounds of the Burmese Revolution*, The Hague, Martinus Nijhoff, 1965.

Sarkisyanz, M. "The Social Ethics of Buddhism and the Socio-Economic Development of Southeast Asia," in Martin Rudner (ed.), *Society and Development in Asia: Asian and African Studies* 6, Jerusalem, Israel Oriental Society, 1970.

Silverstein, Josef. "Burma," in George McT. Kahin (ed.), *Governments and Politics in Southeast Asia,* Ithaca, New York, Cornell University Press, 1959.

Silverstein, Josef. "First Steps in the Burmese Way to Socialism," *Asian Survey,* 1964.

Silverstein, Josef. "Ne Win's Revolution Considered," *Asian Survey,* 1966.

Silverstein, Josef. "Burma Socialist Program Party and its Rivals: A One Plus Party System," *Journal of Southeast Asian History,* 1967.

Smith, Donald E. *Religion and Politics in Burma,* Princeton, Princeton University Press, 1965.

Solomon, R.L. "Saya San and the Burmese Rebellion," *Modern Asian Studies,* 1969.

Stifel, L.D. "Economics of the Burmese Way to Socialism," *Asian Survey,* 1971.

Stifel, L.D. "Burmese Socialism: Economic Problems of the First Decade," *Pacific Affairs,* 1972.

Thompson, J.S. "Marxism in Burma," in Frank N. Trager (ed.), *Marxism in Southeast Asia,* Stanford, Stanford University Press, 1959.

Thompson, V. "Burma's Communists," *Far Eastern Survey,* 1948.

Trager, Frank. *Building a Welfare State in Burma, 1948-1956,* New York, Institute of Pacific Relations, 1958.

Trager, Frank. *Burma, From Kingdom to Republic,* New York, Praeger, 1966.

Trager, Frank. "Burma, 1967 — A Better Ending than Beginning," *Asian Survey,* 1968.

Trager, Frank. "The Failure of U Nu and the Return of the Armed Forces in Burma," *Review of Politics,* 1963.

Thaung. "Burmese Kingship in Theory and Practice During the Reign of Mindon," *Journal of the Burma Research Society,* 1959.

U Ba U. *My Burma,* New York, 1959.

Wittfogel, Karl A. *Oriental Despotism: A Comparative Study of Total Power,* New Haven, Conn., Yale University Press, 1957.

Walinsky, Louis J. *Economic Development in Burma 1951-1960,* New York, Twentieth Century Fund, 1962.

Walinsky, Louis J. "Burma," in Everett E. Hagen (ed.), *Planning Economic Development,* Homewood, Ill., 1963.

Walinsky, Louis J. "The Rise and Fall of U Nu," *Pacific Affairs,* 1965-1966.

Walinsky, Louis J. "The Role of the Military in Development Planning in Burma," in R.O. Tilman (ed.), *Man, State and Society in Contemporary Southeast Asia,* London, Pall Mall, 1969.

Win, Sein. *The Split Story, An Account of Recent Political Upheaval in Burma with Emphasis on the AFPFL,* Rangoon, 1959.

Wickizer, V.D. & Bennett, M.K. *The Rice Economy of Monsoon Asia,* Stanford, Stanford University Press, 1941.

E. Socialism in Africa

Africa Report, VIII: 5, May 1963. Dedicated to African Socialism.
African Forum, I: 3, 1966. Dedicated to African Socialism.
Afrifa, A.A. *The Ghana Coup – 24th February 1966,* London, Frank Cass, 1967.
Alexandre, P. "Marxisme et Tradition Culturelle Africaine," *L'Afrique et l'Asie,* 1964, pp. 8–25.
Amram, A.K. "African Socialism," *Presence Africaine,* 64, 1967, pp. 6–30.
Andrain, C. "Democracy and Socialism: Ideologies of African Leaders," in D. Apter (ed.), *Ideology and Discontent,* London, 1964, pp. 155–205.
Anglin, D.G. "Ghana, the West and the Soviet Union," *Canadian Journal of Economics and Political Science,* XXIV, 1958, pp. 152–165.
Apter, D.E. *Ghana in Transition,* New York, Atheneum, 1963.
Apter, D.E. "The Role of Traditionalism in the Political Modernization of Ghana and Uganda," *World Politics,* XIII, 1960, pp. 45–74.
Apter, D.E. "Some Reflections on the Role of a Political Opposition in New Nations," *Comparative Studies in Society and History,* June 1962, pp. 154–68.
Arnault, J. *Du Colonilisme au Socialisme,* Paris, Editions Sociales, 1966.
"The Arusha Declaration and TANU's Policy on Socialism and Self-Reliance," Dar es Salaam, TANU Publicity Section, 1967.
Austin, D. "Opposition in Ghana: 1947-1967," *Government and Opposition,* II, 1967, pp. 524–39.
Balandier, G. "De la Négritude au Socialisme," *Jeune Afrique,* Dec. 3, 1962, pp. 28–29.
Bankole, Timothy. *Kwame Nkrumah,* Evanston, Northwestern University Press, 1963.
Beauchamp, K. "African Socialism in Ghana," *Spearhead,* I, 1962, pp. 21–25.
Behrman, L. "Party and State Relations in Guinea," in J. Butler and A.A. Castagno (eds.), *Politics in Africa,* pp. 317–42.
Beichman, A. "Western Socialists and Ghana," *Transition,* VI: 30, 1967, pp. 28–29.
Berg, E.J. "Socialism and Economic Development in Tropical Africa," *Quarterly Journal of Economics,* LXXVIII, 1964, pp. 549–73.
Bhambri, R.S. "Marxist Economic Doctrines and their Relevance to Problems of Economic Development in Nigeria," *Nigerian Journal of Economic and Social Studies,* VI: 2, 1964, pp. 185–98.
Bienin, N. "The Party and the No-Party State: Tanganyika and the Soviet Union," *Transition,* III: 13, 1964, pp. 25–32.
Bienin, N. *Tanzania: Party Transformation and Economic Development,* Princeton, Princeton University Press, 1967.

Bomani, M.O. "Tanzania: Towards a One-Party State," *Civilisation,* XV, 1965, pp. 493–503.

Boyon, J. "Une Idéologie Africaine: Le Nkrumaisme," *Revue Française de Science Politique,* XIII, 1963, pp. 68–87.

Bretton, H.L. *The Rise and Fall of Kwame Nkrumah,* London, 1967.

Brzezinski, Z.K. "Communism and the Emerging Nations," in J.R. Pennock (ed.), *Self Government and Modernizing Nations,* Englewood Cliffs, N.J., Prentice-Hall, 1964.

Brockway, A.F. *African Socialism,* Dufour, 1963.

Caiolli, A. *African Communism,* Lusaka, Kingston's Ltd., 1966.

Calvez, J.Y. "Nouvelle Etape du Socialisme Africaine," *Projet,* I, January 1966, pp. 15–24.

Césaire, Aimé. Sékou-Touré — His Political Thought," *Spearhead,* I, 1962, pp. 9–13.

Charles, B. "Le Socialisme Africaine," *Revue Française des Sciences Politiques,* XV, 5, October 1965.

Clairmonte, F.F. "Cuba and Africa," *Journal of Modern African Studies,* II, 1964, pp. 419–30.

Cliffe, L. "Socialist Education in Tanzania," *Mwazo* (Kampala) I, 2, December 1967.

Cliffe, L. "Tanzanian Socialism — New Emphasis," *Venture,* XIX: 6, June 1967.

Colloque sur les Politiques de Developpement et des Diversses Voies Africaines du Socialisme, *Papers,* Dakar, 1962.

Cook, M. *Nationhood and the African Road to Socialism,* Paris, 1962.

Cory, M. "Reform of Tribal Institutions in Tanganyika," *Journal of African Administration,* XII, 1960, pp. 77–84.

Cox, I. "Africa and Socialism," *World Marxist Review,* IX: 2, 1966, pp. 30–34.

Cox, I. *Socialist Ideas in Africa,* London, 1966.

Diarra, I. "The Mass Party and Socialist Construction," *World Marxist Review,* January, 1967, pp. 30–34.

Dowse, R.E. "Ghana: One Party or Totalitarianism," *British Journal of Sociology,* XVIII, 1967, pp. 251–68.

Drake, St. .C. "Pan-Africanism, Negritude, and the African Personality," *Boston University Graduate Journal,* X, 1961, pp. 38–51.

Ehrlich, C. "Some Aspects of Economic Policy in Tanganyika," *Journal of Modern African Studies,* II, 1964, pp. 265–77.

Emerson, R. and Kilson, M. (eds.). *The Political Awakening of Africa,* Englewood Cliffs, N.J., Prentice-Hall, 1965.

Fanon, F. *Toward the African Revolution.* New York, Grove Press, 1968.

Fanret, J. "Le Traditionalism par Excès de Modernité," *Archives Européennes de Sociologies,* I, 1967, pp. 71–93.

Ferkiss, V.G. *Africa's Search for Identity,* New York, 1966.

Fisher, G. "Quelques Aspects de la Doctrine Politique Guinéene," *Civilisation,* IX, 1959, pp. 457–78.

Fitch, B. and Oppenheimer, M. *Ghana: End of an Illusion.* New York, Monthly Review Press, 1966.

Fougey Rollas, P. *Modernisation des Hommes: L'Examplê du Senegal,* Paris, 1967.

Friedland, W.H. and Rosberg, C.G. (eds.). *African Socialism,* Stanford, Stanford University Press, 1964.

Ghai, Y. "Kenya's Socialism," *Transition,* V:20, 1965.

Gingyera-Pinyewa, A.G.G. "Prospects for One-Party System in Uganda," *East Africa,* X, 1968, pp. 15—23.

Green, R.H. "Four African Development Plans: Ghana, Kenya, Nigeria, and Tanzania," *Journal of Modern African Studies,* III, 1965, pp. 249—79.

Gregor, A.J. *Contemporary Radical Ideologies,* New York, Random House, 1967, esp. Chapter VII on African Socialism.

Gregor, A.J. "African Socialism, Socialism and Fascism," *Review of Politics,* XXIX, 1967, pp. 324—53.

Grundy, K.W. "The Class Struggle in Africa," *Journal of Modern African Studies,* II, 1964, pp. 379—93.

Grundy, K.W. "Nkrumah's Theory of Underdevelopment," *World Politics,* XV, 1963, pp. 438—54.

Guerin, D. "Trade Unionism and Socialism in Ghana," *Presence Africaine,* XXIII: 51, 1964, pp. 16—25.

Guibert, A. *Léopold Sédar Senghor: L'Homme et 'Oeuvre,* Paris, 1962.

"Guinea After Five Years," *World Today,* XX, 1964, pp. 113—21.

Hamon, L. "La Voie Africaine du Socialisme selon la Pensée Socialiste Sénégalaise," *Penant,* LXXIII, Part I, January-March, 1963, pp. 13—30; Part II, April-May, 1963, pp. 168—81.

Hapgood, D. "Guinea's First Five Years," *Current History,* XLV, 1963.

Hodgkin, T. "Note on the Language of African Nationalism," *St. Anthony's Papers,* X, pp. 39—40.

Holman, J. "Y-a-t-il une Voie Africaine du Socialisme? " *Presence Africaine,* 1964, pp. 50—64.

Hooker, J.R. *Black Revolutionary: George Padmore's Path from Communism to Pan-Africanism,* London, Pall Mall Press, 1967.

Hopkins, N.S. "Socialism and Social Change in Rural Mali," *Journal of Modern African Studies,* VII, 3, October 1969, pp. 457—69.

Hymans, J.L. "Origins of Leopold Senghor's African Road to Socialism," *Géneve-Afrique,* VI, 1967, pp. 33—48.

Janvier, J. "Géographie et Socialism en Afrique Noire," *Mois en Afrique,* November, 1966, pp. 28—55.

July, R.W. *The Origins of Modern African Thought.* London, Faber and Faber, 1968.

Keita, M. "Le Parti Unique en Afrique," *Presence Africaine,* 30, 1960, pp. 3—24.

Kenya, Government of. "African Socialism and its Application to Planning in Kenya," Nairobi, Government Printer, 1965.

Kilson, M. "Authoritarianism and Single-Party Tendencies in African Politics," *World Politics,* 1960, pp. 262–94.

Kilson, M. "Tensions and Dynamics of African Single-Party Systems: Case of the Erstwhile Convention Peoples Party," Harvard, 1968.

Kouyaté, S.B. "Politiques de Développement et Voies Africaines du Socialisme," *Presence Africaine,* 1963, pp. 59–72.

Kraus, J. "On the Politics of Nationalism and Social Change in Ghana," *Journal of Modern African Studies,* VII, 1969, pp. 109–30.

Lazitch, B. *L'Afrique les lecons de l'Expérience Communiste,* Paris, 1961.

Legum, C. "Single Party Democracy," *World Today,* XXI, 1965, pp. 526ff.

Legum, C. "What Kind of Radicalism for Africa," *Foreign Affairs,* XLIII, 1964, pp. 237–50.

Mboya, T. "African Socialism," *Transition,* III, 8, 1963.

Mboya, T. *Freedom and After,* Deutsch, 1963.

Mboya, T. "The Future of Kenya," *African Affairs,* LXII, 1964, pp. 6–12.

Mboya, T. "Trade-Unionism in Kenya," *Africa South,* I, 1957, pp. 77–85.

McRae, D.G. "Nkrumahism: Past and Future of an Ideology," *Government and Opposition,* I, 1965-1966, pp. 535–45.

Mazrui, A.A. "Nkrumah: The Leninist Czar," *Transition,* VI, 1967, pp. 9–18.

Mazrui, A.A. *Towards a Pax Africana: A Study of Ideology and Ambition,* London, Weidenfeld and Nicolson, 1967.

McAuslan, P. "Kenyan Socialism," *Venture,* XVII, 8, 1965, pp. 25–28.

McAuslan, P. "Socialism in Tanzania – One Party Puritanism," *Round Table,* LVII, 1967, pp. 312–18.

Melady, T.P. "African Socialism: A Bibliographic Essay," *African Forum,* 1, 3 1966, pp. 61–65.

Miller, N.N. "The Modern Survival of African Traditional Leaders: Political Syncretism in Tanzania," Paper Presented at African Studies Association Convention, New York, 1967.

Mohiddin, A. "Ujamaa: A Commentary on Nyerere's Vision of Tanzanian Society," *African Affairs,* LXVII, 1968, pp. 130–43.

Morgenthau, R.S. "French Guinea's RDA Folk Songs," *West African Review,* VIII, 1958.

Morgenthau, R.S. *Political Parties in French-Speaking West Africa,* Oxford, Oxford University Press, 1964.

Morgenthau, R.S. "Single Party Systems in West Africa," *American Political Science Review,* June 1961, pp. 247–307.

Nkrumah, K. *Challenge of the Congo,* New York, International Publishers Co., 1967.

Nkrumah, K. *Consciencism: Philosophy and Ideology for Decolonization and Development,* New York, 1965.

Nkrumah, K. "Le Consciencisme," *Presence Africaine,* 1964, pp. 8–35.

Nkrumah, K. *Ghana: The Autobiography of Kwame Nkrumah,* Edinburgh, 1960.

Nkrumah, K. *I Speak of Freedom.* 1961.

Nkrumah, K. *Neo-Colonialism: The Last Stage of Imperialism,* 1965.

Nkrumah, K. *Towards Colonial Freedom,* London, 1962.

Nyerere, J. "The African and Democracy," in J. Duffy and R. Manners (eds.) *Africa Speaks,* Princeton, Princeton University Press, 1961.

Nyerere, J. "After the Arusha Declaration," Dar es Salaam, Ministry of Information and Tourism, 1967.

Nyerere, J. "Les Fondements du Socialism Africaine," *Presence Africaine,* 1963, pp. 8—17.

Nyerere, J. "Freedom and Unity," *Transition,* IV, 14, 1964, pp. 39—48.

Nyerere, J. *Freedom and Unity: Speeches and Writings, 1952-1965,* Oxford, Oxford University Press, 1967.

Nyerere, J. "The Nationalist View," *International Affairs,* 1960, pp. 43—47.

Nyerere, J. "The Nature and Requirements of African Unity," *African Forum,* 1965.

Nyerere, J. "One Party Government," *Transition,* I, 2, 1961.

Stephens, H.W. *The Political Transformation of Tanganyika,* New York, Praeger, 1968.

Suedson, K.E. "Socialist Problems After the Arusha Declaration," *East Africa Journal,* V, 1967, pp. 9—15.

Obote, A.M. "A Plan for Nationhood," *Transition,* II, 6, 1962.

O'Brien, D.C. "Political Opposition in Senegal," *Government and Opposition,* 1967, pp. 557—66.

O'Connel, J. "Senghor, Nkrumah and Azikiwe," *Nigerian Journal of Economic and Social Studies,* V, i, 1963, pp. 77—93.

Onouma, B. *The Elements of African Socialism,* Deutsch, 1965.

Padmore, G. *Pan-Africanism or Communism,* London, Dobson, 1958.

Phillips, J.F. *Kwame Nkrumah and the Future of Africa,* London, Faber and Faber, 1960.

Potekhin, I. "On African Socialism," *International Affairs* (Moscow), IX, 1963, pp. 71—79.

Sauldie, H.M. "Recent Trends in African Socialism," *African Quarterly,* VII, 3, 1967, pp. 251—56.

Scott, R. *The Development of Trade Unions in Uganda,* Kampala, East Africa Institute of Social Research, 1966.

Senghor, Leopold S. *Nation et Voie Africaine du Socialisme,* Paris, 1961.

Senghor, Leopold S. "Négritude et Civilisation de l'Universel," *Presence Africaine,* 1963, pp. 8—13.

Senghor, Leopold S. "Some Thoughts on Africa: A Continent in Development," *International Affairs,* 1962, pp. 189—195.

Senghor, L.S. "West Africa in Evolution," in P.W. Quigg (ed.), *African Foreign Affairs,* pp. 285—91.

Serreau, J. *Le Développement à la Base au Dahomey et au Sénégal,* Paris, 1966.

"Le Socialisme Africaine: Durcissment de l'Opinion Soviétique," *Revue Africain,* August, 1967, pp. 8—14.

Sigmund, P. (ed.). *The Ideologies of Developing Nations,* New York, Praeger, 1963.

Skurnik, W.A.E. (ed.). *African Political Thought; Lumumba, Nkrumah and Toure,* Denver, University of Denver Press, 1968.

Skurnik, W.A.E. (ed.), "Leopold Sedar Senghor and African Socialism," *Journal of Modern African Studies,* III, 1965, pp. 349–69.

Snyder, F.G. "The Political Thought of Modibo Keita," *Journal of Modern African Studies,* V, 1967, pp. 79–106.

Spark Editors. *Some Essential Features of Nkrumaism,* Accra, Spark Publications, 1964.

Thomas, L.V. *Les Idéologies Negro-Africaines d'Aujourd'hui,* Dakar, 1965.

Thomas, L.V. "Senghor à la Recherche de l'Homme Nègre," *Presence Africaine,* 1965, pp. 7–36.

Thomas, L.V. *Le Socialisme et l'Afrique,* 2 vols., Paris, 1966.

Tordoff, W. *Government and Politics in Tanzania,* Nairobi, East African Publishing House, 1967.

Tordoff, W. "Tanzania: Democracy and the One-Party State," *Government and Opposition,* II, 1967, pp. 599–614.

Touré, A. Sekou. *L'Action Politique du Parti Démocratique du Guinée,* Paris, 1959.

Touré, A. Sekou. *L'Expérience Guinéenne et l'Unité Africaine,* Paris, 1959.

Touré, A. Sekou. "La Guinnée et l'Emancipation Africaine," *Presence Africaine,* 1959, pp. 216–49.

Touré, A. Sekou. "The Republic of Guinea," *International Affairs,* XXXVI, 1960, pp. 168–73.

Traoré, M.R.A. *African Socialism in Guinea,* Conakry, National Institute of Research and Documentation, 1966.

van der Muhl, G. and Koff, D. "Political Socialization in Kenya and Tanzania," *Journal of Modern African Studies,* V, 1968, pp. 13–51.

Wallerstein, I. "L'Idéologie du PDG," *Presence Africaine,* 1962, pp. 44–56.

F.   Socialism in the Arab World

Abdel-Malek, Anovar. *Egypte -- société militaire,* Paris, Editions du Seuil, 1962.

Abdel-Malek, Anovar (ed.). *La pensee politique arabe contemporain,* Paris, Editions du Seuil, 1970.

Agwani, M.S. *Communism in the Arab East,* London, Asia Publishing House, 1969.

Ben-Tsur, Avraham. "Socialism in Egypt," *New Outlook,* Vol. 6, pp. 25–38.

Bertier, F. "L'idéologie sociale de la révolution égyptienne," *Orient,* No. 2, pp. 29–71.

Bill, James D. "Class Analysis and the Dialectics of Modernization in the Middle East," *International Journal of Middle East Studies,* Vol. 3, pp. 417–34.

Binder, Leonard. *The Ideological Revolution in the Middle East,* New York, John Wiley and Sons, 1964.

Dekmejian, R. Hrair. *Egypt under Nasir: A Study in Political Dynamics*, Albany; State University of New York Press, 1971.

Enayat, Hamid. "Islam and Socialism in Egypt," *Middle Eastern Studies*, Vol. 4, pp. 141–72.

Gadalla, Saad M. *Land Reform in Relation to Social Development*, Columbia, University of Missouri Press, 1962.

Gibb, H.A.R. "Social Reform: Factor X" in W.Z. Laqueur (ed.), *The Middle East in Transition*, New York, Praeger, 1958.

Gibb, H.A.R. "The Heritage of Islam in the Modern World," *International Journal of Middle East Studies*, Vol. 1, pp. 3–17, 221–37; Vol. 2, pp. 129–47.

Grunebaum, Gustave E. von. *Modern Islam: The Search for Cultural Identity*, Berkeley and Los Angeles, University of California Press, 1962.

Hafez, Hamdi. *Le socialisme et son application en R.A.U.*, Cairo, 1966.

Hanna, Sami A., and Gardner, George H. *Arab Socialism*, Leiden, E.J. Brill, 1969.

Hoskins, Halford L. "Arab Socialism in the U.A.R.," *Current History*, Vol. 44, pp. 8–12, 53–54.

Hussein, Mahmoud. *La lutte des classes en Egypte de 1945 à 1968*, Paris, F. Maspero, 1971.

Issawi, Charles. *Egypt in Revolution*, London, Oxford University Press, 1963.

Issawi, Charles. "Social Structure and Ideology in Iraq, Lebanon, Syria, and the U.A.R.," *International Affairs*, Vol. 19, pp. 39–46.

Karpart, Kemal H. (ed.). *Political and Social Thought in the Contemporary Middle East*, New York, Praeger, 1948.

Kedourie, Elie. "Anti-Marxism in Egypt," in M. Confino and S. Shamir (eds.), *The U.S.S.R. and the Middle East*, New York, John Wiley & Sons, 1973.

Kerr, Malcom. "Notes on the Background of Arab Socialist Thought," *Journal of Contemporary History*, Vol. III, No. 3, pp. 145–59.

Kerr, Malcom. "The Emergence of a Socialist Ideology in Egypt," *Middle East Journal*, Vol. 16, pp. 127–44.

Khadduri, Majid. *Political Trends in the Arab World: The Role of Ideas and Ideals in Politics*, Baltimore, Johns Hopkins Press, 1970.

Kholi, Lotfi el-. "Une gauche structure dans une Egypte democratique," *Elements*, 7/8, pp. 15–20.

Kotb, Sayed. *Social Justice in Islam*, Washington, D.C., American Council of Learned Societies, 1953.

Koury, Enver M. *The Patterns of Mass Movements in Arab Revolutionary Progressive States*, The Hague, Mouton, 1970.

Leiden, Carl (ed.). *The Conflict of Traditionalism and Modernism in the Muslim Middle East*, Austin, University of Texas Press, 1969.

Lewis, Bernard. "Communism and Islam," *International Affairs*, Vol. 30, pp. 1–12.

O'Brien, Patrick. *The Revolution in Egypt's Economic System from Private Enterprise to Socialism*, London: Oxford University Press, 1966.

Pennar, Jaan. "The Arabs, Marxism and Moscow; A Historical Survey," *Middle East Journal*, Vol. 22, pp. 433–47.

Rodinson, Maxime. *L'Islam et le Marxisme,* Paris.

Said, Abdel Moghny. *Arab Socialism,* London, Blandford Press, 1972.

Sayegh, Fayez. "The Theoretical Structure of Nasser's Arab Socialism," *St. Antony's Papers,* Vol. 17, pp. 9–55.

Smith, Wilfred C. *Islam in Modern History,* Princeton, Princeton University Press, 1957.

Shamir, Shimon. "The Marxists in Egypt: The Doctrine of 'Licensed Infiltration' in Practice," in M. Confino and S. Shamir (eds.), *The U.S.S.R. in the Middle East,* New York, John Wiley & Sons, 1973.

Tibi, Bassam (ed.). *Die arabische Linke,* Frankfurt, Europäische Vertagasamstalt, 1969.

Torrey, G.H., and Devlin, J.F. "Arab Socialism," *International Affairs,* Vol. 19, pp. 47–62.

Ule, Wolfgang. *Der arabische Sozialismus und der zeitgenössische Islam, Dargestellt am Beispiel Aegyptens und des Iraq,* Opladen, C.W. Leske, 1969.

Vatikiotis, P.J. (ed.), *Egypt since the Revolution,* London, George Allen & Unwin, 1968.

Vatikiotis, P.J. (ed.), *La voie égyptienne vers le socialisme,* Cairo, Dar al-Maaref, 1963.

NOTES ON THE CONTRIBUTORS

S.N. EISENSTADT, Professor of Sociology at the Hebrew University of Jerusalem, is a 1973 winner of the Israel Prize for his contributions to the field of sociology. He has been visiting professor at a number of major universities in the United States and Europe and received the 1964 McIver Award of the American Sociological Association and the 1969 Rothschild Prize in Social Sciences. Author of six major works, his most recent book is *Tradition, Change, and Modernity* (1973).

YAEL AZMON , co-editor of this volume, studied at the Hebrew University of Jerusalem, where she now teaches in the Department of Sociology. At present a candidate for a doctorate in the Department, she is investigating "mobility" in the governing Labor Party of Israel for her dissertation. She co-authored an earlier study of life in her native country, *Moshava, Kibbutz, and Moshav: Patterns of Jewish Rural Settlement and Development in Palestine* (1969).

GALIA GOLAN   is a Senior Lecturer in Political Science and Russian Studies at the Hebrew University of Jerusalem. She studied at Brandeis University, the University of Geneva, and L'Ecole Pratique des Hautes Etudes in Paris and worked as an East European specialist in the United States before emigrating to Israel where she took a doctorate at the Hebrew University. She is author of *The Czechoslovak Reform Movement: Communism in Crisis 1962-1968* (1971) and *Reform Rule in Czechoslovakia: The Dubcek Era 1968-1969* (1973).

YITZHAK SHICHOR, a *sabra,* studied at the Institute of Asian and African Studies at the Hebrew University of Jerusalem and has taught in the Institute's Department of Chinese and Japanese Studies. Presently a Ph.D. candidate in international relations at the London School of Economics and Political Science, he has written a number of articles on China's foreign policy for Hebrew publications and is joint author of a survey on China submitted to Israel's Parliament.

MARTIN RUDNER, who studied at McGill University and the University of Oxford, is a Research Fellow in Political Science and Southeast Asian Studies at the Hebrew University of Jerusalem where he has received his doctorate. He is coordinator of the Asia Research Unit at the Harry S. Truman Institute, editor of *Society and Development in Asia,* and has contributed articles to the *Journal of Southeast Asian Studies* and *Modern Asian Studies.*

NAOMI CHAZAN, who teaches African studies at the Hebrew University of Jerusalem, spent a year teaching at the University of Ghana, while conducting fieldwork for her doctoral dissertation on "Politics and Youth Organizations in Ghana and the Ivory Coast." She has published numerous articles on West African politics and is presently preparing a comprehensive study of the experiences of Israeli development experts working abroad.

SHIMON SHAMIR is Director of the Shiloah Center for Middle Eastern and African Studies at Tel Aviv University. Rumanian-born, Dr. Shamir studied at the Hebrew University of Jerusalem and Princeton University. He has published works on the Arab lands in the Ottoman period, on Arabic thought and ideologies, and on contemporary Egypt, and was co-editor of the just-published *The U.S.S.R. and the Middle East* (1973).